Collins

Perfect Maths 3

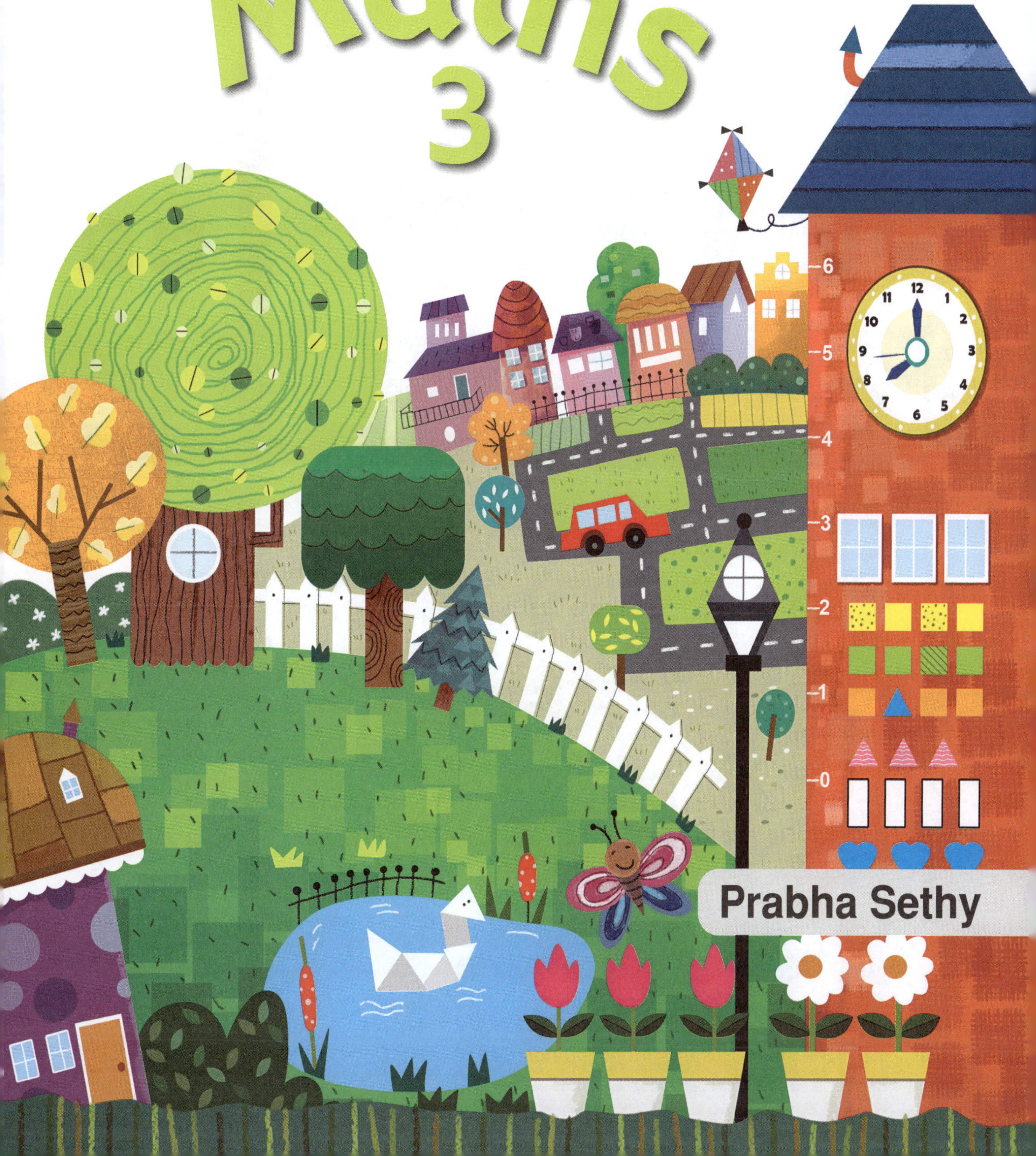

Prabha Sethy

Components of DigiSuite

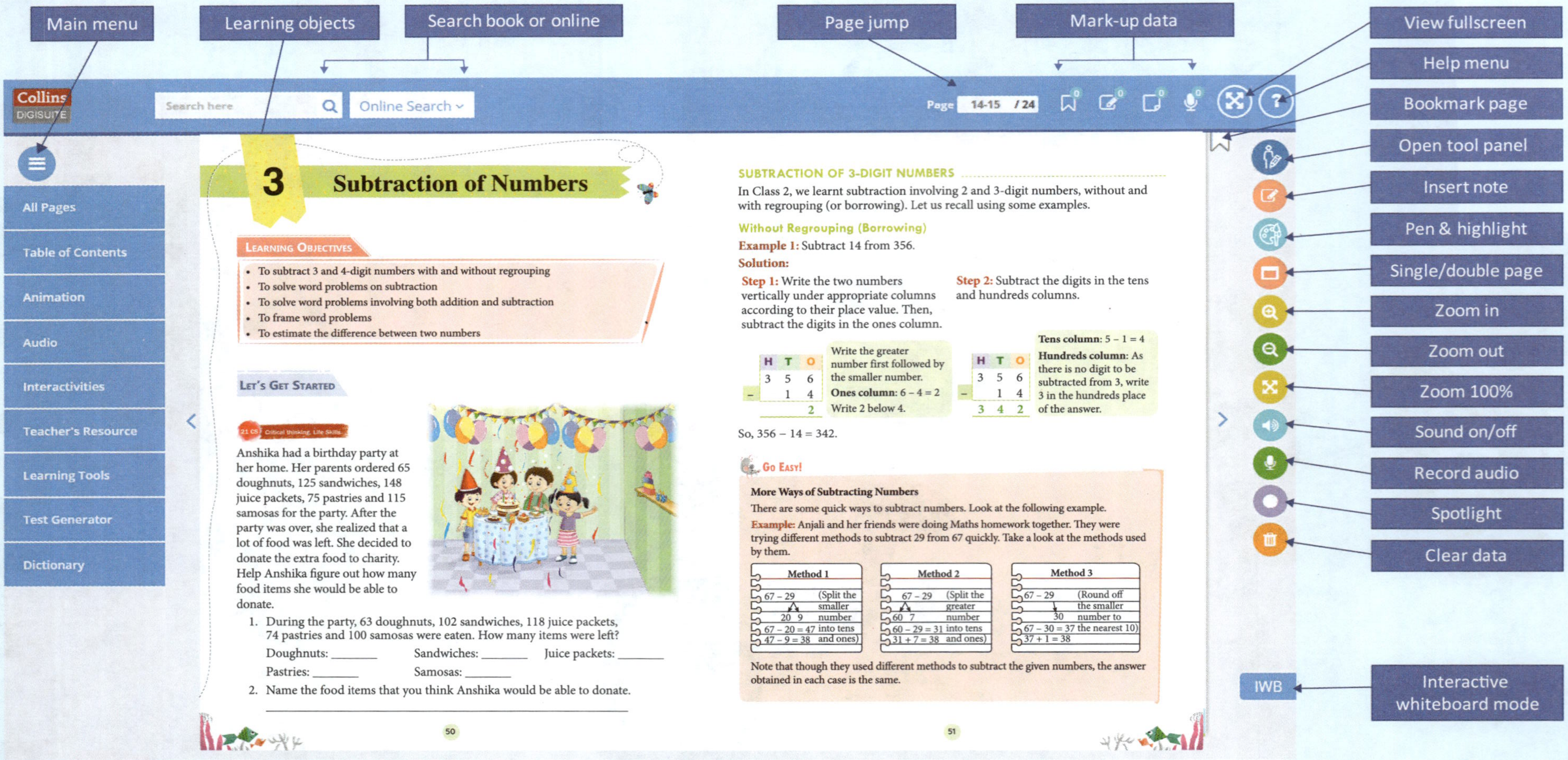

Student + Teacher			Teacher-only	
a animations	**ia** activities	**g** games	**lp** lesson plans	**tn** teacher's notes
ilt instructor-led tutorials	**w** worksheets	**v** videos	**w** worksheets	**ak** answer keys
	audio			

Preface

Perfect Maths is a series of eleven books for Classes Nursery to 8. The books for the Foundational Stage, previously referred to as Grades Nursery, Lower KG and Upper KG, would be the base to make the series complete in providing a strong foundation in numeracy, starting from ECCE till the middle stage. The series adheres to the guidelines of the **National Education Policy (NEP) 2020**, aligns with the vision of the ***National Initiative for Proficiency in Reading with Understanding and Numeracy*** **(NIPUN Bharat)** and aims to make mathematics more relevant to students in a non-threatening way.

The books for Foundational Stage 1 to 3 (Grades Nursery to UKG) are focused on the holistic development of a child. Based on **Numeracy Skills**, **21st Century Skills** and **Multiple Intelligences**, integrated and interdisciplinary approach, experiential learning, the books aim to help a child be "**Happy to Learn**". The unique blend of direct instructions, play-based structured activities, investigations, stories and rhymes provide the children ample opportunities to develop their numeracy and literacy skills.

The books for Classes 1 to 8 follow the ***5E Learning Model***. The 5E Learning Model provides an activity-oriented approach to the series to make mathematics engaging for students through emphasizing connections between mathematics and day-to-day experiences. This series adheres to the guidelines of NEP 2020 completely, with the effective integration of its features with **21st Century Skills**, **Art Integration**, **Experiential Learning**, **Cross-curricular** and **India Focus**. The skill building questions and the varied exposure to situations provided in the pages of this series keep the learners at the centre and focus on making them future-ready. The series also aims to make students aware of the United Nations **Sustainable Development Goals** (SDGs), so that they can become SDG Pioneers, Champions or Ambassadors.

SAFAL in ***Perfect Maths:*** This series also strives to make a shift from rote-learning to competency-based learning, in accordance with **Structured Assessment For Analyzing Learning (SAFAL)**. The components of SAFAL—critical thinking, inquiry-based learning and analysis-based learning—are woven into the features such as Exercises, Mental Maths, Chapter Revision, Skill Up!, Worksheets, Reasoning Worksheets, Review/Assessment Corner and PISA Corner (Classes 6 to 8).

We would like to take this opportunity to thank all the teachers and educationist who reviewed the books and provided their feedback, which helped in improving the quality of the content.

Feedback, invaluable comments and suggestions from users are welcome.

Authors

About the Author

Prabha Sethy, formerly a teacher at Welham Boys' School, Dehradun, with more than 30 years of experience in teaching mathematics, brings in resources from everyday life into her content.

Key Features

The key features of ***Perfect Maths*** are completely aligned with the **National Education Policy (NEP) 2020** and the vision of the **National *Initiative for Proficiency in Reading with Understanding and Numeracy*** (NIPUN Bharat). These meticulously designed features, based on the ***5E Learning Model***, can be used as learning strategies to enhance the understanding of key concepts in mathematics and increase practical learning and problem-solving by bringing in real-life contexts from outside the classroom while providing some form of experiential learning. These key features also aim to help the learners shift from rote-learning to competency-based learning, in accordance with ***Structured Assessment For Analyzing Learning*** (SAFAL).

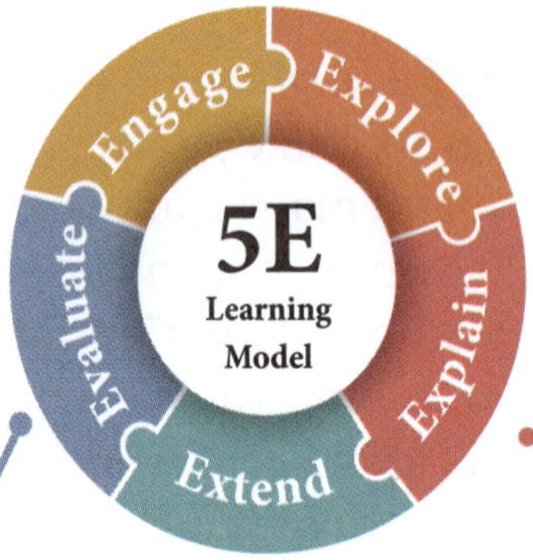

To capture the attention of students, get them mentally engaged and make connections between past and present

- Maths Around Us
- Let's Get Started
- Common Errors
- Go Easy!
- Vedic Maths (Classes 6 to 8)
- Eminent Mathematicians
- Poster

To enable the students to explore the concepts through hands-on activities, investigations, etc.

- Maths Lab Activity
- Crosswords
- Puzzles
- Mental Maths
- Worksheets
- Maths Mela

To enable the students to understand the main ideas of the topics

- Learning Objectives
- Note
- Solved Examples
- Concept Map
- Key Concepts

To enable the students to stimulate thinking and apply prior and current knowledge to real-life situations

- Do You Know?
- Word Problems
- Skill Up!
- SEE Learning

To review, assess and evaluate what students have learned

- Exercises
- Chapter Revision
- Reasoning Worksheet
- Review/Assessment Corner
- PISA Corner (Classes 6 to 8)

Adherence to National Education Policy

21st Century Skills (21 CS)

Learning Skills
- Critical Thinking
- Creativity and Innovation
- Collaboration
- Communication

Life Skills

Literacy Skills
- Information Literacy
- Media Literacy
- Technology Literacy

Art Integration (AI)

Cross Curricular (CC)

India Focus (IF)

Happiness Quotient (HQ)

Experiential Learning (EL)

SUSTAINABLE DEVELOPMENT GOALS

Each feature has been tagged with colour-coded icons to easily identify the type of skills and learning being addressed!

About the Features

Interesting information and activities to connect maths with Indian history, art, culture, real-life situations and financial literacy

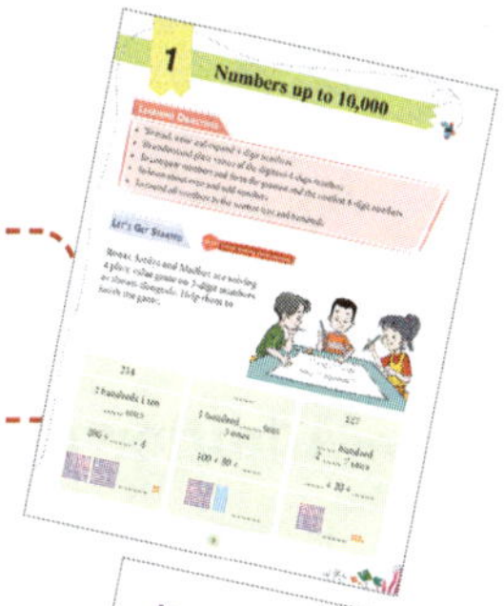

Chapter starter in the form of a picture-based exercise

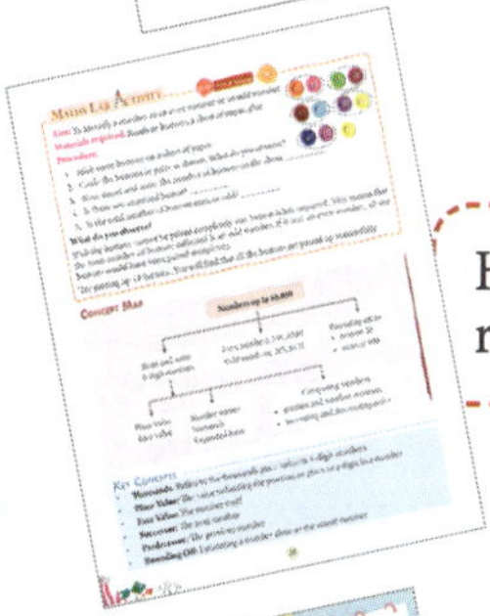

Hands-on activity to help in improving investigation, reinforcement and extension of concepts just learnt

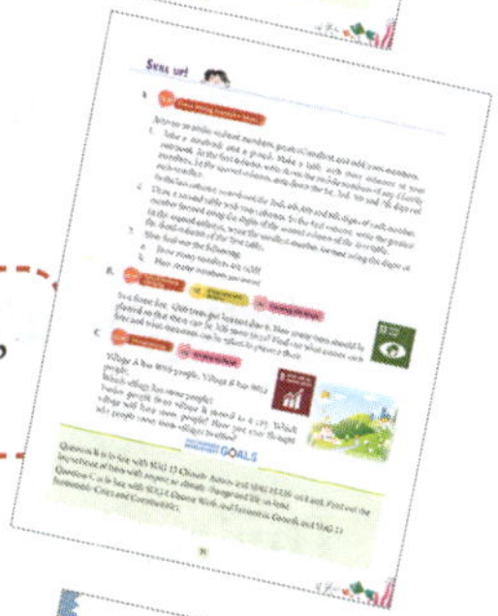

A variety of questions catering to inquiry-based, discovery-based, discussion-based and analysis-based learning

Picture-based, fun, problem-solving questions to reinforce concepts

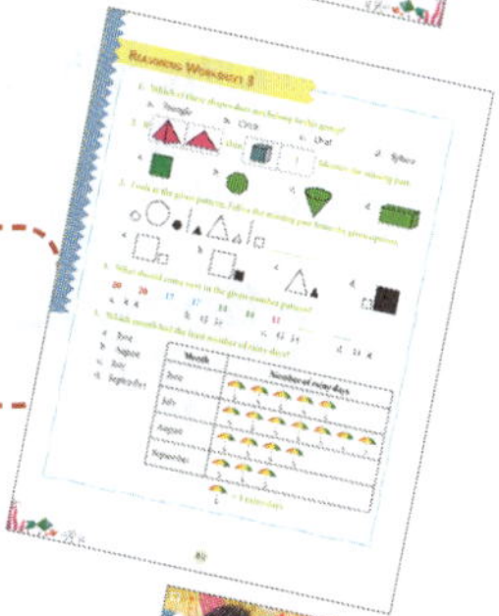

Questions to stimulate rational thinking using mathematical skills

Special stories to promote social, emotional and ethical learning

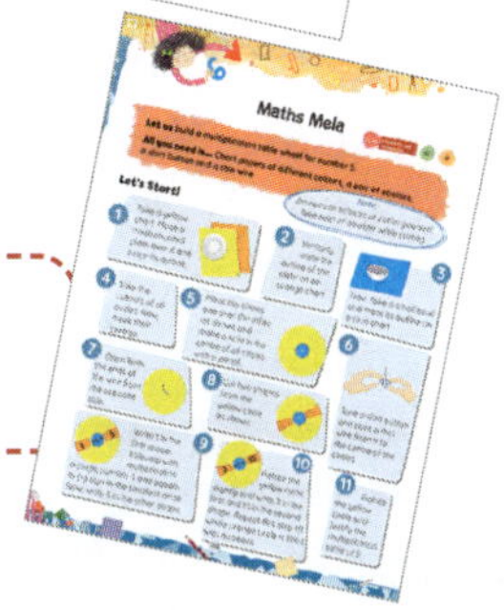

Model making or hands-on project ideas to enhance learning beyond the classroom

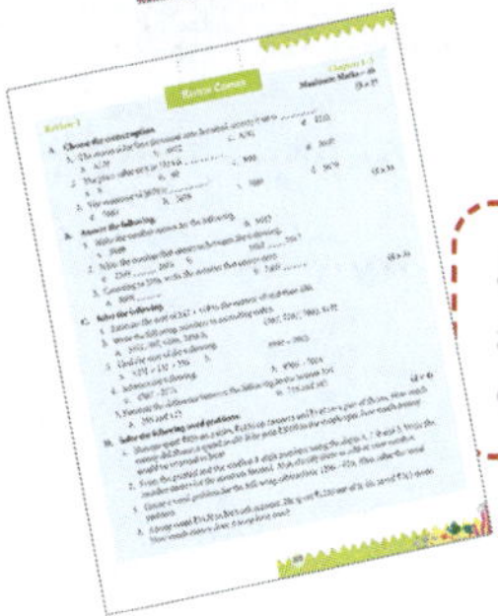

Sample test papers at the end of the book for additional practice (Classes 6 to 8 Assessment Corner based on the New Assessment format)

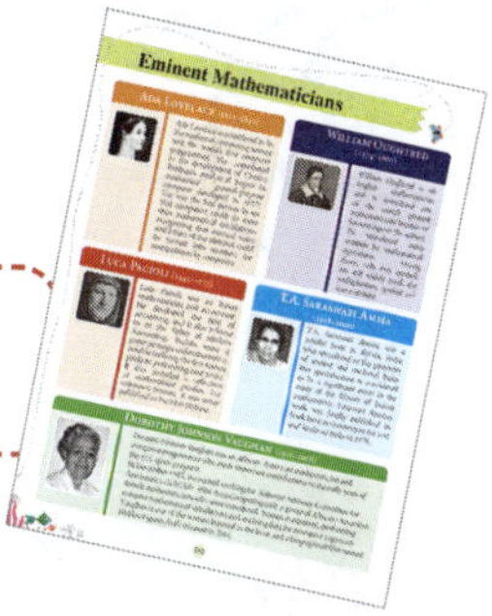

Brief write-ups on eminent mathematicians and their contributions

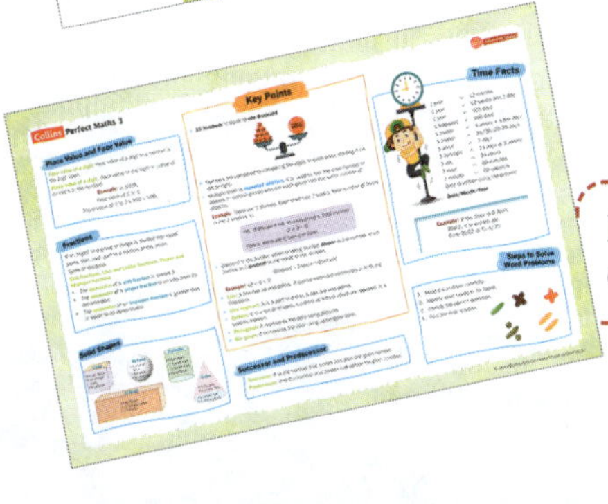

Informative colourful posters to focus on some important concepts or facts

Contents

Maths Around Us

21 CS IF AI CC Integration with Social Studies

SYMMETRY AROUND US

Symmetry means having one half that is exactly the same as or is a mirror image of the other half. Any shape, figure or object is said to be symmetrical if it has mirror halves or equal parts. That is, each half or part must be of the same shape and size as the other. We can observe symmetry all around us—in nature, in patterns, in art and architecture as well as at home.

To find out whether a given shape or object is symmetrical, we can draw an imaginary line through its centre to see if the line divides the shape or object into two identical halves. In addition, we can also fold a figure along this imaginary line to see whether one half overlaps with the other or not.

Most buildings and historical monuments in the world are constructed using symmetry. Symmetry gives strength to these structures and adds to their beauty as well.

India Gate (New Delhi)

Lotus Temple (New Delhi)

Taj Mahal (Agra, Uttar Pradesh)

Qutab Minar (New Delhi)

To understand symmetry better, let us do a hands-on activity.

1. Take a piece of paper (square or rectangular) and fold it perfectly in half (ensure all the edges line up).

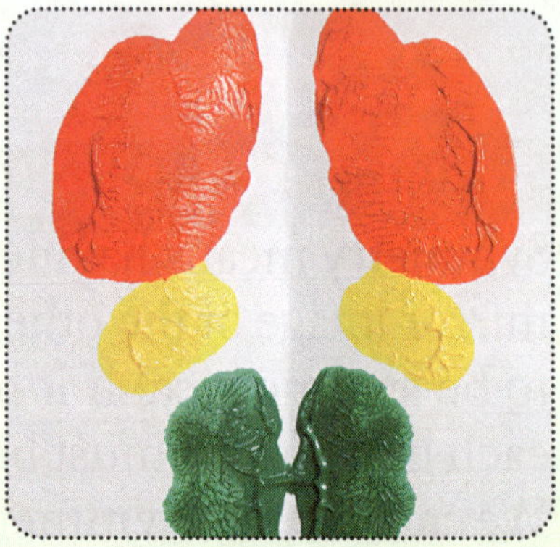

2. Open the paper and place two or three teaspoons of different coloured liquid paint on one half of the paper (preferably near the fold), in a pattern of your choice.
3. Then, fold the paper and slowly rub on top of the paper carefully but thoroughly.
4. Now, open the paper to see the symmetrical design formed. The line of fold in the centre represents the imaginary line.
5. For more fun, you can decorate the design or pattern obtained with glitter glue after they dry up.

Look out for symmetrical objects or things around you. Collect dry flowers or leaves and paste them in the space provided below. Also, draw an imaginary line on each to show their symmetrical halves.

1 Numbers up to 10,000

Learning Objectives

- To read, write and expand 4-digit numbers
- To understand place values of the digits of 4-digit numbers
- To compare numbers and form the greatest and the smallest 4-digit numbers
- To learn about even and odd numbers
- To round off numbers to the nearest tens and hundreds

Let's Get Started

21 CS Critical Thinking, Communication

Ronav, Saniya and Madhav are solving a place value game on 3-digit numbers as shown alongside. Help them to finish the game.

214	____	127
2 hundreds 1 ten ____ ones	1 hundred ____ tens 3 ones	____ hundred 2 ____ 7 ones
200 + ____ + 4	100 + 50 + ____	____ + 20 + ____
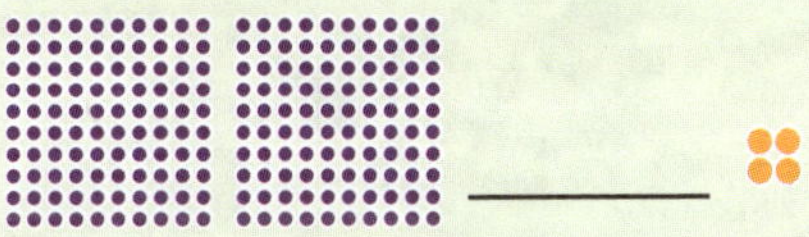 ______	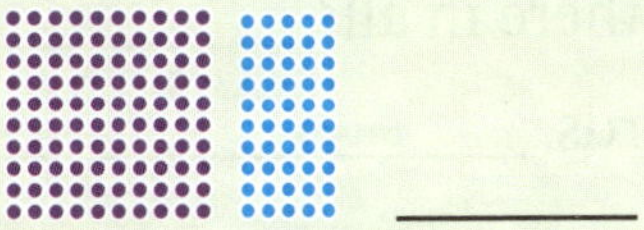 ______	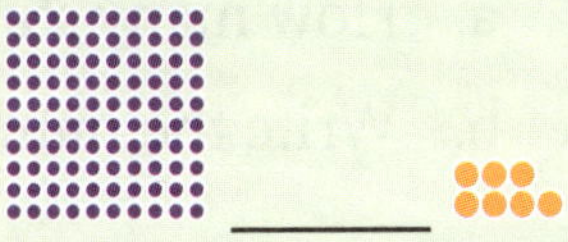 ______

We know that all numbers are formed by combining the digits from 0 to 9.

 = 10 ones = 1 ten

A group of 10 ones is called a **ten**.

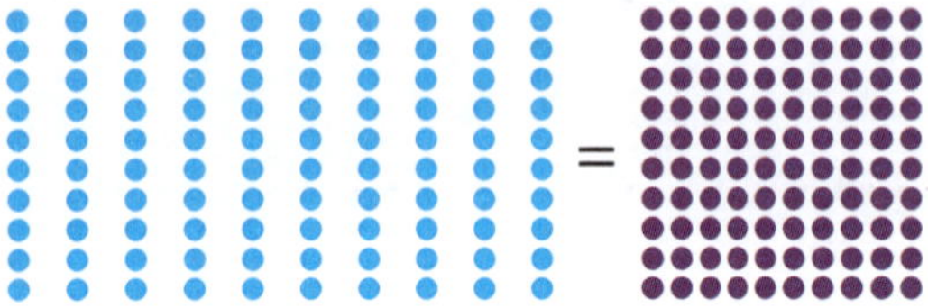

A collection of 10 tens is called a **hundred**.

The smallest 3-digit number is **100**.

The greatest 3-digit number is **999**.

Let us quickly revise numbers up to 999 by solving the following exercise.

EXERCISE 1A

1. Look at the representation given below and answer the questions that follow.

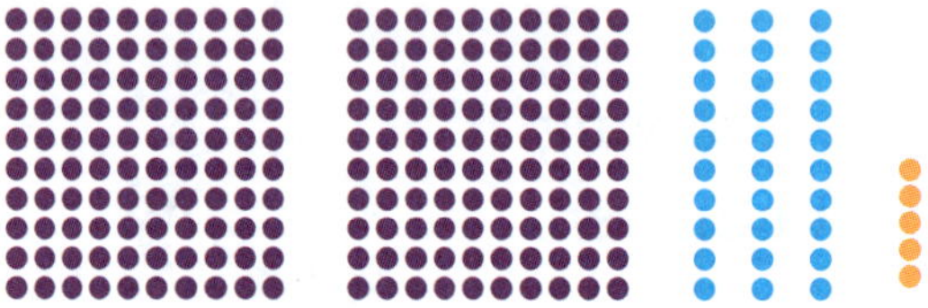

a. Number name: ______________________________

b. Expanded form: ________ + ________ + ________

c. Place values of the digits: ________ hundreds ________ tens ________ ones

d. What is the number just before this number? ________

e. What is the number just after this number? ________

2. Arrange the following numbers as per the order mentioned.

a. Increasing order

659, 284, 971, 364

◯ ◯ ◯ ◯

b. Decreasing order

129, 843, 705, 364

◯ ◯ ◯ ◯

3. Answer the following.

Class 3 of a primary school has a total of (100 + 20 + 5) students.

a. How many students are there in all? ________

b. Write the number in words. ______________________

INTRODUCTION TO 4-DIGIT NUMBERS

The greatest 3-digit number is 999. What comes after 999? Let us find out by adding 1 to 999.

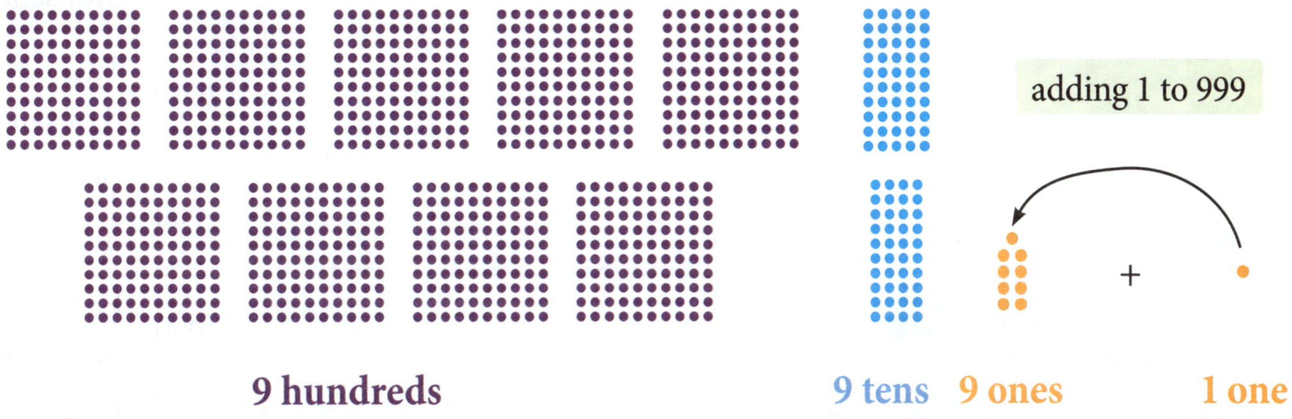

Adding 1 one to 9 ones gives 10 ones. So, we have:

9 hundreds **9 tens** **10 ones** **10 ones = 1 ten**

9 hundreds **10 tens** **10 tens = 1 hundred**

10 hundreds = **1 thousand** or **1000**

So, the number after 999 is 1000. 1000 is the smallest 4-digit number. It is read as one thousand. The number 1000 introduces the **thousands period** to us.

Just after 1000, the counting continues as 1001, 1002, 1003, 1004, 1005, 1006, 1007, 1008, 1009, 1010 and so on. That is, the numbers increase by 1 each time.

We know that 100 can be represented by using a block of 100 small cubes.
So, 10 such blocks placed together represent 1 thousand.

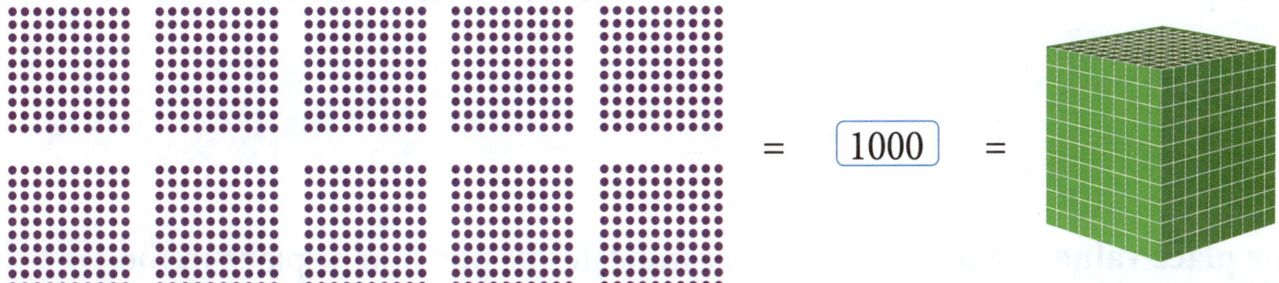

Look at the following table and learn counting by thousands. Also, complete the last column of the table.

	1000	One thousand
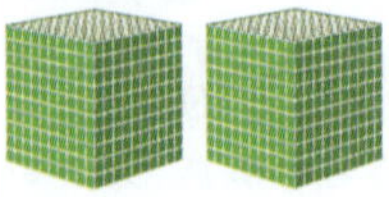	2000	Two thousand
	3000	Three thousand
	4000	Four thousand
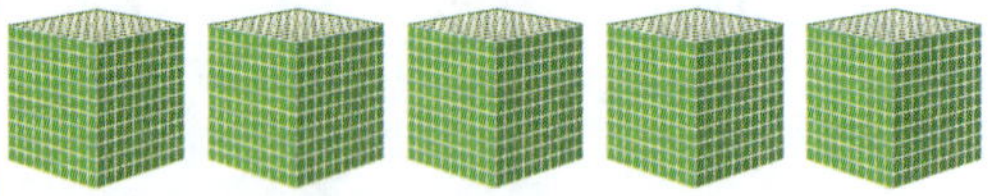	5000	Five thousand
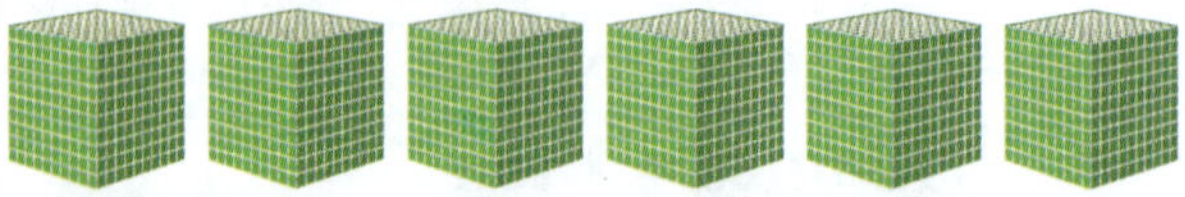	6000	
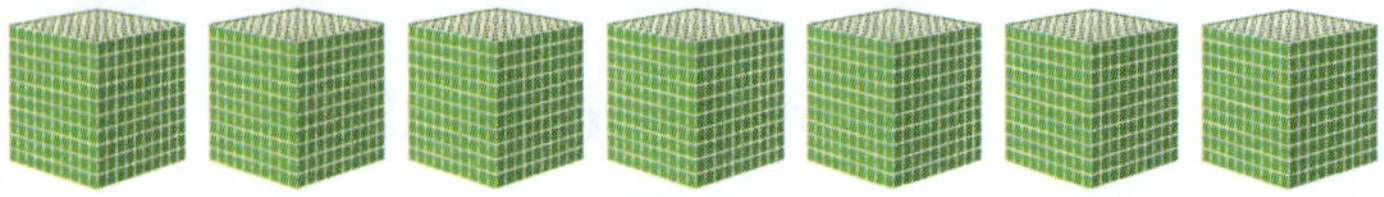	7000	
	8000	
	9000	
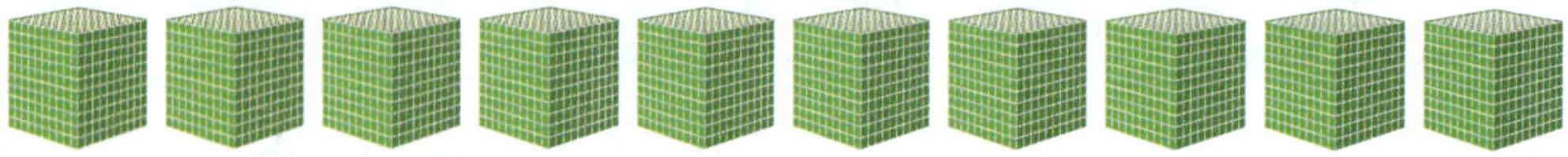	10,000	Ten thousand

Place Value and Face Value

We represent 4-digit numbers by using the following place values.

Thousands	Hundreds	Tens	Ones
↓	↓	↓	↓
Th	H	T	O

The **place value** of a digit in a number indicates its position or place in the number. We can write it in words as well as figures.

The **face value** of a digit in a number is the digit itself.

Go Easy!

An easier way to write the place value is by writing the digit followed by as many zeros as the number of digits on the right side of the digit concerned.

Example: In 7463, the place value of 7 is 7000 (as there are three digits after the digit 7 in the given number).

Consider the number 9638.

Place value of:	Face value of:
9 = 9 thousands or 9000	9 = 9
6 = 6 hundreds or 600	6 = 6
3 = 3 tens or 30	3 = 3
8 = 8 ones or 8	8 = 8

Example: Write the place value and face value of each digit in the number 5839.

	Th	H	T	O
	5	8	3	9
	↓	↓	↓	↓
Place value	5000	800	30	9
Face value	5	8	3	9

Mental Maths

Find the place value and the face value of the underlined digits.

a. 7 5 <u>8</u> 4 b. <u>2</u> 7 3 0

UNDERSTANDING 4-DIGIT NUMBERS

Read and Write 4-Digit Numbers

To read and write the number names for 4-digit numbers:

- First, read the digit in thousands place as per its place value.
- Then, read the digit in hundreds place as per its place value.
- Finally, read the digits in tens and ones places together.

Note

In a 4-digit number, if there are no digits in the hundreds and tens places, we do not mention them in the number name.

Consider the following 4-digit numbers.

Th	H	T	O
2	9	7	6
Two thousand	nine hundred	seventy-six	

Th	H	T	O
5	0	0	9
Five thousand		nine	

2976: Two thousand nine hundred seventy-six   5009: Five thousand nine

Writing Numerals for Number Names

Consider the number name four thousand, seven hundred, sixty-one.

The numeral for it is

Th	H	T	O
4	7	6	1

The numeral for the number name nine thousand eight hundred fifty is

Th	H	T	O
9	8	5	0

More About 4-Digit Numbers

Look at the following representation of a 4-digit number. Count the number of thousands, hundreds, tens and ones, respectively.

Thousands	Hundreds	Tens	Ones
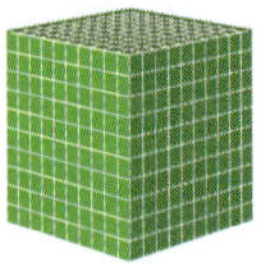	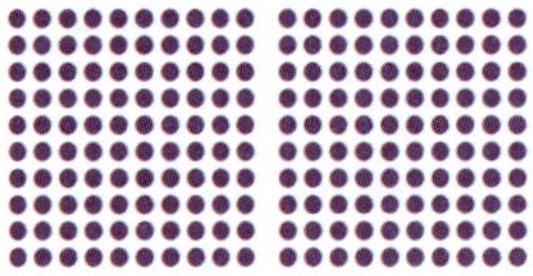	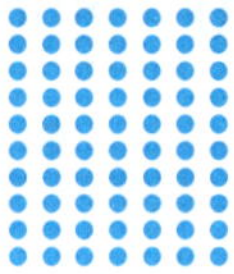	
1 thousand	**2 hundreds**	**7 tens**	**9 ones**

So, the number is 1279.

This is called the **standard form** of a number.

Number name: One thousand two hundred seventy-nine.

This way of representing a number is also called its **word form**.

We can write the number in terms of its place value as follows:

1279 = 1 thousand 2 hundreds 7 tens 9 ones

or

1000 + 200 + 70 + 9

This way of representing a number is called its **expanded form**.

Exercise 1B

1. **Write the place values and face values of the underlined digits.**

   a. 5<u>6</u>29: Place value __________, Face value __________

   b. <u>7</u>341: Place value __________, Face value __________

   c. 81<u>9</u>0: Place value __________, Face value __________

2. **Write the numeral and the number name for the number represented by the following.**

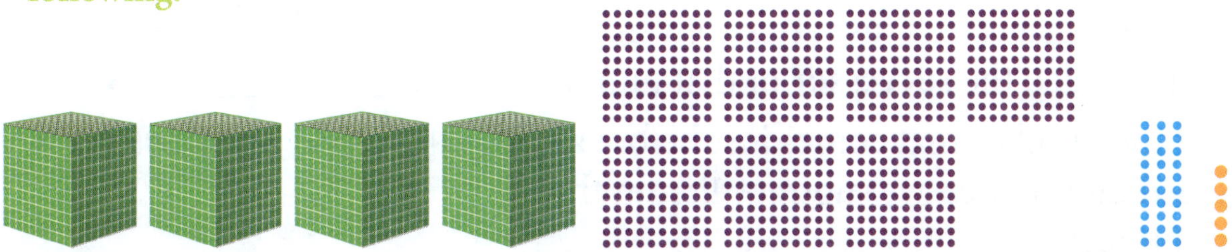

   Numeral = __________ Number name = ____________________________

3. **Write the number names for the following.**

   a. 5689 ____

   b. 2107 ____

   c. 6000 ____

4. **Write the numerals for the following.**

   a. Six thousand two hundred eighty-one ____________

   b. Nine thousand three hundred sixty-seven ____________

   c. Eight thousand one hundred fifty-four ____________

5. **Write the expanded form of the following numbers.**

   a. 4029 = _________ + _________ + _________ + _________

   b. 8572 = _________ + _________ + _________ + _________

   c. 1364 = _________ + _________ + _________ + _________

6. **Write the numerals.**

   a. 6000 + 400 + 20 + 9 = _________ b. 5000 + 100 + 30 + 8 = _________

   c. 3000 + 200 + 40 + 0 = _________ d. 8000 + 600 + 50 + 3 = _________

7. **Fill in the blanks.**

   a. Seven thousand six hundred ninety-five people lived in a village.
   Write that in numerals: __________________________

   b. Out of them, the number of men was equal to the place value of 7.
   Number of men = __________________________

   c. The number of children was equal to the sum of the place values of 9 and 5.
   Number of children = __________________________

NUMBER AFTER, BEFORE OR IN BETWEEN

To find the number that comes just after any given 4-digit number, we add 1 to the given number.

Example: Write the number that comes just after each of the following.

a. 2964 ⟶ <u>2965</u> b. 3718 ⟶ <u>3719</u>

The number that comes just **after** a given number is called the **successor** of that number.

To find the number that comes just before any given 4-digit number, we subtract 1 from the given number.

> **MENTAL MATHS**
>
> What comes just after:
>
> a. 7218 ____________
>
> b. 3429 ____________
>
> What comes just before:
>
> a. ____________ 7246
>
> b. ____________ 3950

Example: Write the number that comes just before each of the following.

a. <u>5293</u> ⟵ 5294 b. <u>7385</u> ⟵ 7386

The number that comes just **before** a given number is called the **predecessor** of that number.

The number **in between** two given numbers is the number that comes between the numbers. It will be the successor of the first number and the predecessor of the second number.

Example: Find the number in between the given numbers.

a. 2596, <u>2597</u>, 2598 b. 7103, <u>7104</u>, 7105

COUNTING NUMBERS IN 10s, 100s AND 1000s

Counting Numbers in 10s

When we count numbers in 10s, we add 10 each time.

Example: Write the next four numbers by counting in 10s.

2730 $\xrightarrow{+10}$ 2740 $\xrightarrow{+10}$ 2750 $\xrightarrow{+10}$ 2760 $\xrightarrow{+10}$ 2770

Counting Numbers in 100s

When we count numbers in 100s, we add 100 each time.

Example: Write the next four numbers by counting in 100s.

3280 $\xrightarrow{+100}$ 3380 $\xrightarrow{+100}$ 3480 $\xrightarrow{+100}$ 3580 $\xrightarrow{+100}$ 3680

Counting Numbers in 1000s

When we count numbers in 1000s, we add 1000 each time.

Example: Write the next four numbers by counting in 1000s.

$$1903 \xrightarrow{+1000} 2903 \xrightarrow{+1000} 3903 \xrightarrow{+1000} 4903 \xrightarrow{+1000} 5903$$

Exercise 1C

1. **Write the successors of the following numbers.**

   a. 3815 ____________ b. 2067 ____________ c. 9149 ____________

2. **Write the predecessors of the given numbers.**

   a. ____________ 5893 b. ____________ 2078 c. ____________ 1430

3. **Write the number in between the given numbers.**

   a. 1672 ______ 1674 b. 3048 ______ 3050 c. 7165 ______ 7167

4. **Fill in the blanks by counting in 10s.**

   a. 7430, ____________, ____________, ____________, ____________

   b. 2581, ____________, ____________, ____________, ____________

5. **Fill in the blanks by counting in 100s.**

   a. 2100, ____________, ____________, ____________, ____________

   b. 9236, ____________, ____________, ____________, ____________

6. **Fill in the blanks by counting in 1000s.**

   a. 3000, ____________, ____________, ____________, ____________

   b. 5929, ____________, ____________, ____________, ____________

COMPARISON OF NUMBERS

Comparing Numbers With Different Number of Digits

A mango orchard had 786 trees and an apple orchard had 2600 trees. Which orchard had more trees?

Here, compare 786 and 2600.

H	T	O
7	8	6

This number has 3 digits.

Th	H	T	O
2	6	0	0

This number has 4 digits.

786 < 2600

So, the apple orchard has more trees.

> **NOTE**
>
> Symbols for:
> Greater than: >
> Less than: <
> Equal to: =
>
> Greater number is on this side > Smaller number is on this side

Comparing Numbers With the Same Number of Digits

Let us learn to compare numbers with the same number of digits using the following examples.

SOLVED EXAMPLES

Compare the given numbers and write >, < or =.

Example 1:

Th	H	T	O
7	2	9	0

Th	H	T	O
3	8	7	5

Solution: We first check the digits in the thousands place of both the numbers.

Thousands place: 7 > 3

So, 7290 > 3875

Example 2:

Th	H	T	O
4	6	2	8

Th	H	T	O
4	9	7	8

Solution: First, check the digits in the thousands place. As both the numbers have the same digit (4), check the digits in the hundreds place.

Hundreds place: 6 < 9

So, 4628 < 4978

Example 3:

Th	H	T	O
5	2	3	0

Th	H	T	O
5	2	3	7

Solution: The digits in the thousands, hundreds and tens places of both the numbers are the same. So, check the digits in the ones place.

Ones place: 0 < 7

So, 5230 < 5237

Example 4:

Th	H	T	O
4	1	0	9

Th	H	T	O
4	1	0	9

Solution: The digits in all the four places of both the numbers are the same. So, both the numbers are equal.

So, 4109 = 4109

Greatest and Smallest Numbers

Vibha has 3617 books in her library, Amit has 2458 books, Sachin has 1800 books and Shalini has 3099 books.

Who has the maximum number of books? Who has the least number of books?

Finding the Greatest Number

To find the maximum number of books, we need to find the greatest number out of the four given numbers.

Th	H	T	O
3	6	1	7

Th	H	T	O
2	4	5	8

Th	H	T	O
1	8	0	0

Th	H	T	O
3	0	9	9

First, check the digits in the thousands place. The greatest digit determines the greatest number.

The numbers 3617 and 3099 have 3 in the thousands place. The other two numbers (2458 and 1800) have smaller thousands digits (2 and 1, respectively).

Th	H	T	O
3	6	1	7

Th	H	T	O
3	0	9	9

Check the hundreds digits in the numbers 3617 and 3099.

Since 6 > 0, 3617 > 3099.

So, Vibha has the maximum number of books.

Finding the Smallest Number

To find the least number of books, we need to find the smallest number out of the four given numbers.

Th	H	T	O	Th	H	T	O	Th	H	T	O	Th	H	T	O
3	6	1	7	2	4	5	8	1	8	0	0	3	0	9	9

First, check the digits in the thousands place. The smallest digit determines the smallest number.

As 1 is the smallest digit, 1800 is the smallest number.

So, Sachin has the least number of books.

SOLVED EXAMPLES

Example 5: Find the greatest number among the following groups of numbers.

a. 5624 5639 5670 5681

b. 7358 7352 7356 7354

Solution a: In this case, the digits in the thousands and hundreds places are the same in all the numbers. So, check the digits in the tens place.

Th	H	T	O	Th	H	T	O	Th	H	T	O	Th	H	T	O
5	6	2	4	5	6	3	9	5	6	7	0	5	6	8	1

The greatest digit in the tens place determines the greatest number.

So, 5681 is the greatest number.

Solution b: Here, the digits in the thousands, hundreds and tens places are the same. So, check the digits in the ones place.

Th	H	T	O	Th	H	T	O	Th	H	T	O	Th	H	T	O
7	3	5	8	7	3	5	2	7	3	5	6	7	3	5	4

The greatest digit in the ones place determines the greatest number.

So, 7358 is the greatest number.

Example 6: Find the smallest number out of the given numbers.

6732 6815 6279 6485

Solution: In all the numbers, the digits in the thousands place are the same. So, we check the digits in the hundreds place.

Th	H	T	O	Th	H	T	O	Th	H	T	O	Th	H	T	O
6	7	3	2	6	8	1	5	6	2	7	9	6	4	8	5

So, the smallest number is 6279.

EXERCISE 1D

1. Compare the numbers. Write >, < or =.

   a. 46 ☐ 351 b. 2436 ☐ 999 c. 6384 ☐ 6329 d. 8901 ☐ 8901

2. Circle the greatest number out of the given numbers.

   a. 2854, 3179, 7264, 6543   b. 3192, 8407, 1889, 7108

3. Circle the smallest number out of the given numbers.

   a. 5329, 1001, 9214, 6372   b. 7128, 8593, 2105, 7469

Order of Numbers

Ascending Order

Ascending order means arranging numbers from the smallest to the greatest.

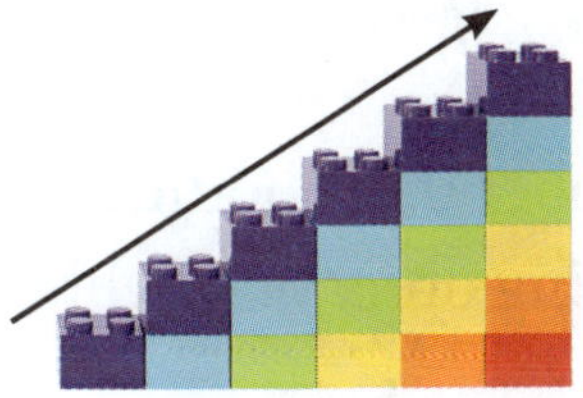

Descending Order

Descending order means arranging numbers from the greatest to the smallest.

To write numbers in **ascending order**, compare them and then write them from the smallest to the greatest.

Example 7: Arrange the following numbers in the ascending order.

5123   4709   8352   4627

Solution:

First, check the number of digits in each number. All the numbers have 4 digits.

Next, check the digits in the thousands place. The smallest digit determines the smallest number.

Here, 4627 and 4709 have the smallest digit in the thousands place, which is 4.

As 4709 and 4627 have the same digit (4) in the thousands place, we check the digits in the hundreds place.

Compare 4 7 0 9 and 4 6 2 7.

In the hundreds place, 6 < 7. So, 4627 becomes the smallest number and 4709 is the second greater number.

Now, compare the other two numbers 5 123 and 8 352. Here, 5 < 8.

So, the third greater number is 5123 and the greatest number is 8352.

③	②	④	①
5123,	4709,	8352,	4627

So, by arranging the numbers in ascending order, we get:

4627 < 4709 < 5123 < 8352

NOTE

Remember to write on top of each number its position to indicate their order, that is, increasing or decreasing.

Example 8: Arrange the following numbers in descending order.

1340, 8457, 6219, 9738

Solution:

First, check the number of digits of each number. All the numbers have 4 digits. Then, check the digits in the thousands place of all the numbers. 9738 has the greatest digit in the thousands place. So, it is the greatest number.

Looking at the thousands digits and arranging the numbers in descending order, we get:

①		②		③		④
9738	>	8457	>	6219	>	1340

MENTAL MATHS

1. Number these bottles in the ascending order of height.

____ ____ ____ ____

2. Number these pine trees in the descending order of height.

____ ____ ____ ____

FORMING THE GREATEST AND THE SMALLEST NUMBERS OUT OF THE GIVEN DIGITS

Samar has 4 cards. Each card has a digit on it. Help Samar make the greatest number out of these digits.

3	5	1	7

a. To form the **greatest number** out of these digits, write the greatest digit first, then the next greater digit and so on.

The greatest 4-digit number using the given digits is 7531.

7	5	3	1

b. To form the **smallest number** out of these digits, write the smallest digit first, then the next smaller digit and so on.

1	3	5	7

EVEN AND ODD NUMBERS

Even numbers are those numbers that can be paired completely.

4 is an even number.

Even numbers end with or have 0, 2, 4, 6 or 8 in their ones place.

Examples: 430, 6574, 2068

Odd numbers are those numbers that cannot be paired completely.

5 is an odd number.

Odd numbers end with or have 1, 3, 5, 7 or 9 in their ones place.

Examples: 431, 6575, 2067

COMMON ERRORS

Write the greatest and the smallest numbers with the following digits.

5, 8, 0, 3

Greatest number 8530

Smallest number: 0358 ✗

3058 ✓

A number never begins with a zero. Zero has no value at the beginning of a number. We start with the next smallest digit and then write 0.

DO YOU KNOW?

While counting numbers in sequence, even and odd numbers appear alternately.

Odd Odd Odd Odd

1 2 3 4 5 6 7...

Even Even Even

MENTAL MATHS

1. Smallest and largest numbers formed by 2, 8, 0, 6 are __________ and __________.
2. Is 342 an odd number? __________
3. Is 4408 an even number? __________

EXERCISE 1E

1. **Write each group of numbers in the ascending order.**

a. 9621	1580	7643	4891
b. 6432	2814	1782	5962
c. 2431	5143	3849	2058

2. **Write each group of numbers in the descending order.**

a. 7068	8726	7592	8251
b. 5728	4205	4816	6214
c. 9100	7640	7381	9432

3. **Write the greatest and the smallest numbers formed by the given digits.**

				Greatest	Smallest
a. 2,	8,	5,	4	________	________
b. 3,	9,	1,	0	________	________
c. 5,	3,	8,	2	________	________

4. **Write the last digit to make these numbers even.**

a.

Th	H	T	O
5	7	3	

b.

Th	H	T	O
6	1	4	

5. **Write the last digit to make these numbers odd.**

a.

Th	H	T	O
5	1	3	

b.

Th	H	T	O
7	0	8	

ROUNDING OFF NUMBERS

Rounding off a number is a method used when we do not know the exact number but come close to the actual number. This method helps us to do our calculations faster and easily.

For instance, if there are 18 children in a park, we can say that there are about 20 children in the park.

Let us learn how to round off a number to its nearest 10 or 100.

Rounding off Numbers to the Nearest 10

To round off a number to the nearest 10, we look at the digit at the ones place.

- If the digit at the ones place is less than 5 (i.e., 0, 1, 2, 3 or 4), we retain the tens digit as it is and change the ones digit to 0.
- If the digit at the ones place is equal to or greater than 5 (i.e., 5, 6, 7, 8 or 9), we add 1 to the tens digit and change the ones digit to 0.

Rules of rounding off to the nearest 10

Rounded down	Numbers from		Rounded up
0 ←	0 to 4	5 to 9	→ 10
10 ←	10 to 14	15 to 19	→ 20
20 ←	20 to 24	25 to 29	→ 30
30 ←	30 to 34	35 to 39	→ 40
40 ←	40 to 44	45 to 49	→ 50
50 ←	50 to 54	55 to 59	→ 60
60 ←	60 to 64	65 to 69	→ 70
70 ←	70 to 74	75 to 79	→ 80
80 ←	80 to 84	85 to 89	→ 90
90 ←	90 to 94	95 to 99	→ 100

This can also be explained on a number line.

Let us round off the number 33 to the nearest 10 using the number line.

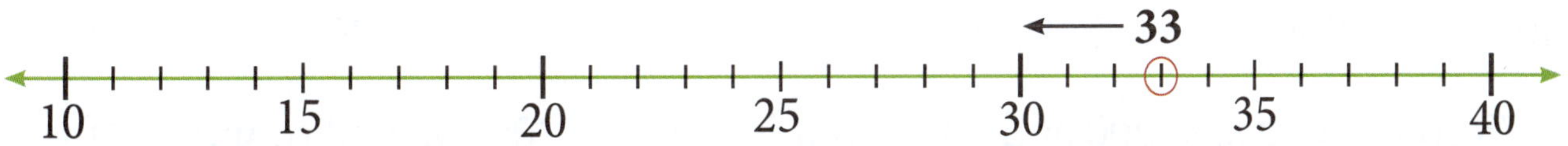

As 33 comes between 30 and 40 and it is more closer to 30 than 40. So, we will round it off to 30.

Rounding off Numbers to the Nearest 100

To round off a number to the nearest 100, we look at the digit at the tens place.

- If the digit at the tens place is less than 5 (i.e., 0, 1, 2, 3 or 4), we retain the hundreds digit as it is and change the tens and ones digits to 0.
- If the digit at the tens place is equal to or greater than 5 (i.e., 5, 6, 7, 8 or 9), we add 1 to the hundreds digit and change the tens and ones digits to 0.

Rules of rounding off to the nearest 100

Rounded down	Numbers from		Rounded up
0 ←	0 to 49	50 to 99	→ 100
100 ←	100 to 149	150 to 199	→ 200
200 ←	200 to 249	250 to 299	→ 300
300 ←	300 to 349	350 to 399	→ 400
400 ←	400 to 449	450 to 499	→ 500
500 ←	500 to 549	550 to 599	→ 600
600 ←	600 to 649	650 to 699	→ 700
700 ←	700 to 749	750 to 799	→ 800
800 ←	800 to 849	850 to 899	→ 900
900 ←	900 to 949	950 to 999	→ 1000

Consider the number 278 and round it off to the nearest 100 using the number line.

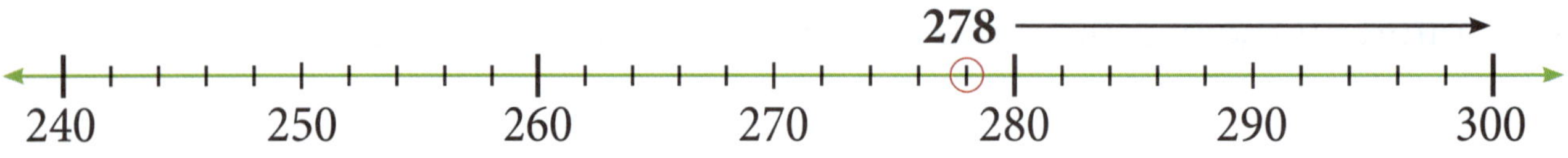

As 278 comes between 200 and 300 and it is closer to 300, we will round it off to 300.

SOLVED EXAMPLES

Example 9: Round off the following numbers to the nearest 10.

Solution:

a. 11 → 10 b. 28 → 30 c. 32 → 30
d. 52 → 50 e. 69 → 70

Example 10: Round off the following numbers to the nearest 100.

Solution:

a. 125 → 100 b. 172 → 200 c. 236 → 200
d. 294 → 300 e. 307 → 300

EXERCISE 1F

1. **Round off the following numbers to the nearest 10.**

   a. 625 _______ b. 421 _______

   c. 5346 _______ d. 8579 _______

2. **Round off the following numbers to the nearest 100.**

   a. 542 _______ b. 1643 _______

   c. 6089 _______ d. 7132 _______

PUZZLE!

1. On sports day, the students were given numbers before the race. The numbers were stuck to their T-shirts.

They were asked to stand in ascending order from left to right according to their number. Write down the names of the students in that order.

2. Given below are some famous personalities and their year of birth. Identify them and write their names in the descending order of the year of their birth.

1869 1910 1889 1931 1929

Maths Lab Activity

21 CS Critical Thinking AI

Aim: To identify a number as an even number or an odd number.

Materials required: Beads or buttons, a sheet of paper, glue

Procedure:

1. Stick some buttons on a sheet of paper.
2. Circle the buttons in pairs as shown. What do you observe?
3. Now, count and write the number of buttons on the sheet. __________
4. Is there any unpaired button? __________
5. Is the total number of buttons even or odd? __________

What do you observe?

If all the buttons cannot be paired completely, one button is left unpaired. This means that the total number of buttons collected is an odd number. If it was an even number, all the buttons would have been paired completely.

Try pairing up 14 buttons. You will find that all the buttons get paired up successfully.

Concept Map

Numbers up to 10,000

- Read and write 4-digit numbers
  - Place value
    Face value
  - Number names
    Numerals
    Expanded form
  - Comparing numbers
    - greatest and smallest numbers
    - ascending and descending order
- Even numbers: 246, 6530
  Odd numbers: 245, 6531
- Rounding off to
  - nearest 10
  - nearest 100

Key Concepts

- **Thousands:** Refers to the thousands place value in 4-digit numbers
- **Place Value:** The value indicating the position or place of a digit in a number
- **Face Value:** The number itself
- **Successor:** The next number
- **Predecessor:** The previous number
- **Rounding Off:** Estimating a number close to the actual number

Chapter Revision

A. Choose the correct answer.

1. The greatest number out of the following.
   a. 5968 b. 1296 c. 9897 d. 3604
2. The smallest number out of the following.
   a. 9108 b. 1563 c. 4706 d. 1547
3. The even number out of the following.
   a. 7563 b. 2466 c. 1281 d. 5127
4. The odd number out of the following.
   a. 1052 b. 4843 c. 2006 d. 8154

B. Write the number represented by the following.

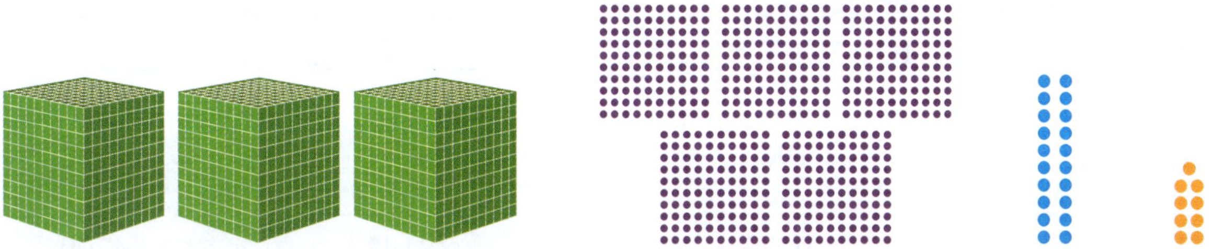

Thousands **Hundreds** **Tens** **Ones**

__________ __________ ____ ____

Number name: ______________________________________

Expanded form: ______ thousands ______ hundreds ______ tens ______ ones

or

__________ + __________ + __________ + __________

C. Write the next four numbers.

1. 3591, __________, __________, __________, __________
2. 2763, __________, __________, __________, __________
3. 6747, __________, __________, __________, __________
4. 8003, __________, __________, __________, __________

D. Write the number names for the following.

1. 7329: ______________________________________
2. 1468: ______________________________________
3. 3214: ______________________________________
4. 8352: ______________________________________

E. Write the numerals for the following number names.

1. Four thousand thirteen __________
2. Seven thousand six __________

3. Two thousand eight hundred ninety-three ____________
4. Five thousand seven hundred forty-two ____________

F. Fill in the blanks.

1. The successor of 3592 is ____________.
2. The predecessor of 9280 is ____________.
3. The greatest 4-digit number is ____________.
4. The place value of 6 in 3658 is ____________.
5. The face value of 6 in 6003 is ____________.

G. Write >, < or =.

1. 5964 ☐ 2135 2. 6192 ☐ 6192 3. 1935 ☐ 1972

H. Write the next four numbers as per the instructions.

1. Counting in 10s: 2430, _______, _______, _______, _______
2. Counting in 100s: 1295, _______, _______, _______, _______
3. Counting in 1000s: 3947, _______, _______, _______, _______

I. Write the following in the ascending order.

1. 3425 1960 8237 9054
____________, ____________, ____________, ____________
2. 1673 9046 8153 4700
____________, ____________, ____________, ____________
3. 7140 1542 6208 9873
____________, ____________, ____________, ____________

J. Write the following in the descending order.

1. 2064 8471 9300 6702
____________, ____________, ____________, ____________
2. 6400 5710 9876 3498
____________, ____________, ____________, ____________
3. 4382 3420 5921 3596
____________, ____________, ____________, ____________

K. Write the greatest and the smallest numbers formed by the given digits.

	Greatest	Smallest
1. 7, 9, 6, 3	__________	__________
2. 5, 8, 4, 1	__________	__________
3. 2, 0, 4, 7	__________	__________

L. Round off the given numbers to the nearest 10 and 100.

	Nearest 10	Nearest 100
1. 6504	__________	__________
2. 1703	__________	__________
3. 9909	__________	__________

Skill up!

A. 21 CS Critical Thinking, Information Literacy

Activity to revise ordinal numbers, greatest/smallest and odd/even numbers:

1. Take a notebook and a pencil. Make a table with three columns in your notebook. In the first column, write down the mobile numbers of any 4 family members. In the second column, note down the 1st, 3rd, 5th and 7th digits of each number.

   In the last column, note down the 2nd, 4th, 6th and 8th digits of each number.
2. Draw a second table with two columns. In the first column, write the greatest number formed using the digits of the second column of the first table.

   In the second column, write the smallest number formed using the digits of the third column of the first table.
3. Also, find out the following:
   a. How many numbers are odd?
   b. How many numbers are even?

B. 21 CS Critical Thinking, Life Skills CC Integration with Science HQ Coexisting with Nature

In a forest fire, 4200 trees got burned down. How many trees should be planted so that there can be 100 more trees? Find out what causes such fires and what measures can be taken to prevent them.

13 CLIMATE ACTION

15 LIFE ON LAND

C. 21 CS Critical Thinking HQ Knowing my Needs

8 DECENT WORK AND ECONOMIC GROWTH

11 SUSTAINABLE CITIES AND COMMUNITIES

Village A has 9010 people.
Village B has 9012 people.
Which village has more people?
Twelve people from village B moved to a city. Which village will have more people? Have you ever thought why people move from villages to cities?

SUSTAINABLE DEVELOPMENT GOALS

Question B is in line with SDG 13 Climate Action and SDG 15 Life on Land. Find out the importance of trees with respect to climate change and life on land.

Question C is in line with SDG 8 Decent Work and Economic Growth and SDG 11 Sustainable Cities and Communities.

Worksheet 1

21 CS Critical Thinking, Information Literacy AI

Look at the numbers given here. Colour the objects by following the instructions given.

1. **Red:** if there is a 7 in the hundreds place.
2. **Orange:** if there is a 0 in the ones place.
3. **Blue:** if there is a 3-digit number with all 3 digits < 5.
4. **Brown:** if there is a 5 in the thousands place.
5. **Yellow:** if the number has the smallest 4-digit number among all the given numbers.
6. **Purple:** if any object, with number on it, is left to be coloured.

2 Addition of Numbers

Learning Objectives

- To add two or three 3-digit numbers with and without regrouping
- To add two or three 4-digit numbers with and without regrouping
- To solve word problems on addition
- To estimate the sum of two numbers

Let's Get Started

21 CS Creativity and Innovation, Collaboration | EL | HQ Happiness My Goal

For the Annual School Fair, students were asked to put up stalls. The fair was for two days.

The following is a list of stalls put up by 3 students – Sachin, Farzana and Jamie – along with the number of items sold by them on each day.

Students and their stalls	Number of items sold	
	Day 1	Day 2
Sachin – Ice cream stall	75	95
Farzana – Toy stall	80	105
Jamie – Cupcake stall	110	150

a. What is the total number of items sold by each student?

Sachin ____________

Farzana ____________

Jamie ____________

b. Who sold the maximum number of items? ____________

We learnt the addition of 2-digit numbers with and without regrouping in the previous class. Let us revise that using a few examples.

Example 1: Find the sum of 45, 11 and 22.

Solution:

Step 1: First, write the numbers vertically under appropriate columns; in this case, ones and tens columns.

	T	O
	4	5
	1	1
+	2	2

Step 2: Add the digits in the ones column first and then in the tens column.

	T	O
	4	5
	1	1
+	2	2
	7	8

So, 45 + 11 + 22 = 78.

Example 2: Add 78 and 13. Regroup if required.

Solution:

Step 1: Write the numbers vertically. Add the digits in the ones column.

	T	O
	1	
	7	8
+	1	3
		1

8 + 3 = 11
Write '1' of 11 in the ones column and carry forward the other '1' to the tens column. Write this 1 above 7 in the tens column.

Step 2: Now, add the digits in the tens column.

	T	O
	1	
	7	8
+	1	3
	9	1

7 + 1 + 1 (carried forward) = 9

So, 78 + 13 = 91.

NOTE

Addition Facts:

- When we add 0 to a number, the answer is the number itself; that is, the value of the number does not change.
  Example: 56 + 0 = 56
- When we add 1 to a number, the answer is 1 more than the number.
  Example: 72 + 1 = 73
- In addition, we can add the numbers in any order. The order does not affect the answer. This property is called the commutative property of addition.
  Example: 36 + 3 = 3 + 36 = 39

ADDITION OF 3-DIGIT NUMBERS WITHOUT REGROUPING

Now, we will learn to add 3-digit numbers. Let us understand this through a few examples.

Addition of 3-Digit and 2-Digit Numbers

Example 3: Add 256 and 13.

Solution:

Step 1: Write the numbers vertically as shown below.

	H	T	O
	2	5	6
+		1	3

Step 2: Add the digits in ones, tens and hundreds columns.

	H	T	O
	2	5	6
+		1	3
	2	6	9

The hundreds column has the digit 2 only. So, we write 2 in the hundreds place of the answer.

Thus, 256 + 13 = 269.

Addition of Two 3-Digit Numbers

Example 4: Add 413 and 265.

Solution:

Step 1: Write the numbers vertically. Add the digits in the ones column.
3 + 5 = 8
Write 8 below 5.

	H	T	O
	4	1	3
+	2	6	5
			8

Step 2: Next, add the digits in the tens column.
1 + 6 = 7
Write 7 below 6.

	H	T	O
	4	1	3
+	2	6	5
		7	8

Step 3: Now, add the digits in the hundreds column.
4 + 2 = 6
Write 6 below 2.

	H	T	O
	4	1	3
+	2	6	5
	6	7	8

Thus, 413 + 265 = 678.

> **COMMON ERRORS**
>
> Add 256 and 13.
>
> | | H | T | O |
> |---|---|---|---|
> | | 2 | 5 | 6 |
> | + | 1 | 3 | |
>
> | | H | T | O |
> |---|---|---|---|
> | | 2 | 5 | 6 |
> | + | | 1 | 3 |
>
> Always start writing the numbers from the ones column and move towards the left.

Example 5: Add 728 and 251.

Solution:

	H	T	O
	7	2	8
+	2	5	1
	9	7	9

728 + 251 = 979

> **COMMON ERRORS**
>
> Add 143 and 206.
>
> | | H | T | O |
> |---|---|---|---|
> | | 3 | 4 | 1 |
> | + | 6 | 0 | 2 |
>
> | | H | T | O |
> |---|---|---|---|
> | | 1 | 4 | 3 |
> | + | 2 | 0 | 6 |
>
> Always write the digit on the extreme right under the ones and then move towards the left.

Exercise 2A

Add the following.

1.

	H	T	O
	6	1	3
+		2	4

2.

	H	T	O
	8	3	5
+		2	1

3.

	H	T	O
	2	1	4
+	7	5	3

4.

	H	T	O
	5	2	6
+	3	4	1

Addition of Three 3-Digit Numbers

The addition of three 3-digit numbers is done in the same way as the addition of two 3-digit numbers. Look at the following examples.

Example 6: Add 135, 212 and 321.

Solution:

	H	T	O
	1	3	5
	2	1	2
+	3	2	1
	6	6	8

Columns:
Ones: 5 + 2 + 1 = 8
Tens: 3 + 1 + 2 = 6
Hundreds: 1 + 2 + 3 = 6

Thus, 135 + 212 + 321 = 668.

Example 7: Add 210, 548 and 141.

Solution:

	H	T	O
	2	1	0
	5	4	8
+	1	4	1
	8	9	9

Thus, 210 + 548 + 141 = 899.

Exercise 2B

Find the sum of the following.

1.

	H	T	O
	3	2	1
	4	0	3
+	1	5	1

2.

	H	T	O
	5	3	6
	2	4	1
+	1	1	2

3.

	H	T	O
	7	5	2
	1	0	0
+	1	2	1

4.

	H	T	O
	6	4	3
	2	1	2
+	1	1	3

Mental Maths

If 3 + 1= 4 and 30 + 10 = 40, then add the following.

	T	O
	2	0
+	1	0

	T	O
	4	0
	2	0
+	1	0

	H	T	O
	3	0	0
+	5	0	0

	H	T	O
	1	0	0
	6	0	0
+	2	0	0

ADDITION OF 3-DIGIT NUMBERS WITH REGROUPING

NOTE

Regrouping means when we split the sum obtained and move one of the two digits to the column on the left. In other words, **regrouping** is done when the sum of two or three single digits is a two-digit number. Then, we keep one digit in that column and carry forward the other digit to the column on the left.

Carry forward means to move a digit of the sum to the next column on the left.

Regrouping From Ones to Tens

Let us now learn how to add 3-digit numbers with regrouping from ones to tens by simplifying the following examples.

Example 8: Add 207, 138 and 213.

Solution:

Step 1: Write the numbers vertically first. Add the digits in the ones column.

7 + 8 + 3 = 18. Write '8' of 18 under 3 in the ones column and carry forward '1'. Write 1 above 0 in the tens column.

	H	T	O
		1	
	2	0	7
	1	3	8
+	2	1	3
			8

Step 2: Add the digits in the tens column.

0 + 3 + 1 + 1 (carried forward) = 5. Write 5 under 1 in the tens column.

	H	T	O
		1	
	2	0	7
	1	3	8
+	2	1	3
		5	8

Step 3: Add the digits in the hundreds column.

2 + 1 + 2 = 5 . Write 5 under 2 in the hundreds column.

	H	T	O
		1	
	2	0	7
	1	3	8
+	2	1	3
	5	5	8

Thus, 207 + 138 + 213 = 558.

EXERCISE 2C

Add the following.

1.

	H	T	O
	3	1	5
	2	2	4
+	4	1	3

2.

	H	T	O
	1	7	9
	2	0	3
+	1	1	4

3.

	H	T	O
	2	5	6
	1	3	4
+	4	0	3

4.

	H	T	O
	1	2	8
	2	0	5
+	3	6	1

Regrouping From Tens to Hundreds

Example 9: On Sunday, 143 people went to the town fair by cars and 295 people went by buses. What is the total number of people who went by cars and buses?

Solution:

		H	T	O
		1		
People by cars		1	4	3
People by buses	+	2	9	5
		4	3	8

Ones column: 3 + 5 = 8
Tens column: 4 + 9 = 13
Write 3 in the tens column and carry forward 1 to the hundreds column.
Hundreds column:
1 + 2 + 1 (carried forward) = 4

Thus, the total number of people who went by cars and buses is 438.

Regrouping Hundreds

Example 10: There are 723 students in School A and 546 students in School B. What is the total number of students in both the schools?

Solution:

		Th	H	T	O
School A			7	2	3
School B	+		5	4	6
		1	2	6	9

Ones column: 3 + 6 = 9
Tens column: 2 + 4 = 6
Hundreds column: 7 + 5 = 12
Write 1 in the thousands column.

Thus, the total number of students is 1269.

Regrouping From Ones to Tens to Hundreds

Example 11: A bookseller sold 297 books in the first week and 186 books in the second week. How many books did he sell in both the weeks?

Solution:

		H	T	O
		1	1	
First week		2	9	7
Second week	+	1	8	6
		4	8	3

Ones column: 7 + 6 = **13**
Carry forward **1** to the tens column.
Tens column: 9 + 8 + 1 (carried forward) = **18**
Carry forward **1** to the hundreds column.
Hundreds column: 2 + 1 + 1 (carried forward) = 4

Thus, the bookseller sold 483 books.

Regrouping Ones, Tens and Hundreds

Example 12: Add 235, 168 and 721.

Solution:

We write the sum as:

	Th	H	T	O
		1	1	
		2	3	5
		1	6	8
+		7	2	1
	1	1	2	4

Ones column: 5 + 8 + 1 = **14**
Carry forward **1** to the tens column.
Tens column: 3 + 6 + 2 + 1 (carried forward) = **12**
Carry forward **1** to the hundreds column.
Hundreds column: 2 + 1 + 7 + 1 (carried forward) = **11**
Write **1** in the thousands column.

Thus, 235 + 168 + 721 = 1124.

Exercise 2D

Add the following.

1.

	H	T	O
	2	4	6
	1	8	3
+	3	2	5

2.

	H	T	O
	1	7	3
	3	2	5
+	4	1	4

3.

	H	T	O
	2	3	9
	1	7	4
+	3	0	5

4.

	H	T	O
	4	2	8
	1	7	2
+	2	3	5

ADDITION OF 4-DIGIT NUMBERS WITHOUT REGROUPING

We add 4-digit numbers in the same way as 3-digit numbers.

Example 13: 2564 + 3125

Solution:

	Th	H	T	O
	2	5	6	4
+	3	1	2	5
	5	6	8	9

Ones column: 4 + 5 = 9
Tens column: 6 + 2 = 8
Hundreds column: 5 + 1 = 6
Thousands column: 2 + 3 = 5

Thus, 2564 + 3125 = 5689.

Mental Maths

What is the total of these numbers?

100 + 5000 + 3000

____

Example 14: 1624 + 2130 + 5201

Solution:

	Th	H	T	O
	1	6	2	4
	2	1	3	0
+	5	2	0	1
	8	9	5	5

Ones column: 4 + 0 + 1 = 5
Tens column: 2 + 3 + 0 = 5
Hundreds column: 6 + 1 + 2 = 9
Thousands column: 1 + 2 + 5 = 8

Thus, 1624 + 2130 + 5201 = 8955.

ADDITION OF 4-DIGIT NUMBERS WITH REGROUPING

We have already learnt to add 2-digit and 3-digit numbers with regrouping (carrying). We use the same method to add 4-digit numbers.

Example 15: 2563 + 1785 + 3916

Solution:

	Th	H	T	O
	2	1	1	
	2	5	6	3
	1	7	8	5
+	3	9	1	6
	8	2	6	4

Write the numbers vertically and add the digits.
Ones column: 3 + 5 + 6 = **14**
Carry forward **1** to the tens column.
Tens column: 6 + 8 + 1 + 1 (carried forward) = **16**
Carry forward **1** to the hundreds column.
Hundreds column: 5 + 7 + 9 + 1 (carried forward) = **22**
Carry forward **2** to the thousands column.
Thousands column: 2 + 1 + 3 + 2 (carried forward) = 8

Thus, 2563 + 1785 + 3916 = 8264.

EXERCISE 2E

Find the sum.

1.

	Th	H	T	O
	2	5	8	4
+	6	0	1	4

2.

	Th	H	T	O
	3	7	5	6
+	2	2	9	8

3.

	Th	H	T	O
	1	5	7	9
	2	4	8	6
+	1	3	6	5

4.

	Th	H	T	O
	1	9	3	6
	2	0	5	4
+	3	7	2	8

WORD PROBLEMS

We add when:

- A quantity increases by the amount given.
- We need to find the sum or total.

Let us look at a few examples.

Go Easy!

Look out for the **addition words** to solve word problems easily: sum, altogether, all, in all, together, total, total number, add, increase, increased by, more than, etc.

Example 16: In a sports club, 158 children like to play cricket and 143 children like to play tennis. How many children like to play cricket and tennis?

Solution:

		H	T	O
		1	1	
Cricket =		1	5	8
Tennis =	+	1	4	3
		3	0	1

Thus, 301 children like to play cricket and tennis.

Example 17: A car manufacturing company sold 185 cars in January, 246 cars in February and 314 cars in March. What is the total number of cars sold in these three months?

Solution:

		H	T	O
		1	1	
Cars sold in January =		1	8	5
Cars sold in February =		2	4	6
Cars sold in March =	+	3	1	4
		7	4	5

Thus, the company sold 745 cars in these three months.

EXERCISE 2F

Solve the following word problems.

1. 243 people went to see a flower show on Monday and 125 people went to see the show on Tuesday. How many people went to see the flower show on Monday and Tuesday?

		H	T	O
Monday =				
Tuesday =	+			

_____________ people went to see the flower show on Monday and Tuesday.

2. Ajoy has 138 orange marbles, 264 green marbles and 321 blue marbles. What is the total number of marbles with Ajoy?

		H	T	O
Orange marbles =				
Green marbles =				
Blue marbles =	+			

The total number of marbles with Ajoy is _____________.

3. Deep had ₹1035. His father gave him ₹418 more. How much money does Deep have now?

		Th	H	T	O
Money with Deep =					
Money given by father =	+				

Deep has ₹ _____________ now.

4. 246 people went to the movie hall on Monday, 135 people went on Tuesday and 324 people went on Wednesday. What is the total number of people who went to the movie hall on these three days?

	Th	H	T	O
Monday =				
Tuesday =				
Wednesday = +				

____________ people went to the movie hall on these three days.

ESTIMATION

Estimation is a method used when we do not know the exact value, but we guess a value reasonably close to it. Estimation is done by rounding off numbers, which we learnt in Chapter 1. We learnt to round off numbers to the nearest 10 or 100.

NOTE

Rounding off is a type of estimation.

Estimating the Sum of Two Numbers

To estimate the sum of two numbers, we round off the numbers to their estimated value and then add them.

SOLVED EXAMPLES

Example 18: Estimate the sum of 19 and 7 to the nearest 10.

Solution: Rounding off 19 to the nearest 10 gives 20.

Rounding off 7 to the nearest 10 gives 10.

	T	O
	2	0
+	1	0
	3	0

Estimated sum: 30

Actual sum:

	T	O
	1	
	1	9
+		7
	2	6

26 is quite close to the estimated value 30.

Example 19: Estimate the sum of 891 and 116 to the nearest 100.

Solution: Rounding off 891 to the nearest 100 gives 900.

Rounding off 116 to the nearest 100 gives 100.

	Th	H	T	O
		9	0	0
+		1	0	0
	1	0	0	0

Estimated sum: 1000

Actual sum:

	Th	H	T	O
		1		
		8	9	1
+		1	1	6
	1	0	0	7

1007 is quite close to the estimated value 1000.

MENTAL COMPUTATION OF SUM OF 2-DIGIT AND 3-DIGIT NUMBERS

To quickly add two 2-digit or 3-digit numbers, we first write the expanded form of the numbers and then add them.

Example 20: Add 25 and 36.

Solution:

25 + 36
= 20 + 5 + 30 + 6
= (20 + 30) + (5 + 6)
= 50 + 11
= 61

Thus, 25 + 36 = 61.

Steps:

1. Write the expanded form of both the numbers.
2. Add the tens separately and the ones separately.
3. Add the two sums.

Check:

	T	O
	1	
	2	5
+	3	6
	6	1

Example 21: Add 357 and 124.

Solution:

357 + 124
= 300 + 50 + 7 + 100 + 20 + 4
= (300 + 100) + (50 + 20) + (7 + 4)
= 400 + 70 + 11
= 400 + 81 = 481

Thus, 357 + 124 = 481.

Check:

	H	T	O
		1	
	3	5	7
+	1	2	4
	4	8	1

EXERCISE 2G

1. **Estimate the sums to the nearest 10.**

 a. 15 + 8 b. 25 + 18 c. 38 + 22 d. 45 + 37

2. **Estimate the sums to the nearest 100.**

 a. 765 + 112 b. 354 + 211 c. 159 + 130 d. 145 + 121

DO YOU KNOW?

There are 14 mountains in the world, with a height of over 8000 metres and are known as the Eight-thousanders. Following are a few among that list:

- Mount Everest - 8849 m
- Kangchenjunga - 8586 m (highest in India)
- Nanga Parbat - 8126 m
- K2 - 8611 m
- Lhotse - 8516 m
- Annapurna - 8091 m

PUZZLE!

Fill in the Christmas trees. Each number is the sum of the two numbers below it. One has been done for you.

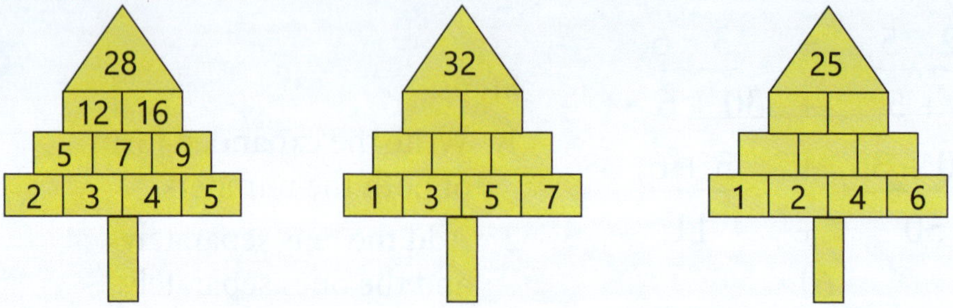

MATHS LAB ACTIVITY

21 CS Critical Thinking, Collaboration AI

Aim: To reinforce the concept of addition with regrouping using coloured stars.

Materials required: Stars of different colours (red, blue, green, etc.), a chart paper and a pen

Procedure: This can be performed as a group activity.

1. Let each group pick some stars of each colour, a chart paper and a pen.
   Each ★ (red) is equal to a hundred. Each ★ (blue) is equal to a ten. Each ★ (green) is equal to a one.
2. Now, on a chart paper make a table as shown.

   Consider the sum 293 + 148. To add the two numbers, put the stars in the correct columns as shown. Then, add the stars under each column separately.

Number	Hundreds	Tens	Ones
293	★★	★★★★★★★★★	★★★
148	★	★★★★	★★★★★★★★
Total	★★★ (which is equal to 3 hundreds or 300)	★★★★★★★★★★★★★ (which is equal to 13 tens or 130)	★★★★★★★★★★★ (which is equal to 11 ones or 11)

3. Start with the ones column. As **10 ones = 1 ten**, remove 10 green stars and add 1 blue star to the tens column. Now, we have 14 blue stars and 1 green star.

Hundreds	Tens	Ones
★★★	★★★★★★★★★★★★★★	★~~★★★★★★★★★★~~

Add 1 ★ star

4. In the tens column, as **10 tens = 1 hundred**, remove 10 blue stars and add 1 red star to the hundreds column. Now, we have 4 blue stars and 4 red stars.

Hundreds	Tens	Ones
★★★	~~★★★★★★★★★★~~★★★★	★

Add 1 ★ star

5. Your chart will look like this.

Hundreds	Tens	Ones
★★★★	★★★★	★

This gives you the answer as 441.

Try adding more 3-digit numbers using this activity and 4-digit numbers as well.

Concept Map

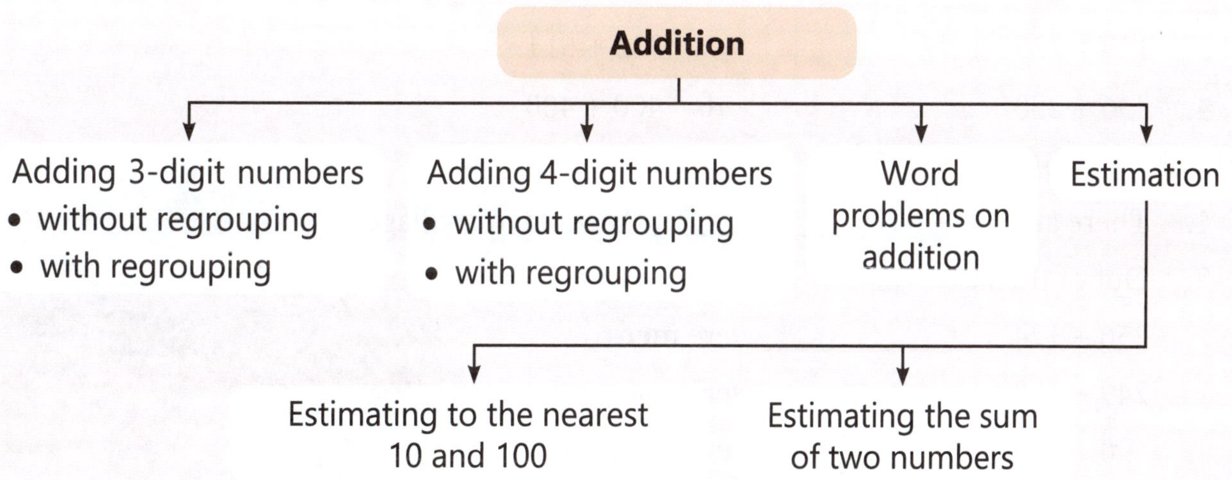

Key Concepts

- **Addition:** When we combine two or more numbers, the result we get is called the sum
- **Regrouping:** When the sum is a 2-digit number, then we split the digits and carry forward one of the digits to the place value on the left
- **Estimation:** When we do not know the exact answer but guess a number reasonably close to it

A. Write T for True and F for False.

1. 200 + 300 = 700
2. 529 + 246 = 775
3. 314 + 598 = 813
4. 2051 + 3101 = 5002

B. Match the following.

	Column A		Column B
1.	520 + 416	a.	293 + 161
2.	200 + 600	b.	514 + 172
3.	129 + 325	c.	322 + 614
4.	436 + 250	d.	400 + 400

C. Fill in the blanks.

1. There are 300 + 649 = ____________ people in a village.
2. Out of them,

256 + 124 = ____________ were men.

249 + 150 = ____________ were women.

90 + 80 = ____________ were children.

D. Add the following.

1.

	H	T	O
	5	3	4
+	2	1	2

2.

	H	T	O
	9	3	2
+		4	1

3.

	H	T	O
	5	0	0
+	3	0	0

4.

	H	T	O
	4	2	0
	1	1	5
+	3	1	2

5.

	H	T	O
	2	2	5
	2	1	7
+	3	4	3

6.

	H	T	O
	1	0	3
	2	1	5
+	3	4	0

7.

	Th	H	T	O
	2	5	9	4
	3	4	7	8
+		1	5	6

8.

	Th	H	T	O
	4	3	2	8
	1	6	7	5
+	2	5	9	4

9.

	Th	H	T	O
	2	5	6	2
	1	4	2	4
+	3	0	0	6

E. Answer the following.

1. There are 246 tables and 178 chairs in a school. What is the total number of tables and chairs in the school?

		H	T	O
Tables =				
Chairs =	+			

The total number of tables and chairs is ____________.

2. In a rose garden, there are 368 plants of red roses and 273 plants of pink roses. How many rose plants are there in all?

		H	T	O
Red roses =				
Pink roses =	+			

There are ____________ rose plants in all.

3. A shop sold 342 T-shirts in January, 169 T-shirts in February and 273 T-shirts in March. What is the total number of T-shirts that the shop sold in these three months?

		H	T	O
January =				
February =				
March =	+			

The total number of T-shirts sold is ____________.

4. A baker sold 1025 loaves of bread in the first month and 929 loaves in the second month. How many loaves of bread did he sell in the two months?

		Th	H	T	O
First month =					
Second month =	+				

He sold ____________ loaves of bread in the two months.

Skill up!

A. 21 CS Collaboration, Communication | EL | AI

Let the students make 3 cards each for digits from 0 to 9. Place the cards upside down. Make two teams. Let each team take out 2 sets of 3 cards each. These cards will make two 3-digit numbers. Let each team add their two numbers. The team that gets a greater sum wins!

1	2	3
4	5	6
7	8	9
	0	

Team A

	H	T	O
	1	1	
	2	4	8
+	1	5	3
	4	0	1

Team B

	H	T	O
	1		
	3	1	5
+	2	9	4
	6	0	9

Team B will win because

609 > 401

B. 21 CS Critical Thinking, Life Skills | CC Integration with Science and Physical Education | HQ Harmony in the Self

3 GOOD HEALTH AND WELL-BEING

The total number of bones in a human body is 206. The total number of muscles in a human body is about 650.

What is the total number of bones and muscles in the human body? Is it important to play games and to exercise? Why?

C. 21 CS Critical Thinking

Alladin found a chest of treasure which had a number lock. He found a sheet of paper which gave hints to find the code for the number lock.
Can you help Alladin to find the code?

Unlock the code!!

1. The first digit is 1 less than 3.
2. The second digit is double of the first digit.
3. The sum of all the three digits is 12.

SUSTAINABLE DEVELOPMENT GOALS

Question B is in line with SDG 3 Good Health and Well-Being. How important is it to be in good health? How can you ensure you have a healthy life?

WORKSHEET 2

21 CS Critical Thinking, Information Literacy

Find the right route!

Neel plans to meet his friends at a park. The path to meet them has two routes. Each path has wooden boards with addition problems and number boards with some numbers.

Step 1: First, solve all the sums given on each wooden board along the two paths.

Step 2: Observe that the number board at each crossing bears a few numbers.

Step 3: If the sums found in Step 1 matches with the numbers on the number boards at each crossing, then take a left, else take a right.

Step 4: Draw the path to meet Neel's friends.

3 Subtraction of Numbers

Learning Objectives

- To subtract 3- and 4-digit numbers with and without regrouping
- To solve word problems on subtraction
- To solve word problems involving both addition and subtraction
- To frame word problems
- To estimate the difference between two numbers

Let's Get Started

21 CS Critical Thinking, Life Skills HQ Understanding Values in Relationships

Anshika had a birthday party at her home. Her parents ordered 65 doughnuts, 125 sandwiches, 148 juice packets, 75 pastries and 115 samosas for the party. After the party was over, she realized that a lot of food was left. She decided to donate the extra food to charity. Help Anshika figure out how many food items she would be able to donate.

1. During the party, 63 doughnuts, 102 sandwiches, 118 juice packets, 74 pastries and 100 samosas were eaten. How many items were left?

   Doughnuts: ________ Sandwiches: ________ Juice packets: ________

   Pastries: ________ Samosas: ________

2. Name the food items that you think Anshika would be able to donate.

   ____

SUBTRACTION OF 3-DIGIT NUMBERS

In Class 2, we learnt subtraction involving 2- and 3-digit numbers, without and with regrouping (or borrowing). Let us recall using some examples.

Without Regrouping (Borrowing)

Example 1: Subtract 14 from 356.

Solution:

Step 1: Write the two numbers vertically under appropriate columns according to their place value. Then, subtract the digits in the ones column.

	H	T	O
	3	5	6
–		1	4
			2

Write the greater number first followed by the smaller number.

Ones column: 6 – 4 = 2

Write 2 below 4.

Step 2: Subtract the digits in the tens and hundreds columns.

	H	T	O
	3	5	6
–		1	4
	3	4	2

Tens column: 5 – 1 = 4

Hundreds column: As there is no digit to be subtracted from 3, write 3 in the hundreds place of the answer.

So, 356 – 14 = 342.

Go Easy!

More Ways of Subtracting Numbers

There are some quick ways to subtract numbers. Look at the following example.

Example: Anjali and her friends were doing Maths homework together. They were trying different methods to subtract 29 from 67 quickly. Take a look at the methods used by them.

Method 1

67 – 29 (Split the smaller number into tens and ones)

20 9

67 – 20 = 47

47 – 9 = 38

Method 2

67 – 29 (Split the greater number into tens and ones)

60 7

60 – 29 = 31

31 + 7 = 38

Method 3

67 – 29 (Round off the smaller number to the nearest 10)

30

67 – 30 = 37

37 + 1 = 38

Note that though they used different methods to subtract the given numbers, the answer obtained in each case is the same.

NOTE

Subtraction Facts:

- When we subtract 0 from a number, the value of the number does not change.

  Example: 9 – 0 = 9; 425 – 0 = 425
- When we subtract 1 from a number, the answer is 1 less than the number.

  Example: 8 – 1 = 7; 984 – 1 = 983
- When we subtract a number from itself, the answer is always 0.

  Example: 5 – 5 = 0; 294 – 294 = 0

MENTAL MATHS

Subtract the following.

1. 629 – 0 = ____________
2. 714 – 1 = ____________
3. 385 – 385 = ____________

DO YOU KNOW?

Minus is a Latin word which means 'less'.

Johannes Widmann is believed to be the first person to use both plus and minus signs in his first printed book in 1489.

With Regrouping (Borrowing)

Regrouping From Tens to Ones

Example 2: Subtract 6 from 283.

Solution:

Step 1: Write the two numbers vertically, first the greater number followed by the smaller number.

	H	T	O
		7	13
	2	~~8~~	~~3~~
–			6
			7

Ones column: 3 < 6; borrow 1 ten from 8 tens in the tens column. So, 8 becomes 7 in the tens place and 3 becomes 13 in the ones place.

So, 13 – 6 = 7.

Step 2: Subtract the digits in the tens and hundreds columns.

	H	T	O
		7	13
	2	~~8~~	~~3~~
–			6
	2	7	7

Tens and hundreds columns: There are no numbers to be subtracted from 7 and 2. So, write 7 in the tens place and 2 in the hundreds place of the answer.

So, 283 – 6 = 277.

COMMON ERRORS

Subtract 6 from 283.

	H	T	O
			13
	2	8	~~3~~
–			6
	2	8	7

	H	T	O
		7	13
	2	~~8~~	~~3~~
–			6
	2	7	7

Subtract 14 from 365.

	H	T	O
		1	4
–	3	6	5

	H	T	O
	3	6	5
–		1	4

Regrouping From Hundreds to Tens

Example 3: Subtract 485 from 656.

Solution: Write the two numbers vertically, first the greater number, followed by the smaller number. Subtract the digits.

	H	T	O
	5	15	
	~~6~~	~~5~~	6
–	4	8	5
	1	7	1

Ones column: 6 – 5 = 1
Tens column: 5 < 8; borrow 1 hundred from 6 hundreds. 6 becomes 5 in the hundreds place and 5 becomes 15 in the tens place. So, 15 – 8 = 7.
Hundreds column: 5 – 4 = 1

Thus, 656 – 485 = 171.

COMMON ERRORS

Subtract 485 from 656.

	H	T	O
		15	
	6	~~5~~	6
–	4	8	5
	2	7	1

	H	T	O
	5	15	
	~~6~~	~~5~~	6
–	4	8	5
	1	7	1

Regrouping From Tens and Hundreds (Twice)

Example 4: Subtract 189 from 726.

Solution: Write the two numbers vertically, first the greater number followed by the smaller number. Subtract the digits.

	H	T	O
		11	
	6	~~1~~	16
	~~7~~	~~2~~	~~6~~
–	1	8	9
	5	3	7

Ones column: 6 < 9; borrow 1 ten from 2 tens. 2 becomes 1 in the tens place and 6 becomes 16 in the ones place. So, 16 – 9 = 7.
Tens column: 1 < 8; borrow 1 hundred from 7 hundreds. 7 becomes 6 in the hundreds place and 1 becomes 11 in the tens place. So, 11 – 8 = 3.
Hundreds column: 6 – 1 = 5

Thus, 726 – 189 = 537.

EXERCISE 3A

1. **Solve the following.**

a.

	T	O
	5	7
–	4	1

b.

	H	T	O
	6	9	5
–	2	1	0

c.

	H	T	O
	9	2	3
–	1	6	5

d.

	H	T	O
	4	7	1
–		8	6

2. **Out of 527 students in a school, 259 are boys. How many are girls?**

__________ students are girls.

SUBTRACTION OF 4-DIGIT NUMBERS

To subtract 4-digit numbers, we use the same method as used to subtract 3-digit numbers. Let us look at the following examples for a better understanding.

Without Regrouping (Borrowing)

Example 5: Find the difference between 8569 and 1241.

Solution: Write the two numbers vertically, with the greater number above the smaller number. Subtract the digits.

	Th	H	T	O
	8	5	6	9
–	1	2	4	1
	7	3	2	8

Ones column: 9 – 1 = 8
Tens column: 6 – 4 = 2
Hundreds column: 5 – 2 = 3
Thousands column: 8 – 1 = 7

Thus, 8569 – 1241 = 7328.

With Regrouping (Borrowing)

Regrouping From Tens to Ones

Example 6: Subtract 436 from 6954.

Solution: Write the two numbers vertically, with the greater number above the smaller number. Subtract the digits.

	Th	H	T	O
			4	14
	6	9	~~5~~	~~4~~
–		4	3	6
	6	5	1	8

Ones column: 4 < 6; borrow 1 ten from 5 tens. 5 becomes 4 in the tens place and 4 becomes 14 in the ones place. So, 14 – 6 = 8.
Tens column: 4 – 3 = 1
Hundreds column: 9 – 4 = 5
Thousands column: There is no digit to be subtracted from 6. Write 6 in the thousands place of the answer.

Thus, 6954 – 436 = 6518.

Regrouping From Hundreds to Tens

Example 7: Subtract 1393 from 2573.

Solution: Write the two numbers vertically, with the greater number above the smaller number. Subtract the digits.

	Th	H	T	O
		4	17	
	2	~~5~~	~~7~~	3
–	1	3	9	3
	1	1	8	0

Ones column: 3 – 3 = 0
Tens column: 7 < 9; borrow 1 hundred from 5 hundreds. 5 becomes 4 in the hundreds place and 7 becomes 17 in the tens place. So, 17 – 9 = 8.
Hundreds column: 4 – 3 = 1
Thousands column: 2 – 1 = 1

Thus, 2573 – 1393 = 1180.

Regrouping From Thousands to Hundreds

Example 8: Subtract 4911 from 5445.

Solution: Write the two numbers vertically, with the greater number above the smaller number. Subtract the digits.

	Th	H	T	O
	4	14		
	~~5~~	~~4~~	4	5
–	4	9	1	1
	0	5	3	4

Ones column: 5 – 1 = 4
Tens column: 4 – 1 = 3
Hundreds column: 4 < 9; borrow 1 thousand from 5 thousands. 5 becomes 4 in the thousands place and 4 becomes 14 in the hundreds place. So, 14 – 9 = 5.
Thousands column: 4 – 4 = 0

Thus, 5445 – 4911 = 534.

Regrouping From Tens, Hundreds and Thousands (Thrice)

Example 9: Subtract 1957 from 8326.

Solution: Write the two numbers vertically, with the greater number above the smaller number. Subtract the digits.

	Th	H	T	O
		12	11	
	7	~~2~~	~~1~~	16
	~~8~~	~~3~~	~~2~~	~~6~~
–	1	9	5	7
	6	3	6	9

Ones column: 6 < 7; borrow 1 ten from 2 tens. 2 becomes 1 in the tens place and 6 becomes 16 in the ones place. So, 16 – 7 = 9.
Tens column: 1 < 5; borrow 1 hundred from 3 hundreds. 3 becomes 2 in the hundreds place and 1 becomes 11 in the tens place. So, 11 – 5 = 6.
Hundreds column: 2 < 9; borrow 1 thousand from 8 thousands. 8 becomes 7 in the thousands place and 2 becomes 12 in the hundreds place. So, 12 – 9 = 3.
Thousands column: 7 – 1 = 6

Thus, 8326 – 1957 = 6369.

SUBTRACTING WITH ZEROS AND ONES

Example 10: Subtract 2768 from 8615.

Solution: Write the two numbers vertically, greater number above the smaller number. Subtract the digits.

	Th	H	T	O
		15	10	
	7	~~5~~	~~0~~	15
	~~8~~	~~6~~	~~1~~	~~5~~
–	2	7	6	8
	5	8	4	7

Ones column: 5 < 8; borrow 1 ten from 1 tens. 1 becomes 0 in the tens place and 5 becomes 15 in the ones place. So, 15 – 8 = 7.
Tens column: We cannot subtract 6 from 0. Borrow 1 hundred from 6 hundreds. 6 becomes 5 in the hundreds place and 0 becomes 10 in the tens place. So, 10 – 6 = 4.
Hundreds column: 5 < 7; borrow 1 thousand from 8 thousands. 8 becomes 7 in the thousands place and 5 becomes 15 in the hundreds place. So, 15 – 7 = 8.
Thousands column: 7 – 2 = 5

Thus, 8615 – 2768 = 5847.

Example 11: Subtract 3527 from 8005.

Solution: Write the two numbers vertically, with the greater number above the smaller number. Subtract the digits.

	Th	H	T	O
	7	10		
	~~8~~	~~0~~	0	5
–	3	5	2	7

Ones column: 5 < 7; we cannot borrow from 0 in the tens and hundreds places. So, we borrow from the thousands place.
Thousands and hundreds columns: Borrow 1 thousand from 8 thousands and add it to the hundreds place. Then, 8 becomes 7 in the thousands place and 0 becomes 10 in the hundreds place.
Tens column: Borrow 1 hundred from 10 hundreds and add it to the tens place. 10 becomes 9 in the hundreds place and 0 becomes 10 in the tens place.
Ones column again: Borrow 1 ten from 10 tens and add it to the ones place. 10 becomes 9 in the tens place and 5 becomes 15 in the ones place.

	Th	H	T	O
		9	9	
	7	~~10~~	~~10~~	15
	~~8~~	~~0~~	~~0~~	~~5~~
–	3	5	2	7
	4	4	7	8

Thus, 8005 – 3527 = 4478.

Now, subtract:
Ones column: 15 – 7 = 8 **Tens column:** 9 – 2 = 7
Hundreds column: 9 – 5 = 4 **Thousands column:** 7 – 3 = 4

COMMON ERRORS !

	Th	H	T	O
			7	10
	5	6	~~8~~	~~1~~
–	2	4	3	7
	3	2	4	3

	Th	H	T	O
			7	11
	5	6	~~8~~	~~1~~
–	2	4	3	7
	3	2	4	4

EXERCISE 3B

1. **Find the difference.**

a.

	Th	H	T	O
	5	9	6	8
–	3	2	5	1

b.

	Th	H	T	O
	7	5	4	2
–	1	2	3	9

c.

	Th	H	T	O
	6	2	2	5
–	2	8	6	1

d.

	Th	H	T	O
	5	4	6	1
–	4	5	7	9

e.

	Th	H	T	O
	9	6	0	5
–	4	7	6	8

f.

	Th	H	T	O
	8	0	1	4
–	6	8	9	5

2. **Solve the following in your notebook.**

a. 8659 – 2105 b. 4372 – 1204 c. 7217 – 3189 d. 8017 – 5128

CHECKING THE RESULT OF SUBTRACTION

We can check the result of subtraction problems with the help of addition. Consider the following examples to find out how we can do this.

Example: Sonia and her mother went to a grocery store. The total bill amount of the purchased items was ₹1232. Her mother gave ₹1555 to the grocer and got ₹323 as balance.

Sonia checked whether the grocer gave the correct balance amount to her mother or not.

Let us check the calculations done by Sonia.

First, Sonia subtracted the bill amount from the original amount paid by her mother.

	Th	H	T	O
	1	5	5	5
−	1	2	3	2
	0	3	2	3

To check, she added the balance amount and the bill amount together. If she gets the original amount paid as the answer, then the grocer's calculation is correct.

	Th	H	T	O
	1	2	3	2
+		3	2	3
	1	5	5	5

As the two amounts match or are the same, the subtraction done by the grocer is correct.

Example 12: The teacher had 2568 school diaries to give to all the students. She gave a diary each to 2400 students. How many diaries were left with her?

Solution:

Subtraction

	Th	H	T	O
	2	5	6	8
−	2	4	0	0
		1	6	8

Check

	Th	H	T	O
	2	4	0	0
+		1	6	8
	2	5	6	8

As 2400 + 168 = 2568, so the subtraction is correct.

Thus, 168 diaries were left with her.

EXERCISE 3C

Subtract the following and check your answer.

1.

	Th	H	T	O
	7	3	8	9
–	2	1	5	7

Check

	Th	H	T	O
–				

2.

	Th	H	T	O
	9	5	0	8
–	1	3	6	7

Check

	Th	H	T	O
–				

3.

	Th	H	T	O
	6	3	2	9
–	1	0	5	8

Check

	Th	H	T	O
–				

WORD PROBLEMS

Word problems on subtraction with 3-digit and 4-digit numbers are solved in the same way as subtraction with 2-digit numbers.

GO EASY!

Look out for **subtraction words**: difference, fewer, left, less, need to, remains, subtract, how many more, how much more, etc.

Example 13: Ramesh has ₹6295. Zehra has ₹2595 lesser than Ramesh. How much money does Zehra have?

Solution:

		Th	H	T	O
		5	12		
Amount Ramesh has		~~6~~	~~2~~	9	5
Amount less than Ramesh	–	2	5	9	5
		3	7	0	0

Thus, Zehra has ₹3700.

NOTE

We subtract when we need:

- to find out how much is **left**;
- to find out **how much less or more** is one number than another;
- to find out the **difference** between two numbers;
- to find out a number which is **less than** another number by a given amount.

Example 14: An ice cream vendor sold 5700 ice creams in June and 2850 ice creams in July. How many less ice creams did he sell in July than in June?

Solution:

		Th	H	T	O
			16		
		4	~~6~~	10	
Ice creams sold in June		~~5~~	~~7~~	~~0~~	0
Ice creams sold in July	–	2	8	5	0
		2	8	5	0

Thus, he sold 2850 less ice creams in July than in June.

WORD PROBLEMS INVOLVING TWO STEPS

In some situations, we may need more than one operation to solve a problem. Let us work out a few problems involving two steps, that is, addition and subtraction or twice addition or twice subtraction.

Example 15: 9420 people lived in a village. 3310 people left the village. 1985 more people came to live in the village. Now, how many people are there in the village?

Solution: Step 1:

		Th	H	T	O
People in the village		9	4	2	0
People left	–	3	3	1	0
People remaining		6	1	1	0

Step 2:

		Th	H	T	O
		1			
People remaining		6	1	1	0
People came to live	+	1	9	8	5
		8	0	9	5

Now, there are 8095 people in the village.

Example 16: A library had 3900 books. 1200 books got spoilt. The library gave away 900 books. How many books are there in the library now?

Solution: Step 1:

		Th	H	T	O
Books library had		3	9	0	0
Books got spoilt	–	1	2	0	0
Books left		2	7	0	0

Step 2:

		Th	H	T	O
		1	17		
Books left		~~2~~	~~7~~	0	0
Books given away	–		9	0	0
		1	8	0	0

Now, the library has 1800 books.

EXERCISE 3D

1. There were 8675 apple trees in an orchard. 2134 trees were cut down. How many trees were left in the orchard?

		Th	H	T	O
Total number of trees					
Trees cut down					

________ trees were left in the orchard.

2. A factory manufactured 5436 watches. It sold 1782 watches. How many watches were not sold?

_____________ watches were not sold.

3. Amit had ₹6270. Sudhir had ₹3920 less than Amit. How much money did Sudhir have?

Sudhir had _______________ .

4. There were 8500 students in a school. 500 students left the school. 398 more students joined the school. How many students are there in the school now?

There are _____________ students in the school now.

5. A bookshop had 9450 books. It sold 4220 books in one month and 2910 books in the next month. How many books are left in the bookshop?

_____________ books are left in the bookshop.

6. 9500 people came to a Book Fair in the morning. By the afternoon, 2000 people left. By the evening, 1600 more people came. How many people were there at the Book Fair in the evening?

In the evening, there were ___________ people at the Book Fair.

FRAMING WORD PROBLEMS

To frame a word problem on subtraction questions, we should follow the given steps.

1. Look at the numbers and think of what they could relate to in our daily life.
2. Frame the word problems accordingly.

Example: Frame a word problem on the given subtraction.

	H	T	O
	8	7	9
–	5	3	4
	3	4	5

Step 1: Think of what these 3-digit figures could relate to in our daily life.

Step 2: These could be the number of students in a school or the number of cars parked outside an airport.

Step 3: Frame the word problems.

Given below are two word problems.

1. There are 879 students in a school. Out of these, 534 are boys. How many are girls?

2. There were 879 cars parked outside the airport in the morning. By the evening, 534 cars left. How many cars were left in the parking?

ESTIMATING THE DIFFERENCE BETWEEN TWO NUMBERS

We learnt about the method of rounding off in Chapter 1 and estimation in Chapter 2. Estimation can be used for subtraction as well.

To estimate the difference of two numbers, we have to first round off the numbers to their estimated value and then subtract.

Less than 5					Equal to or more than 5				
0	1	2	3	4	5	6	7	8	9
← rounded down					rounded up →				

Example 17: Estimate the difference between 678 and 521 to the nearest 10.

Solution: 678 is rounded off to 680 (as 8 > 5).

521 is rounded off to 520 (as 1 < 5).

	H	T	O
	6	8	0
–	5	2	0
	1	**6**	**0**

Estimated difference: 160

Actual difference:

	H	T	O
	6	7	8
–	5	2	1
	1	**5**	**7**

157 is quite close to the estimated value 160.

Example 18: Estimate the difference between 891 and 116 to the nearest 100.

Solution: 891 is rounded off to 900.

116 is rounded off to 100.

	H	T	O
	9	0	0
–	1	0	0
	8	**0**	**0**

Estimated difference: 800

Actual difference:

	H	T	O
		8	11
	8	~~9~~	~~1~~
–	1	1	6
	7	**7**	**5**

775 is quite close to the estimated value 800.

EXERCISE 3E

1. Frame word problems for the following subtraction questions.

a.

	H	T	O
	4	3	8
–	1	5	7

b.

	Th	H	T	O
	3	9	8	5
–	1	4	7	2

c.

	Th	H	T	O
	8	7	0	2
–	4	5	9	6

2. Estimate the difference between the given numbers to the nearest 10 and then 100. Check your answers with actual subtraction.

a. 935 – 472 b. 870 – 216 c. 618 – 134 d. 593 – 417

PUZZLE!

Subtract the following to decode the answer.

I LOVE ____ ____ ____ ____ ____ ____ ____

Code
355 = B
412 = S
812 = N
511 = R
241 = U
441 = E
129 = M

 =

	H	T	O
	5	6	5
–	2	1	0

 =

	H	T	O
	7	8	2
–	3	4	1

 =

	H	T	O
	7	1	4
–	3	0	2

 =

	H	T	O
	2	5	9
–	1	3	0

 =

	H	T	O
	6	3	8
–	1	2	7

 =

	H	T	O
	5	4	9
–	3	0	8

 =

	H	T	O
	9	6	2
–	1	5	0

MATHS LAB ACTIVITY

21 CS Creativity and Innovation, Collaboration AI

Aim: To reinforce the concept of subtraction with regrouping

Materials required: Colour pencils (in bundles of 100 and 10 pencils each, loose pencils)

Procedure: This can be performed as a group activity.

1. Arrange the class into groups. Consider a subtraction problem. For example, subtract 148 from 353.
2. To solve this, first represent the greater number using bundles of pencils and loose pencils.

	H	T	O
	3	5	3
–	1	4	8

3. Each group needs to make 3 bundles of 100 pencils each (for the hundreds place), 5 bundles of 10 pencils each (for the tens place) and 3 loose pencils (for the ones place).
4. In the ones column, 3 < 8. So, borrow 1 bundle of 10 pencils from the tens place and add them to 3 pencils in the ones place.

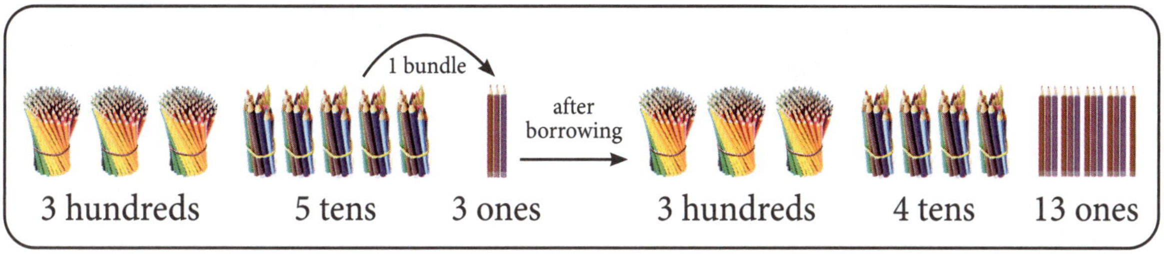

5. After borrowing, remove (take away) from:

   Ones column: 8 pencils from 13 pencils

   Tens column: 4 bundles from 4 bundles of 10 pencils each

   Hundreds column: 1 bundle from 3 bundles of 100 pencils each.
6. After subtraction, 2 bundles of 100 pencils each and 5 loose pencils are left. So, we get 205 as the answer.

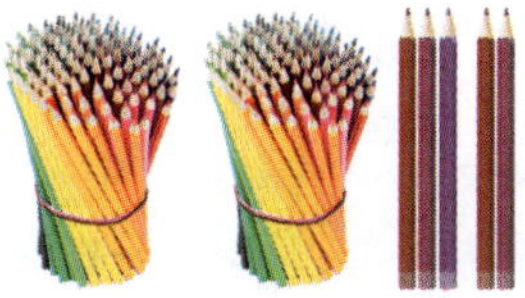

Check the answer by actual subtraction:

	H	T	O
		4	13
	3	~~5~~	~~3~~
−	1	4	8
	2	0	5

Try subtracting more 3-digit numbers like this and 4-digit numbers as well.

Concept Map

Subtraction

- Subtracting 3-digit numbers
  - without regrouping
  - with regrouping
- Subtracting 4-digit numbers
  - without regrouping
  - with regrouping
- Solving word problems
  - on subtraction
  - involving two steps
- Framing word problems
- Estimating difference between two numbers

Key Concepts

- **Subtraction:** Taking away and reducing the quantity
- **Difference:** The answer we get after subtraction
- **Estimation:** Guessing a number close to the actual answer

A. Choose the correct option.

1.

	H	T	O
	9	7	8
–	5	1	3

a. 485
b. 1491
c. 465
d. 513

2.

	H	T	O
	7	3	2
–	1	8	6

a. 846
b. 546
c. 746
d. 146

3.

	Th	H	T	O
	6	8	7	5
–	3	2	6	1

a. 3614
b. 9614
c. 9136
d. 3136

4.

	Th	H	T	O
	9	1	3	8
–	2	7	5	6

a. 7382
b. 9382
c. 2382
d. 6382

B. Match the following.

Column A	Column B
1. 478 – 125	a. 8299
2. 9651 – 1352	b. 1921
3. 608 – 153	c. 4347
4. 5347 – 1000	d. 455
5. 2222 – 301	e. 353

C. Subtract the following.

1.

	H	T	O
	7	9	5
–	2	0	4

2.

	H	T	O
	3	9	6
–		3	1

3.

	H	T	O
	6	1	7
–	4	3	1

4.

	Th	H	T	O
	5	0	1	4
–	3	2	0	1

5.

	Th	H	T	O
	7	3	2	4
–	1	9	5	7

6.

	Th	H	T	O
	6	4	3	5
–	2	5	8	9

D. Write T for true and F for false.

1. If a shirt costs ₹896 and Amit has only ₹538, he needs ₹358 more. ☐
2. Out of 3500 students, if 2750 students came wearing sports uniform, then the number of students who did not come wearing sports uniform is 750. ☐
3. A florist has 380 flowers to sell. Out of these, if 250 flowers are roses, then 275 flowers are not roses. ☐
4. Sachin has 500 stickers. If he gives 275 stickers to his brother, then 350 stickers are left with him. ☐
5. If Sanjay spends ₹5800 out of ₹9200, then he has ₹3400 left with him. ☐

E. Answer the following.

1. A shop had 5240 cycles. It sold 4185 cycles. How many cycles were left in the shop?

   ______________ cycles were left in the shop.

2. Rajan earned ₹9800 in March. He earned ₹3950 less in April. How much did he earn in April?

   He earned ₹______________ in April.

3. There were 2700 ducks in a farm. By June, 520 ducks died. By December, 645 more ducks were born. How many ducks were there in the farm in December?

   There were ______________ ducks in the farm in December.

4. 4500 people went to the fair. 1986 people left early. How many people were still at the fair?

   Check your answer after subtraction.

   ______________ people were still at the fair.

F. Tick (✓) the correct estimated value.

1.	596 – 105	a. 690 ☐	b. 490 ☐	c. 190 ☐	d. 290 ☐
2.	323 – 123	a. 200 ☐	b. 560 ☐	c. 180 ☐	d. 310 ☐
3.	642 – 187	a. 880 ☐	b. 730 ☐	c. 120 ☐	d. 450 ☐
4.	1562 – 1289	a. 270 ☐	b. 580 ☐	c. 1200 ☐	d. 1100 ☐
5.	4689 – 1723	a. 3500 ☐	b. 6840 ☐	c. 3000 ☐	d. 1200 ☐

(To the nearest 100)

SKILL UP!

A. 21 CS Information Literacy | HQ Why Education

Take all your school textbooks and write down the total number of pages in each book.

What is the difference in the number of pages between your

a. English and Maths textbooks?

b. English and Hindi textbooks?

c. Maths and Hindi textbooks?

B. 21 CS Critical Thinking, Life Skills | CC Integration with Social Studies | HQ Cooperation and Collaborative Living

2 ZERO HUNGER

6 CLEAN WATER AND SANITATION

13 CLIMATE ACTION

Children of Class 3 were collecting money for flood relief. They needed to collect ₹9000. Given below are the amounts they collected in the first three days.

Days	Money collected
Day 1	₹1400
Day 2	₹2000
Day 3	₹3200

How much more money do they need to collect to make it ₹9000?

SUSTAINABLE DEVELOPMENT GOALS

Question B is in line with SDG 2 Zero Hunger, SDG 6 Clean Water and Sanitation, SDG 13 Climate Action. How does a flood occur? What happens when there is a flood? What can you do to help in such situations? Climate change may lead to flood. Flood leads to shortage of food and clean water. Helping others by providing flood relief would help in fighting zero hunger. Your flood relief could also help in providing clean drinking water. Most SDGs are related, as you can see from this question.

WORKSHEET 3

21 CS Information Literacy

HQ Cooperation and Collaborative Living

Subtract the problems and follow the path that has an even number as the answer to guide the tourists to reach their destination.

4 Multiplication of Numbers

Learning Objectives

- To recall multiplication tables and learn multiplication facts
- To multiply 2- and 3-digit numbers by 1- and 2-digit numbers
- To multiply 4-digit numbers by 1-digit numbers
- To multiply numbers by lattice method
- To solve word problems on multiplication
- To frame word problems
- To estimate the product of two numbers

Let's Get Started

21 CS Communication, Information Literacy

HQ Understanding Values in Relationships

Shairiz is helping her mother in baking some cookies. Her mother asked her to arrange the cookies on baking trays.

At first, Shairiz prepared 3 trays for baking, with 12 cookies on each tray.

a. How many cookies were baked by Shairiz in the beginning?

____

b. If Shairiz prepared two more trays of cookies for baking, then how many cookies would be baked in the second round?

____

c. Find out the number of cookies baked by Shairiz in total.

____

In Class 2, we learnt about multiplication. Let us quickly recall what we had learnt.

The method of adding the same number to itself a number of times is called **multiplication**. In other words, multiplication is the same as **repeated addition**.

3 + 3 + 3 + 3 + 3	is same as	5×3
5 + 5 + 5 + 5 + 5 + 5 + 5 + 5	is same as	8×5

NOTE

The sign of multiplication is ×.

Also, when there are many groups and each group has the same number of objects, we use multiplication to calculate the total number of objects.

GO EASY!

We can add 10 seven times to find the answer.

10 + 10 + 10 + 10 + 10 + 10 + 10

But it will be a long method. So, we multiply the numbers for faster calculation.

Example 1: Michelle bought 7 packets of bows. Each packet has 10 bows. How many bows does Michelle have in total?

Solution: Number of packets = 7

Number of bows in each packet = 10

Total number of bows with Michelle = 7×10

$7 \times 10 = 70$ — Multiplication statement

7 → Number of groups

10 → Number of objects in each group

70 → Total number of objects

So, Michelle has 70 bows in total.

RECALL MULTIPLICATION TABLES

Table of 6	Table of 7	Table of 8	Table of 9	Table of 10
$1 \times 6 = 6$	$1 \times 7 = 7$	$1 \times 8 = 8$	$1 \times 9 = 9$	$1 \times 10 = 10$
$2 \times 6 = 12$	$2 \times 7 = 14$	$2 \times 8 = 16$	$2 \times 9 = 18$	$2 \times 10 = 20$
$3 \times 6 = 18$	$3 \times 7 = 21$	$3 \times 8 = 24$	$3 \times 9 = 27$	$3 \times 10 = 30$
$4 \times 6 = 24$	$4 \times 7 = 28$	$4 \times 8 = 32$	$4 \times 9 = 36$	$4 \times 10 = 40$
$5 \times 6 = 30$	$5 \times 7 = 35$	$5 \times 8 = 40$	$5 \times 9 = 45$	$5 \times 10 = 50$
$6 \times 6 = 36$	$6 \times 7 = 42$	$6 \times 8 = 48$	$6 \times 9 = 54$	$6 \times 10 = 60$
$7 \times 6 = 42$	$7 \times 7 = 49$	$7 \times 8 = 56$	$7 \times 9 = 63$	$7 \times 10 = 70$
$8 \times 6 = 48$	$8 \times 7 = 56$	$8 \times 8 = 64$	$8 \times 9 = 72$	$8 \times 10 = 80$
$9 \times 6 = 54$	$9 \times 7 = 63$	$9 \times 8 = 72$	$9 \times 9 = 81$	$9 \times 10 = 90$
$10 \times 6 = 60$	$10 \times 7 = 70$	$10 \times 8 = 80$	$10 \times 9 = 90$	$10 \times 10 = 100$

MULTIPLICATION FACTS

1. In any multiplication statement,

$$2 \times 5 = 10$$

Multiplicand (the number to be multiplied) — 2

Multiplier (the number of times the multiplicand is to be multiplied) — 5

Product (the answer obtained after multiplying) — 10

2. When a number is multiplied by 0, the product is always equal to 0.

   Example: $65 \times 0 = 0$

3. When a number is multiplied by 1, the product is the number itself.

   Example: $14 \times 1 = 14$

4. If the order of the numbers that are being multiplied is changed, the product does not change.

   That is, the order in which we multiply the given numbers does not matter. The answer still remains the same.

   Example: $2 \times 10 = 20$ is the same as $10 \times 2 = 20$.

   This is also called the **commutative property** of multiplication.

EXERCISE 4A

1. **Identify the multiplicand, multiplier and product in the given multiplication statements.**

	Multiplicand	Multiplier	Product
a. $2 \times 9 = 18$	______	______	______
b. $15 \times 3 = 45$	______	______	______
c. $6 \times 7 = 42$	______	______	______

2. **Write T for true or F for false.**
   a. Multiplication is repeated addition. ☐
   b. A number multiplied by 0 is always equal to the number itself. ☐
   c. When a number is multiplied by 1, the product is 0. ☐
   d. It does not matter in which order the given numbers are multiplied. ☐

3. **Fill in the blanks.**
   a. $4 \times 9 =$ ____
   b. ____ $\times 11 = 0$
   c. $8 \times 8 =$ ____
   d. $1 \times 22 =$ ____
   e. $6 \times 13 = 13 \times$ ____
   f. $7 \times 3 =$ ____

MULTIPLICATION OF 3-DIGIT NUMBERS

Let us learn how to multiply 3-digit numbers by 1-digit numbers.

Without Regrouping (Carrying Over)

Example 2: 123 × 3

Solution: Step 1: Multiply the ones.

	H	T	O
	1	2	3
×			3
			9

3 × 3 = 9

Step 2: Multiply the tens.

	H	T	O
	1	2	3
×			3
		6	**9**

3 × 2 = 6

Step 3: Multiply the hundreds.

	H	T	O
	1	2	3
×			3
	3	**6**	**9**

3 × 1 = 3

So, 123 × 3 = 369.

With Regrouping (Carrying Over)

Regrouping Ones

Example 3: 116 × 4

Solution:

Step 1: Multiply the ones and regroup ones into tens.

	H	T	O
		2	
	1	1	6
×			4
			4

4 × 6 = 24 ones (= 2 tens and 4 ones)
Write **4** of **24** in the ones column below 4.
Carry forward **2** of **24** to the tens column and write it above 1.

So, 116 × 4 = 464.

Step 2: Multiply the tens and then hundreds.

	H	T	O
		2	
	1	1	6
×			4
	4	**6**	**4**

Tens: 4 × 1 = 4; now add 2 (carried forward). Thus, 4 + 2 = 6.
Write this 6 in the tens column, before 4.
Hundreds: 4 × 1 = 4
Write this 4 in the hundreds column, before 6.

Regrouping Tens

Example 4: 361 × 2

Solution:

	H	T	O
	1		
	3	6	1
×			2
	7	**2**	**2**

Step 1: Multiply the ones. 2 × 1 = 2.
Step 2: Multiply the tens and regroup tens into hundreds.
2 × 6 = 12 tens (= 1 hundred and 2 tens)
Carry forward **1** of **12** to the hundreds column and write 2 in the tens column.
Step 3: Multiply the hundreds.
2 × 3 = 6; now add 1 (carried forward). Thus, 6 + 1 = 7.
Write 7 in the hundreds column.

So, 361 × 2 = 722.

Regrouping Hundreds

Example 5: 412 × 4

Solution:

	Th	H	T	O
		4	1	2
×				4
	1	6	4	8

Step 1: Multiply the ones first and then the tens.

Ones: 4 × 2 = 8; **Tens:** 4 × 1 = 4

Step 2: Multiply the hundreds and regroup.

4 × 4 = 16 hundreds (= 1 thousand and 6 hundreds)

Write 6 in the hundreds column and 1 in the thousands column.

Thus, 412 × 4 = 1648.

Regrouping Ones, Tens and Hundreds

Example 6: 356 × 3

Solution:

	Th	H	T	O
		1	1	
		3	5	6
×				3
	1	0	6	8

Thus, 356 × 3 = 1068.

Step 1: Multiply the ones and regroup.

3 × 6 = 18 ones (= 1 ten and 8 ones); carry forward **1** of **18** to the tens column. Write 8 in the ones column.

Step 2: Multiply the tens and regroup.

3 × 5 = 15; now add 1 (carried forward). Thus, 15 + 1 = 16 tens (= 1 hundred and 6 tens); carry forward **1** of **16** to the hundreds column and write 6 in the tens column.

Step 3: Multiply the hundreds and regroup.

3 × 3 = 9; now add 1 (carried forward). Thus, 9 + 1 = 10 hundreds (= 1 thousand).

Write 0 in the hundreds column and 1 in the thousands column.

Exercise 4B

1. Multiply the following.

a.

	T	O
	3	2
×		3

b.

	H	T	O
		2	9
×			4

c.

	H	T	O
	2	3	2
×			3

d.

	H	T	O
	1	6	4
×			5

2. Fill in the missing digits.

a. 15 × 6 = __0

b. 49 × 2 = 9__

c. 57 × 3 = 1__1

d. 232 × 3 = 69__

e. 134 × 5 = __7__

f. 423 × 4 = __6__2

MULTIPLICATION BY NUMBERS ENDING WITH ZEROS

Multiplying by 10 and Multiples of 10

- When we multiply a number by 10, we write one zero to the right of the number (i.e., in the ones place) and then multiply the number by 1.

Examples:

a. $3 \times 10 =$

T	O
3	0

b. $26 \times 10 =$

H	T	O
2	6	0

c. $594 \times 10 =$

Th	H	T	O
5	9	4	0

- When we multiply a number by the multiples of 10 (20, 30, 40, 50 and so on), we write 0 at the right end and multiply the remaining digits.

Example 7: 2×40

Solution:

$2 \times 40 = \underline{\quad 0}$

While multiplying 40 by a 1-digit number, first write 0 on the right end of the answer because 40 has one zero.

$2 \times 40 = \underline{80}$

Then, multiply 2 by 4. We get 8, which we write before 0.

MENTAL MATHS

Answer these:

1. $7 \times 2 =$ ____________
2. $7 \times 20 =$ ____________

Example 8: 13×50

Solution: We can do this multiplication vertically as well.

	H	T	O
		1	
		1	3
×		5	0
	6	5	0

Since 50 has one zero, write 0 on the extreme right. Next, multiply 13 by 5 to get 65.

So, $13 \times 50 = 650$.

Multiplying by 100 and Multiples of 100

- When we multiply a number by 100, we write two zeros to the right of the number (i.e., in the ones and tens places) and then multiply the number by 1.

Examples:

a. $2 \times 100 =$

H	T	O
2	0	0

b. 64×100

Th	H	T	O
6	4	0	0

- When we multiply a number by the multiples of 100 (200, 300, 400, 500 and so on), we write 00 at the right end and multiply the remaining digits.

Example 9: 7×200

Solution:

$7 \times 200 = \underline{\quad 00}$

As 200 has two zeros, write 00 at the right end of the answer.

$7 \times 200 = \underline{1400}$

Then, multiply 2 by 7. We get 14, which we write before 00.

Example 10: 36 × 200

Solution:

	Th	H	T	O
			1	
			3	6
×		2	0	0
	7	2	0	0

We write 200 below 36, even though it is a bigger number than 36. This is because without the two zeros, 2 is a single-digit number and smaller than 36. We write 00 at the right end of the answer. Then, multiply 36 by 2 to get 72.

Thus, 36 × 200 = 7200.

EXERCISE 4C

1. **Solve the following.**

   a. 2 × 10 = ____ b. 36 × 10 = ____ c. 4 × 100 = ____ d. 12 × 400 = ____

2. **Multiply the following.**

a.

	H	T	O
			3
×		6	0

b.

	H	T	O
		3	4
×		2	0

c.

	H	T	O
		1	3
×		2	0

d.

	Th	H	T	O
			2	5
×			4	0

MULTIPLICATION OF TWO 2-DIGIT NUMBERS

Let us now learn to multiply a 2-digit number by a 2-digit number.

Without Regrouping

Example 11: 12 × 23

Solution:

Step 1: Multiply the ones.

First, 3 × 2 = 6.
Write 6 below 3.
Next, 3 × 1 = 3.
Write 3 below 2.

	H	T	O
		1	2
×		2	3
		3	6

Step 2: Multiply the tens.

Write 0 below 6 in the ones column.
Then, 2 × 2 = 4; write 4 below 3.
Now, 2 × 1 = 2; write 2 before 4.

	H	T	O
		1	2
×		2	3
		3	6
	2	4	0

Step 3: Add both the products.

Draw a line below 240 and add.
Ones column: 6 + 0 = 6
Tens column: 3 + 4 = 7
Hundreds column: We have only 2.

	H	T	O
		1	2
×		2	3
		3	6
+	2	4	0
	2	7	6

So, 12 × 23 = 276.

With Regrouping

Regrouping Ones

Example 12: 26 × 15

Solution: Step 1: Multiply the ones and regroup.

	H	T	O
		3	
		2	6
×		1	5
	1	3	0

First, 5 × 6 = 30.
Carry forward **3** of **30** to the tens column.
5 × 2 = 10; now add 3 (carried forward). Thus, 10 + 3 = 13.
Write 13 before 0.

Step 2: Multiply the tens.

	H	T	O
		3	
		2	6
×		1	5
	1	3	0
	2	6	0

Write 0 below 0 in the ones column. Then,
1 × 6 = 6
1 × 2 = 2

Step 3: Add both the products.

	H	T	O
		3	
		2	6
×		1	5
	1	3	0
+	2	6	0
	3	9	0

So, 26 × 15 = 390.

Regrouping Ones and Tens

Example 13: 86 × 32

Solution:

	Th	H	T	O
			①	
			1	
			8	6
×			3	2
		1		
		1	7	2
+	2	5	8	0
	2	7	5	2

We have circled 1 to distinguish it from the earlier carried forward number 1.

So, 86 × 32 = 2752.

COMMON ERRORS

- If we write the number carried forward, one on top of the other, then we will not make mistakes.
- When multiplying the tens, first write 0 in the ones column and then multiply the digits.

	H	T	O
		①	
		2	
		2	5
×		3	4
	1	0	0
		7	5
	1	7	5

	H	T	O
		①	
		2	
		2	5
×		3	4
	1	0	0
+	7	5	0
	8	5	0

MULTIPLICATION OF 3-DIGIT NUMBERS BY 2-DIGIT NUMBERS

Let us multiply a 3-digit number by a 2-digit number.

Without Regrouping

Example 14: 121 × 24

Solution:

	Th	H	T	O
		1	2	1
×			2	4
		1		
		4	8	4
+	2	4	2	0
	2	**9**	**0**	**4**

So, 121 × 24 = 2904.

With Regrouping

Example 15: 252 × 36

Solution:

	Th	H	T	O
		①		
		3	1	
		2	5	2
×			3	6
	1			
	1	5	1	2
+	7	5	6	0
	9	**0**	**7**	**2**

So, 252 × 36 = 9072.

MULTIPLICATION OF 4-DIGIT NUMBERS BY 1-DIGIT NUMBERS

Without Regrouping

Example 16: 2313 × 2

Solution:

	Th	H	T	O
	2	3	1	3
×				2
	4	**6**	**2**	**6**

So, 2313 × 2 = 4626.

With Regrouping

Example 17: 1516 × 4

Solution:

	Th	H	T	O
	2		2	
	1	5	1	6
×				4
	6	**0**	**6**	**4**

So, 1516 × 4 = 6064.

EXERCISE 4D

1. Solve the following.

a.

	H	T	O
		2	5
×		1	3

b.

	H	T	O
		1	6
×		2	3

c.

	Th	H	T	O
		2	1	1
×			2	6

d.

	Th	H	T	O
		1	1	3
×			2	6

2. Find the product.

a. 23 × 42 b. 35 × 27 c. 42 × 27

d. 26 × 15 e. 447 × 18 f. 2234 × 3

MULTIPLICATION BY LATTICE METHOD

To multiply numbers using the lattice method, we first need to draw a box with a slanting line as shown below.

This box has a space for the tens digit and a space for the ones digit. It is called a lattice, with 1 column and 1 row.

Look at the following examples to understand multiplication using the lattice method.

SOLVED EXAMPLES

Example 18: Multiply 2 by 8 using the lattice method.

Solution: Draw a lattice with 1 column and 1 row as shown below.

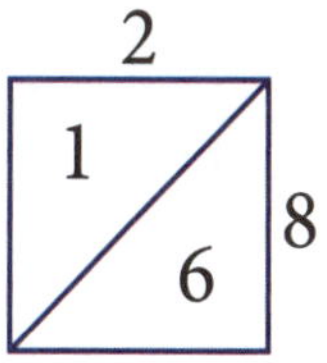

Write 2 and 8 outside the box as shown.
Multiply 2 by 8: 2 × 8 = 16.
Write 6 of 16 in the ones space and 1 in the tens space inside the box as shown.

Example 19: Multiply 54 by 3 using the lattice method.

Solution: Make a lattice with 2 columns and 1 row as shown below.

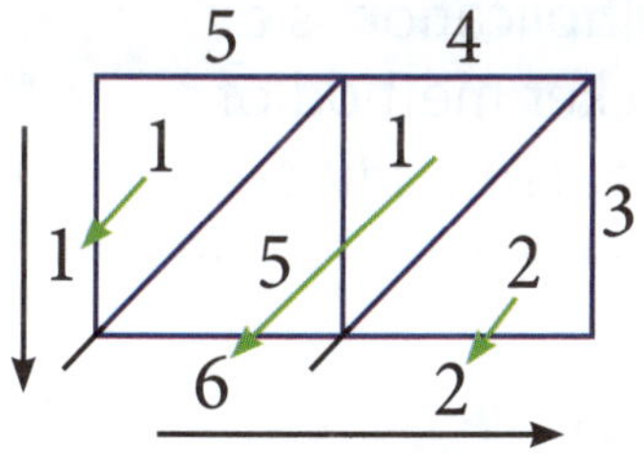

Multiply:
3 × 4 = 12. Write 12 as shown.
3 × 5 = 15. Write 15 as shown.
Add the numbers diagonally, as shown by the green arrows.

To calculate the answer, read down the left side and across the bottom, as indicated by black arrows.

So, 54 × 3 = 162.

Example 20: Multiply 34 by 12 using lattice method.

Solution: We will make a lattice with 2 columns and 2 rows as given below.

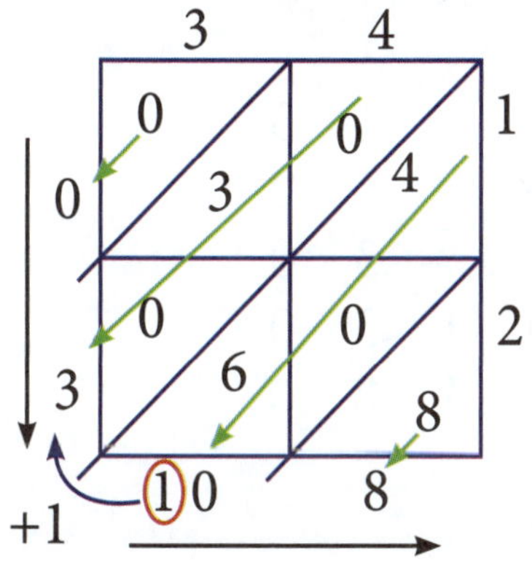

Multiply:
1 × 4 = 4. Write it as 04 as shown.
1 × 3 = 3. Write it as 03 as shown.
2 × 4 = 8. Write it as 08 as shown.
2 × 3 = 6. Write it as 06 as shown.
Add the numbers diagonally.

When we get a 2-digit number on adding, keep the ones digit there and add the tens digit to the number on the left. In this case, add 1 of 10 to 3 (3 + 1 = 4).

Read down the left side and across the bottom.

So, 34 × 12 = 408.

> **Do you know?**
> Lattice multiplication is also known as the Italian method, Chinese method, Chinese lattice, *gelosia* multiplication, sieve multiplication, *shabakh* or Venetian squares. This method was first founded in the 10th century in India.

Exercise 4E

Find the products of the following using the lattice method.

1. 23 × 2
2. 13 × 21
3. 35 × 5
4. 42 × 22

WORD PROBLEMS

In word problems, we multiply when:

- The answer increases multiple times by the given number;
- The value of one item is given and we need to find out the values of more items;
- We have to find the product.

> **Note**
> Multiplication is a quicker method of repeated addition.

Example 21: A *kurti* costs ₹325. A saree costs four times the *kurti*. How much does the saree cost?

Solution: 1 *kurti* costs ₹325.

1 saree costs 4 × ₹325 = ₹1300.

So, the cost of the saree is ₹1300.

	Th	H	T	O
		1	2	
		3	2	5
×				4
	1	3	0	0

Example 22: In one box, I can keep 15 pens. How many pens can I keep in 12 boxes?

Solution: In 1 box I can keep 15 pens.

In 12 boxes, I can keep 15 × 12 pens.

So, I can keep 180 pens in 12 boxes.

	H	T	O
		1	
		1	5
×		1	2
		3	0
+	1	5	0
	1	8	0

Framing Word Problems

Follow the given steps to frame word problems on the given multiplication:

1. First, study the calculation and make a note of the numbers used, whether they are in tens, hundreds or thousands.
2. Think of what these numbers could relate to, in our everyday life.
3. Frame the word problem accordingly.

Example 23: Frame word problems on the given multiplication: 55 × 12.

Solution:

	T	O
	5	5
×	1	2

Step 1: Think of what these 2-digit numbers could relate to.

Step 2: These could be the number of toffees in a packet or the number of passengers travelling in a bus.

Step 3: Now, frame the word problem.

Based on the given multiplication, two word problems have been framed as follows:

There are 55 toffees in a packet. Renji bought 12 packets of toffees. What is the total number of toffees with her?

A tourist bus can carry 55 passengers in one trip. How many passengers will it carry in 12 trips?

ESTIMATION OF PRODUCT OF TWO NUMBERS

We have learnt that estimation is a method used to find a value or number that is close enough to the exact right answer. In other words, estimation is a rough or an approximate calculation of a value or a quantity.

To estimate a number, we can round it off to its nearest 10 or 100. For example, if the cost of a brownie is ₹17, we can say that it costs around ₹20. So, if one has ₹20, it would be enough to buy the brownie.

To **estimate the product** of two numbers, we first round off the two numbers to their nearest 10 or 100 and then multiply them.

Example 24: Estimate the product of 32 and 49.

Solution: Round off 32 to the nearest 10: 30

Round off 49 to the nearest 10: 50

Now multiply: $30 \times 50 = 1500$

Estimated product: 1500

So, the actual product is 1568, which is close to the estimated product 1500.

Check:

	Th	H	T	O
			1	
			3	2
×			4	9
		1		
		2	8	8
+	1	2	8	0
	1	**5**	**6**	**8**

Actual product: **1568**

Exercise 4F

1. **Solve the following word problems.**

   a. Sachin has 25 marbles. Kunal has 13 times the number of marbles that Sachin has. How many marbles does Kunal have?

   Kunal has ____________ marbles.

   b. One box of chocolate has 24 pieces in it. How many pieces of chocolates are there in 15 such boxes?

   There are ____________ pieces of chocolates in 15 such boxes.

   c. If I can put 35 books on one shelf, how many books can I put in 17 shelves?

   I can put ____________ books in 17 shelves.

   d. One shirt costs ₹250. How much do 15 shirts cost?

   15 shirts cost ₹____________.

2. **Frame word problems for the following multiplication.**

   a. 32×5 b. 100×4 c. 250×3

3. **Estimate the following products.**

   a. 12×47 b. 39×62 c. 181×19

Go Easy!

Multiplication Tricks

Multiplication Table of 9

Here is a trick which helps us to write the table of 9 very easily. Let us see how.

- First, write down the multiplication part of the table.
- For the first digit part (i.e., tens digit) of the answer, write numbers from 0 to 9 vertically (top to bottom) as shown.
- For the second digit (i.e. ones digit) of the answer, write numbers from 9 to 0 vertically (top to bottom) next to each first digit.

Using this trick, we could write the complete table of 9 so quickly, without having to memorize the table.

Step 1:	Step 2:
9 × 1 = 0	9 × 1 = 09
9 × 2 = 1	9 × 2 = 18
9 × 3 = 2	9 × 3 = 27
9 × 4 = 3	9 × 4 = 36
9 × 5 = 4	9 × 5 = 45
9 × 6 = 5	9 × 6 = 54
9 × 7 = 6	9 × 7 = 63
9 × 8 = 7	9 × 8 = 72
9 × 9 = 8	9 × 9 = 81
9 × 10 = 9	9 × 10 = 90

Multiplying 2-digit Numbers by 11

Consider the following examples to understand the trick.

Example 25: 27 × 11 = ?

Solution: To find the answer, add 2 and 7 to get **9**.

Then, write 9 in between the digits of 27, that is, 297.

So, 27 × 11 = **297**.

Example 26: 78 × 11 = ?

Solution: First, add 7 and 8 to get 15.

Then, write **5** in between the digits of 78 and add 1 to 7, that is, 858.

So, 78 × 11 = **858**.

Mental Maths

1. 5 × 10 = ____________
2. 32 × 10 = ____________
3. 694 × 10 = ____________
4. 5 × 100 = ____________
5. 37 × 100 = ____________
6. 111 × 2 = ____________

MATHS LAB ACTIVITY

21 CS Creativity and Innovation, Communication EL AI

Aim: To try multiplication of numbers with the help of paper strips

Materials required: Chart papers of different colours including white, a black sketch pen, scissors

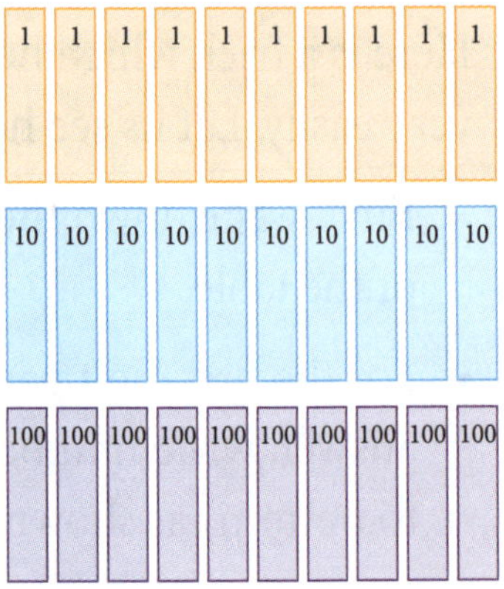

Procedure:

1. Take chart papers of different colours and cut them in long strips of 3 cm width.
2. Make 10 strips of each colour and write the different place values, as shown alongside.
3. Consider the example 234 × 5. Place the coloured strips vertically, as shown.

234 = 2 hundreds 3 tens 4 ones

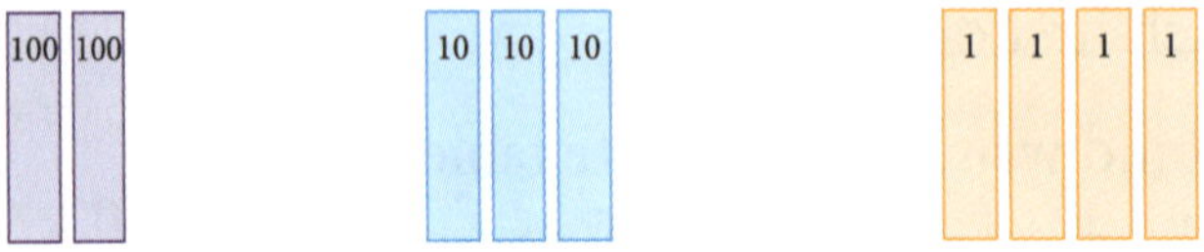

4. To multiply 234 by 5, put 5 strips (of white colour) horizontally on top of the vertical strips and mark using a black sketch pen all the meeting points (put a cross mark), as shown here.

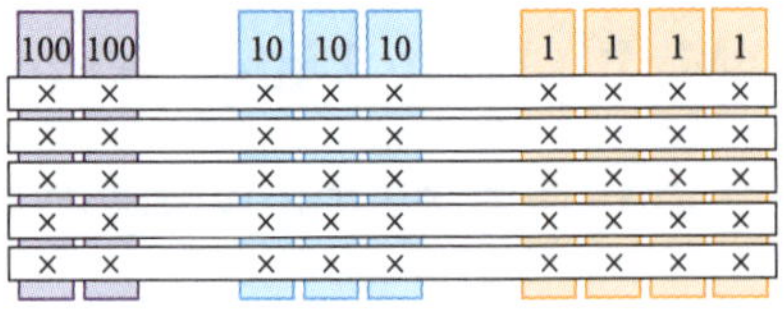

5. Now, count all the meeting points for each place value as given below.

		Th	H	T	O
10 × 100 =		1	0	0	0
15 × 10 =			1	5	0
20 × 1 =	×			2	0
		1	1	7	0

Then, add all the products.
So, 234 × 5 = 1170.

To verify the answer, check by actual multiplication.

Try more multiplication problems using this method. Explain the method to your friend.

Concept Map

Multiplication

Multiplication facts:
- Multiplicand × multiplier = product
- Number × 0 = 0
- Number × 1 = Same number
- Order of numbers does not matter
  15 × 3 = 3 × 15 = 45

Multiplication of numbers (without and with regrouping):
- 3-digit by 1-digit
- 2-digit by 2-digit
- 3-digit by 2-digit
- 4-digit by 1-digit

Multiplication with numbers ending with zeros
- 10, multiples of 10
- 100, multiples of 100

Estimate product of 2 numbers by rounding off the numbers to the nearest 10 or 100

- Solve word problems on multiplication
- Frame word problems

Multiplication using lattice method

Key Concepts

- **Multiplication:** The method of adding the same number to itself a number of times
- **Multiplicand:** The number to be multiplied
- **Multiplier:** The number of times the multiplicand is to be multiplied
- **Product:** The answer obtained after multiplying the multiplier and the multiplicand
- **Lattice Method:** A method of doing multiplication by drawing boxes and diagonal lines
- **Estimation:** A rough or an approximate calculation of a value or number that is close enough to the exact answer

CHAPTER REVISION

A. Write T for true and F for false.

1. The number to be multiplied is called the product. ☐
2. 2 × 30 = 60. ☐
3. 235 × 0 = 235. ☐
4. 1413 × 6 = 8466. ☐
5. The estimated product of 29 and 52 is 1500. ☐

B. Fill in the blanks.

1. 7 × 5 = ________
2. 9 × 9 = ________
3. 6 × 8 = ________
4. 12 × 4 = ________
5. 5 × 40 = ________
6. 15 × 20 = ________

C. Match the questions in Column A to the answers in Column B.

	A		B
1.	27 × 10	a.	830
2.	83 × 10	b.	9200
3.	695 × 10	c.	500
4.	92 × 100	d.	270
5.	5 × 100	e.	6950

D. Multiply the following.

1.

	H	T	O
	1	3	2
×			3

2.

	H	T	O
	2	0	3
×			2

3.

	H	T	O
	4	3	0
×			2

4.

	H	T	O
		1	5
×		2	6

5.

	H	T	O
	1	3	4
×			6

6.

	Th	H	T	O
	1	1	2	5
×				6

E. Solve the following in your notebook.

1. 24 × 35
2. 43 × 27
3. 347 × 2
4. 198 × 11
5. If one book costs ₹398, what is the cost of 2 books?
6. If there are 25 students in a class, how many students are there in 13 classes?
7. How much money do 5 children collect, if each child brings ₹125?
8. Frame a word problem for 20 × 42. Also, solve the word problem.

SKILL UP!

A. 21 CS Critical Thinking, Information Literacy

Observe the pattern in the multiplication table of 8 and complete the table.

1 × 8 = 8	(10 – 2)
2 × 8 = 16	(20 – 4)
3 × 8 = 24	(30 – 6)
4 × 8 = 32	(40 – ___)
5 × 8 = 40	(50 – ___)
6 × 8 = 48	(60 – ___)
7 × 8 = ___	(70 – ___)
8 × 8 = ___	(80 – ___)
9 × 8 = ___	(90 – ___)
10 × 8 = ___	(100 – ___)

Are there any other numbers whose multiplication tables follow a pattern? Find out.
If yes, write them in your notebook and explain the pattern being followed.

B. 21 CS Critical Thinking, Life Skills HQ Understanding Values in Relationships

Sonam brought a packet of biscuits to school which had 15 × 2 = _______ biscuits.

Out of which, Sonam and her friends ate 7 × 3 = _____ biscuits.

They threw the remaining biscuits in the waste bin.

1. How many biscuits did they throw in the bin?
2. Is it fine to waste food? Justify.

2 ZERO HUNGER

C. 21 CS Information Literacy EL

Multiplication by 4: Instead of multiplying a number by 4, we can first find the double of the number and again double the result obtained. (Two times any number doubles the number.)

Consider the example 6 × 4. Instead of multiplying 6 by 4, we can find:

Double of 6 = 12 (6 × 2 = 12)

Then, double of 12 = 24 (12 × 2 = 24)

When we multiply 6 by 4, we get 24.

Try this method with the following:

1. 3 × 4 2. 5 × 4 3. 7 × 4 4. 9 × 4

SUSTAINABLE DEVELOPMENT GOALS

Question B is in line with SDG 2 Zero Hunger. Have you ever thought of children who do not have enough food to eat and go hungry every day? What can you do with your leftover food?

WORKSHEET 4

21 CS Critical Thinking, Communication   HQ Happiness My Goal

Let us play a multiplication tic-tac-toe game. Two players are required to play this game. Follow the given steps:

1. Take turns to solve the multiplication questions given in each grid.
2. Each player needs to choose a symbol from ✗ and ○ to mark on the questions attempted.
3. In each grid, there are three same answers in a row (horizontal, vertical or slanting).
4. The player who gets a row of three same answers first wins the game.

16 × 6	32 × 4	112 × 2
100 × 11	32 × 3	50 × 6
205 × 2	16 × 10	24 × 4

105 × 6	1231 × 4	112 × 2
25 × 6	150 × 1	2 × 75
5 × 12	391 × 2	200 × 3

1010 × 6	32 × 4	101 × 2
101 × 20	505 × 4	1010 × 2
444 × 0	765 × 1	50 × 50

64 × 22	99 × 2	268 × 3
2002 × 2	41 × 3	201 × 4
11 × 12	10 × 10	67 × 12

5 Division of Numbers

Learning Objectives

- To revise the concept of division and division facts
- To understand the relation between multiplication and division
- To learn to divide using short and long division methods
- To understand the concept of remainder
- To divide 2- and 3-digit numbers by 1-digit numbers
- To solve and frame word problems on division

Let's Get Started

21 CS Creativity and Innovation, Information Literacy AI

Class 3 students planned to do something special on Teacher's day.

A group of 6 students were asked to make 'Thank you' cards for all the teachers. There were 18 teachers in all.

If each student made equal number of cards, then how many cards did each one of them make?

Total number of teachers = _______

Number of students in the group = _______

Number of cards made by each student = _______

Now, write a message for your favourite teacher on the card given here.

RECALL DIVISION

We have learnt in Class 2 that the concept of division is used when we need to share, distribute or group things equally. Let us revise that.

Division as Equal Sharing

At times, we need to share things equally among people.

Anjali has 12 cupcakes. She wants to share them equally with her three friends. How many cupcakes will each child get?

When 12 cupcakes are shared equally among 4 children (Anjali and her 3 friends), each child gets **3 cupcakes** and no cupcakes are left.

12 ÷ 4 = 3 ⟵ Division statement

Division as Equal Grouping

We also use division when we have to put things into equal groups.

There are 21 flowers. 7 flowers are put in one vase.
How many vases will be needed to put all the flowers?

One vase has 7 flowers. Therefore, 21 ÷ 7 = 3.

So, 3 vases will be needed to put all the flowers.

Division as Repeated Subtraction

Division is the result of repeated subtraction.
Rajat's mother gave him ₹30. If he spends ₹5 every day, for how many days will his money last?
We need to find the number of times 5 can be subtracted from 30 till we get 0.
So, the money will last for 6 days.
Instead of using the above method, we can divide 30 by 5 to get the answer.

30 – 5 = 25 ①
25 – 5 = 20 ②
20 – 5 = 15 ③
15 – 5 = 10 ④
10 – 5 = 5 ⑤
5 – 5 = 0 ⑥

30 ÷ 5 = 6

DIVISION FACTS AND PROPERTIES

1. The sign for division is ÷.
2. In a division statement:

30 ÷ 5 = 6

Dividend: It is the number to be divided. (30)

Divisor: It is the number which divides. (5)

Quotient: It is the answer obtained or result of division. (6)

3. When a number is divided by itself, the quotient is always equal to 1.
Example: $53 \div 53 = 1$

4. When a number is divided by 1, the quotient is the number itself.
Example: $47 \div 1 = 47$

5. Dividing 0 by any number is equal to 0.
Example: $0 \div 4 = 0$

6. Dividing a number by 0 is not possible.
Example: $15 \div 0$ is not possible.

Relation Between Multiplication and Division

Division is related to multiplication.
When 15 toffees are shared equally by 3 children, we write $15 \div 3 = 5$.
The division statement $15 \div 3 = 5$ gives the multiplication statement $5 \times 3 = 15$. This comes in the table of 3.
With the same division statement, we can also write $3 \times 5 = 15$. This comes in the table of 5.
So, for each division statement, there are two multiplication statements.
Also, for each multiplication statement, there are two division statements.

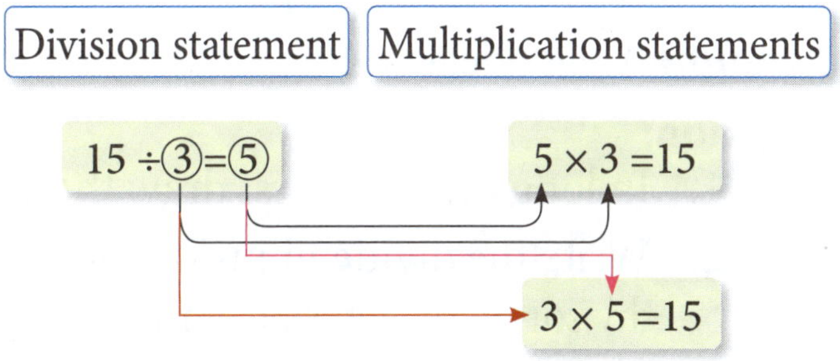

$3 \times 5 = 15 \longrightarrow 15 \div 3 = 5$ and $15 \div 5 = 3$

NOTE
Multiplication is the opposite of division. Also, division is the opposite of multiplication.

EXERCISE 5A

1. Share the following objects equally and write the division statement.

a. 27 sandwiches among 9 children
Each child will get __________ sandwiches.

b. 20 pencils among 5 boxes
Each box will have __________ pencils.

2. Put the objects in groups and write the division statement.

a. There are 15 pastries. 5 pastries are put on one plate.
Number of plates = __________ Division statement:

b. There are 30 balloons. 3 balloons are given to each child.
Number of children = __________ Division statement:

3. Complete the division statement and write the multiplication statements.

a. $16 \div 2 =$ ______ Multiplication statements: ____________ ____________

b. $24 \div 8 =$ ______ Multiplication statements: ____________ ____________

SHORT DIVISION

We can solve division problems by the short division method, as shown here.

Example: Divide 6 by 2 using the short division method.

Write the divisor here. → 2 | 6 ← Write the dividend here.

3 ← Write the quotient here.

$6 \div 2 = 3$

LONG DIVISION

Another method used to solve division problems is the long division method. Look at the following example.

Example 1: Divide: $8 \div 4$

Solution:

1. In long division, first draw the symbol (⟌) as shown.
2. Write the dividend inside the symbol and the divisor on the left side of the symbol as shown here.
3. Now, to divide, check the multiplication table of the divisor (4) to see if the dividend (8) comes in its table. The multiplication table of 4 tells us that $4 \times 2 = 8$. So, $8 \div 4 = 2$. (Quotient)
4. Write the quotient above the symbol, as shown.
5. Write the product of the divisor and the quotient below the dividend, as shown. Draw a line below the product (8) and then subtract. Write the difference below the line. In this case, it is 0.

Divisor: 4
2 ← Quotient
4) 8 ← Dividend
− 8 ← $4 \times 2 = 8$
0

If the first digit of the dividend is smaller than the divisor, then we take the first two digits and divide them by the divisor. Look at the example given alongside.

4
4) 16
− 16
0

Therefore, $16 \div 4 = 4$.

Concept of Remainder

In division, we group the objects equally, but sometimes we are unable to create equal groups and are left with some objects. The leftover is known as the remainder. The remainder is always smaller than the divisor.

Example 2: Share 7 ice creams between two children.

Solution: After grouping, each child gets 3 ice creams and 1 ice cream is left.

3
2) 7
− 6
Remainder → 1

Hence, 1 is the leftover here, which is the remainder.

So, $7 \div 2$ gives 3 as the quotient and 1 as the remainder.

Checking Division

We can check the answer of division with the help of multiplication and addition. We need to multiply the quotient and the divisor and then add the remainder (if any) to the product. If the result obtained is equal to the dividend, then our division is correct. That is,

> **Do you know?**
> The long division method was invented in early 1597 by Henry Briggs, who was an English mathematician. He was the first professor of geometry at Gresham College, London.

Dividend = (Divisor × Quotient) + Remainder

Example 3: Divide 16 by 3.

Solution: Dividend = 16 and divisor = 3

After dividing, we get quotient = 5 and remainder = 1.

```
      5
 3 ) 16
   - 15
   ----
Remainder ──→ 1
```

Check: (Divisor × Quotient) + Remainder = (3 × 5) + 1

= 15 + 1 = 16 = Dividend

So, the division is correct.

Exercise 5B

Solve the following by long division method and check your answer.

1. 10 ÷ 2 = ___   2) 10
2. 11 ÷ 3 = ___   3) 11
3. 18 ÷ 9 = ___   9) 18
4. 27 ÷ 6 = ___   6) 27

DIVISION OF 2-DIGIT NUMBERS BY 1-DIGIT NUMBERS

Division without Regrouping and No Remainder

Example 4: Divide 68 by 2.

Solution: Write the division problem as given below.

```
2 ) 6 8
```

```
      3
2 ) 6 8
  - 6
  -----
    0
```

Step 1: Take the first digit of 68, which is 6. Divide it by 2.
So, 6 ÷ 2 = 3 (as 3 × 2 = 6).
Write 3 in the quotient's place, 6 below 6 and subtract.
Draw a line below 6 and write 0 below the line.

```
     3 4
2 ) 6 8
  - 6 ↓
    0 8
  -   8
      0
```

Step 2: Bring 8 down and write it next to 0.
Step 3: Now, divide 8 by 2.
$8 \div 2 = 4$ (as $4 \times 2 = 8$)
Write 4 in the quotient place next to 3 and 8 under 8.
Draw a line below 8 and subtract.
We get 0 as the remainder and 34 as the quotient.

Therefore, $68 \div 2 = 34$, where quotient = 34 and remainder = 0.

Division with Regrouping and no Remainder

Example 5: Divide 74 by 2.

Solution:

```
     3 7
2 ) 7 4
  - 6 ↓
    1 4
  - 1 4
      0
```

Step 1: Divide 7 by 2. We get 3 as quotient and 1 as remainder.
Step 2: Bring down 4 of dividend and write it alongside 1 (remainder). The number we get is 14.
Step 3: Divide 14 by 2. Write 7 in the quotient next to 3 and 14 under 14. Draw a line below 14 and subtract, which gives 0 as the remainder.

Thus, $74 \div 2 = 37$.

Division with Regrouping and Remainder

Example 6: Divide 58 by 3.

Solution:

```
     1 9
3 ) 5 8
  - 3 ↓
    2 8
  - 2 7
      1
```

Step 1: Divide 5 by 3. We get 1 as quotient and 2 as remainder.
Step 2: Bring down 8 of dividend and write it alongside 2. The number we get is 28.
Step 3: Divide 28 by 3. Write 9 in the quotient and 27 under 28. Draw a line below 27 and subtract, which gives 1 as the remainder.

So, the quotient is 19 and the remainder is 1.

Division Involving Zero in the Quotient

Example 7: Divide 40 by 2.

Solution: Write the division problem as shown below.

```
2 ) 4 0
```

```
     2
2 ) 4 0
  - 4
    0
```

Divide the first digit of 40 by 2, which is 4.
$4 \div 2 = 2$ (as $2 \times 2 = 4$)
Write 2 in the quotient and 4 below 4.
Draw a line below 4 and subtract, $4 - 4 = 0$.
Write 0 below the line.

NOTE

After bringing down a digit, if the number to be divided is still smaller than the divisor, or it is 0, then we put 0 in the quotient.

20
2) 40
− 4↓
00
− 00
0

Now, bring down the 0 of 40.
Divide 0 by 2, that is, $0 \div 2 = 0$. Write 0 in the quotient next to 2 and 0 below 0. Subtract 0 from 0, which gives 0 as the remainder.

Thus, Quotient = 20, Remainder = 0.

Exercise 5C

Divide the following 2-digit numbers using the long division method.

1. $24 \div 2$
2. $39 \div 3$
3. $68 \div 6$
4. $72 \div 2$
5. $55 \div 3$
6. $72 \div 6$
7. $85 \div 4$
8. $70 \div 7$

DIVISION OF 3-DIGIT NUMBERS BY 1-DIGIT NUMBERS

Division without Regrouping and No Remainder

Example 8: Solve: $864 \div 2$

Solution:

432
2) 864
− 8↓
06
− 6↓
04
− 4
0

Thus, Quotient = 432, Remainder = 0.

Mental Maths

Fill in the boxes to complete the division.

1□□
3) 396
− 3↓
09
− □↓
0□
− 6
0

Division with Regrouping and No Remainder

Example 9: Solve: $784 \div 4$

Solution:

1
4) 784
− 4↓
38

First divide 7 by 4.
$4 \times 1 = 4$ $4 \times 2 = 8$
As 8 is greater than 7, use 4. Subtract 4 from 7 to get 3.
Bring down the next digit, that is, 8.

```
     1 9
4 ) 7 8 4
  - 4↓
    3 8
  - 3 6↓
      2 4
```

Next, divide 38 by 4.
4 × 9 = 36   4 × 10 = 40
As 40 is greater than 38, use 36.
Then, subtract 36 from 38, we get 2.
Now, bring down the last digit, that is, 4.

```
     1 9 6
4 ) 7 8 4
  - 4↓
    3 8
  - 3 6↓
      2 4
  -   2 4
        0
```

Now, divide 24 by 4.
4 × 6 = 24
Subtract 24 from 24, we get 0.

So, Quotient = 196, Remainder = 0.

Division with Regrouping and Remainder

Example 10: Solve: 597 ÷ 2

Solution:

```
     2 9 8
2 ) 5 9 7
  - 4↓
    1 9
  - 1 8↓
      1 7
  -   1 6
        1
```

So, Quotient = 298, Remainder = 1.

NOTE

Whenever the number to be divided is smaller than the divisor, we write 0 in the quotient and bring down the next digit.

Division Involving Zero in the Quotient

Case 1: When the Dividend Involves 0

Example 11: Solve: 340 ÷ 2

Solution:

```
     1 7 0
2 ) 3 4 0
  - 2↓
    1 4
  - 1 4↓
      0 0
```

When the last digit is 0 and there is nothing left to divide, write a 0 in the quotient.

So, 340 ÷ 2 = 170.

Example 12: Solve: 502 ÷ 5

Solution:

```
     1 0
5 ) 5 0 2
  - 5↓↓
    0 0 2
```

First, divide 5 by 5 to get 1. Next, bring down the 0. As 00 is smaller than the divisor 5, put a 0 in the quotient and bring down the next digit, which is 2.

```
     1 0 0
5 ) 5 0 2
  - 5↓↓
    0 0 2
  -     0
        2
```

Again 2 is smaller than the divisor 5. Write another 0 in the quotient and write 0 below 2 (because 5 × 0 = 0). Now, subtract: 2 – 0 = 2.

So, Quotient = 100, Remainder = 2.

Case 2: When the Dividend Does Not Involve 0

Example 13: Solve: 636 ÷ 6.

Solution:

```
      1 0
   6 ) 6 3 6
     - 6 ↓ ↓
     -------
       0 3 6
```

First, divide 6 by 6 to get 1.
Next, bring down 3.
Here 3 is smaller than the divisor 6. Write 0 in the quotient.
Bring down the next digit, which is 6.

```
       1 0 6
   6 ) 6 3 6
     - 6 ↓ ↓
     -------
       0 3 6
     -   3 6
     -------
         0 0
```

Now, divide 36 by 6.
$6 \times 6 = 36$
So, $36 - 36 = 0$.

So, Quotient = 106, Reminder = 0.

EXERCISE 5D

Solve the following in your notebook using the long division method.

1. 284 ÷ 2	2. 936 ÷ 3	3. 648 ÷ 9	4. 625 ÷ 4
5. 435 ÷ 7	6. 514 ÷ 3	7. 960 ÷ 4	8. 600 ÷ 5

DIVISION BY 10 AND 100

Division by 10

Example 14: Solve: 34 ÷ 10

Solution:

```
          3
   1 0 ) 3 4
       - 3 0
       -----
           4
```

So, Quotient = 3, Remainder = 4.

Example 15 : Solve: 597 ÷ 10

Solution:

```
          5 9
   1 0 ) 5 9 7
       - 5 0 ↓
       -------
           9 7
       -   9 0
       -------
             7
```

So, Quotient = 59, Remainder = 7.

COMMON ERRORS !

```
        2                 1 4
   5 ) 7 0           5 ) 7 0
     - 1 0             - 5 ↓
     -----             -----
       6 0               2 0
                       - 2 0
                       -----
                         0 0
```

- If the first digit is greater than the divisor, we must divide it separately.
- The remainder can never be greater than the divisor.

GO EASY!

H	T	O
5	9	7

We can also solve 597 ÷ 10 by drawing a line between the ones and the tens digits because 10 has one 0.

So, 59, on the left of the line, is the quotient and 7, on the right of the line, is the remainder.

Division by 100

Example 16: Solve: 246 ÷ 100

Solution:

```
        2
100 ) 2 4 6
    - 2 0 0
      -----
        4 6
```

Thus, Quotient = 2, Remainder = 46.

GO EASY!

H	T	O
2	4	6

We can also solve 246 ÷ 100 by drawing a line between the tens and the hundreds digits (2 digits from the right, because 100 has 2 zeros). The 2 on the left is the quotient and 46 on the right is the remainder.

Division by 2-Digit Numbers Ending With 0

Example 17: Solve: 160 ÷ 20.

Solution: 20) 160

1 is smaller than 20. So, consider the first two digits, that is, 16. Again 16 < 20. So, consider all the three digits, that is, 160.

```
       8
20 ) 1 6 0
   - 1 6 0
     -----
         0
```

20 × 5 = 100; as 100 is smaller than 160, try

20 × 6 = 120   20 × 7 = 140   20 × 8 = 160

So, we take 20 × 8 = 160.

Thus, Quotient = 8, Remainder = 0.

Example 18: Solve: 490 ÷ 30

Solution:

```
      1
30 ) 4 9 0
   - 3 0
     -----
     1 9
```

4 is smaller than 30.

So, take 4 and 9 together.

30 × 1 = 30   30 × 2 = 60

60 is greater than 49, so use 30.

Now, solve 49 – 30, we get 19.

```
      1 6
30 ) 4 9 0
   - 3 0↓
     -----
     1 9 0
   - 1 8 0
     -----
       1 0
```

Bring down 0. Now, we get 190.

30 × 6 = 180   30 × 7 = 210

As 210 is greater than 190, use 180.

Now, solve 190 – 180 = 10.

Thus, Quotient = 16, Remainder = 10.

MENTAL MATHS

Fill in the boxes to complete the division.

```
        2 □
20 ) 4 7 5
   - 4 0↓
     -----
       □□
   -   6 0
     -----
       1 5
```

EXERCISE 5E

1. **Fill in the blanks.**

a. 48 ÷ 10 Q = ______ R= ______ b. 573 ÷ 10 Q = ______ R= ______

c. 790 ÷ 100 Q = ______ R= ______ d. 508 ÷ 100 Q = ______ R= ______

2. **Solve the following in your notebook.**

a. 20) 140 b. 30) 360 c. 50) 250 d. 70) 490

WORD PROBLEMS

We can solve word problems by following the steps given below:

1. While solving word problems, we divide when:
   - something is distributed, shared or grouped equally;
   - we know the value of many quantities and we have to find the value of one quantity;
   - the answer is to decrease or will be a smaller number.
2. When we divide, the greater number is written inside the division symbol and the smaller number is written outside the division symbol. Note that this condition is not true when we need to divide a smaller number by a greater number (the concept of decimals about which you will learn in Class 4).

Example 19: 48 doughnuts were distributed among 3 groups. How many doughnuts did each group get?

Solution: Number of doughnuts = 48

Number of groups = 3

Doughnuts with each group = 48 ÷ 3

So, each group got 16 doughnuts.

```
     1 6
  3 ) 4 8
    - 3 ↓
      1 8
    - 1 8
        0
```

Example 20: 634 books were packed in cartons containing 20 books each. How many cartons will be packed and how many books will be left?

Solution: Number of books = 634

Number of books in each carton = 20

Number of cartons packed = 634 ÷ 20

So, 31 cartons will be packed and 14 books will be left unpacked.

```
Cartons packed ←   3 1
              2 0 ) 6 3 4
                  - 6 0 ↓
                      3 4
                   -  2 0
Books left     ←      1 4
```

NOTE

The remainder is always what is left over or remaining.

Framing Word Problems

We can frame word problems on given division questions. Follow the given steps:

1. First, study the question and make a note of the numbers used, whether they are in tens, hundreds or thousands.
2. Think of what these numbers could relate to in everyday life.
3. Frame the word problem accordingly.

Example 21: Frame word problems on division question: 58 ÷ 5.

Solution:

Step 1: Think of what these 2-digit numbers could relate to, in our everyday life.

Step 2: These could be the number of bangles bought or the number of children in a club.

Step 3: Now, frame the word problem.

Based on the given division question, the following word problems have been framed:

Sunaina got 58 colourful bangles from Jaipur. She wants to distribute them among 5 friends. How many bangles will each of her friends get? Will there be any bangles left over?

There are 58 children in a club. The teacher wants to make 5 groups. How many children will be there in each group? Will there be any children left without forming a group?

Exercise 5F

1. **Solve the following word problems.**
   a. 96 books were distributed among 8 children. How many books did each child get?
      Each child got ____________ books.
   b. If 6 people have to collect ₹60, how much money should each person bring?
      Each person should bring ₹____________.
   c. 125 biscuits were packed in packets containing 20 biscuits each. How many packets were made and how many biscuits were left over?
      ____________ packets were made and ____________ biscuits were left over.
2. **Frame word problems on the following division questions.**
   a. 24 ÷ 4
   b. 16 ÷ 3

MIXED WORD PROBLEMS ON FOUR OPERATIONS

In some cases, we have to perform more than one operation to find the answer to a given problem. Let us look at some examples.

Example 22: In Class 3, section A had 25 students, section B had 24 students and section C had 23 students. All the students brought ₹5 to give for charity. How much money was collected by these students?

Solution:

Step 1:

		T	O
		1	
Number of students of Section A =		2	5
Number of students of Section B =		2	4
Number of students of Section C =	+	2	3
Total number of students =		7	2

Step 2:

Money brought by each student = ₹5

Money collected by all students = ₹72 × 5

	H	T	O
		1	
		7	2
×			5
	3	6	0

So, the amount of money collected by all the students is ₹360.

Example 23: In a school, out of 78 teachers, three teachers were absent to attend a workshop. If five teachers can sit on a bench, how many benches would be required to seat all the teachers?

Solution:

Step 1:

		T	O
Total number of teachers =		7	8
Teachers absent =	−		3
Teachers present =		7	5

Step 2:

1 bench can seat = 5 teachers

Benches required for 75 teachers = 75 ÷ 5

$$\begin{array}{r|l} & 15 \\ 5 & 75 \\ & -5\downarrow \\ \hline & 25 \\ & -25 \\ \hline & 0 \end{array}$$

So, 15 benches are required for 75 teachers.

Mental Maths

1. If I have 3 flowers and 3 vases, how many flowers can I put equally in each vase?
2. If 4 × 5 = 20, then 20 ÷ 4 = ______ and 20 ÷ 5 = ______.

PUZZLE!

Solve the division problems and fill in the blank boxes.

28	÷	7	=		
÷				÷	
2	÷		=	2	
=				=	
		20	÷		= 10

Exercise 5G

1. **Three children brought ₹50 each. This money was distributed equally among 10 people. How much money did each person get?**

   Each person got ₹__________.

2. **Priyanka had 120 stamps. Her sister gave her 20 more stamps. Priyanka pasted all the stamps in an album with 5 stamps on each page. How many pages did she use?**

   Priyanka used __________ pages.

3. **Ten children, each from classes 1 to 5, were sent to the playground. These children were divided into 2 groups. How many children were there in each group?**

   There were __________ children in each group.

4. **For Zehra's birthday party, her mother bought 40 red balloons, 30 blue balloons and 30 white balloons. If these balloons are put equally in two different rooms, how many balloons would be there in each room?**

   There are __________ balloons in each room.

Maths Lab Activity

21 CS Creativity and Innovation, Collaboration

EL

Aim: To reinforce the concept of long division and remainder

Materials required: Kidney beans (rajma), transparent jars, paper chits, a bowl

Procedure:

1. Prepare some paper chits (around 50) with one division problem written on each chit. Fold all the chits and keep them in a bowl.
2. Make two teams, say A and B. Give both the teams some kidney beans and few jars.
3. One player from Team A will come forward to pick up a chit and read out the division problem to both the teams. (Teams take turns to pick up a chit.)
4. For instance, if the problem read out is 26 ÷ 3, then both the teams have to divide 26 kidney beans into 3 jars (i.e., in 3 equal groups) and find the quotient and remainder.
5. To form equal groups, put one kidney bean at a time in the 3 jars till all 26 beans are put in them. Then, count the number of beans in each jar to get the quotient and see if any beans are left (in this case, 2 beans), which gives the remainder.

6. The team which comes up with the correct answer first wins a point. One student can record the scores on the board.

Continue the game for 4 or 5 rounds. The team with the most points will be the winner.

Concept Map

Division

Division can be explained as:

- equal sharing
- equal grouping
- repeated subtraction

Relationship between multiplication and division:

- 10 ÷ 2 = 5
  5 × 2 = 10
  2 × 5 = 10
- 5 × 2 = 10
  10 ÷ 2 = 5
  10 ÷ 5 = 2

Division methods:

- Short division
- Long division
  - ➢ Concept of remainder
  - ➢ Check division

Long division by 10, 100 and multiples of 10

Long division of:

- 2-digit numbers by 1-digit numbers
  - ➢ without regrouping: no remainder, with remainder
  - ➢ with regrouping: no remainder, with remainder
- 3-digit numbers by 1-digit numbers
  - ➢ without regrouping: no remainder, with remainder
  - ➢ with regrouping: no remainder, with remainder

Word problems

Solve word problems on

- division
- mixed operations

Frame word problems

Division facts and properties:

- The sign of division is ÷
- Division statement:
  22 ÷ 2 = 11
  22 – Dividend
  2 – Divisor
  11 – Quotient
- 33 ÷ 33 = 1
- 33 ÷ 1 = 33
- 0 ÷ 33 = 0
- 33 ÷ 0 is not possible.

Key Concepts

- **Division:** Operation used to share things equally or make equal groups
- **Short and Long Division:** Methods used to solve division problems
- **Remainder:** The number that is left over from a division problem
- **Checking Division:** Check the answer of division by multiplying the quotient and the divisor and then adding the remainder

CHAPTER REVISION

A. Choose the correct option.

1. Arrange 30 roses in 5 vases. Each vase will have _____ roses.
   a. 5   b. 4   c. 6   d. 9
2. Divide 18 butterflies in equal groups of 6 each. How many groups can be formed?
   a. 4   b. 3   c. 9   d. 2
3. In the division statement 28 ÷ 7 = 4, 7 is the __________.
   a. quotient   b. remainder   c. divisor   d. dividend
4. Division is the result of repeated __________.
   a. addition   b. multiplication   c. subtraction   d. grouping
5. 45 ÷ 5 = _____
   a. 5   b. 40   c. 45   d. 9

B. Fill in the blanks.

1. 42 ÷ 10: Q = _______ R= _______
2. 590 ÷ 10: Q = _______ R= _______
3. 789 ÷ 10: Q = _______ R= _______
4. 526 ÷ 100: Q = _______ R= _______
5. _______ = (Divisor × _____) + Remainder

C. Solve the following in your notebook.

1. $2\overline{)420}$
2. $3\overline{)530}$
3. $4\overline{)549}$
4. $3\overline{)600}$
5. $7\overline{)918}$
6. $40\overline{)746}$
7. $60\overline{)980}$
8. $20\overline{)150}$

D. Answer the following questions.

1. 480 students are made to stand in 3 queues. How many students will be there in 1 queue?
2. Medha paints 3 flowers on one card. She makes 120 such flowers. How many cards does she make?
3. The teacher distributed 240 crayons equally among 20 students. How many crayons did each student get?
4. If a tailor needs 5 buttons for 1 shirt, how many shirts can he make with 35 buttons?
5. Radhika had 305 apples. She put 15 apples in one basket. How many baskets did she fill and how many apples were left over?

6. 325 students went for a picnic in 13 buses. How many students sat in one bus, if each bus had the same number of students?
7. Frame a word problem on division using 40 and 5. Also, solve the word problem.
8. In a park, there are 21 children. A balloon seller brings some balloons to the park. He bursts 11 balloons while trying to inflate them. How many balloons did he bring if each child bought 3 balloons?

SKILL UP!

A. 21 CS Creativity and Innovation | EL | AI

Make a scrapbook of your favourite items. You can collect any of these items for the scrapbook: dried leaves, flowers, bird feathers, buttons of different colours and sizes, shells, stickers, etc. Decorate the pages by drawing or colouring designs along the page borders.

Count the number of items you have and paste them in the scrapbook. While pasting, arrange the items such that there are same number of items on each page. How would you do that?

B. 21 CS Critical Thinking, Life Skills | EL | CC Integration with Physical Education

If Kartik gets 14 hours every week to study and swim, how should he divide his time equally to do both?

Why must we study as well as play sport?

C. 21 CS Critical Thinking, Information Literacy | EL

The teacher divides a class of 25 students into 6 groups.

How many groups does she make? __________

How many children are left? __________

If she wants to make one more group, how many more children does she need?

SUSTAINABLE DEVELOPMENT GOALS

Question B is in line with SDG 3 Good Health and Well-Being and SDG 4 Quality Education. Only when you have good health, you would be able to study well.

WORKSHEET 5

21 CS Critical Thinking, Information Literacy | HQ Why Education

In an amusement park, Yasmin bought tickets to the following game. Help her to finish the game. Solve each division problem and then find the correct answer out of the given choices. That will lead to the next problem to be solved. This way, Yasmin should reach the exit point where her brother is waiting.

Reasoning Worksheet 1

1. What number should come next in the given series?

   201, 202, 204, 207, ______

   a. 208 b. 205 c. 210 d. 211

2. Circle the odd one out.

   a. 8000 + 1000 b. 7000 + 2000 c. 6000 + 1000 d. 5000 + 4000

3. At a cricket match, Sumit was sitting in seat 153. Hazel was sitting to the right of Sumit in seat 154. To the left of Sumit, Gaurav was sitting. Jenny was sitting to the left of Gaurav. What was Jenny's seat number?

   a. 151 b. 154 c. 155 d. 156

4. The distance between Sameer's house and Roshan's house is 1200 m. How much distance will Sameer cover if he walks from his house to Roshan's house and then back to his house?

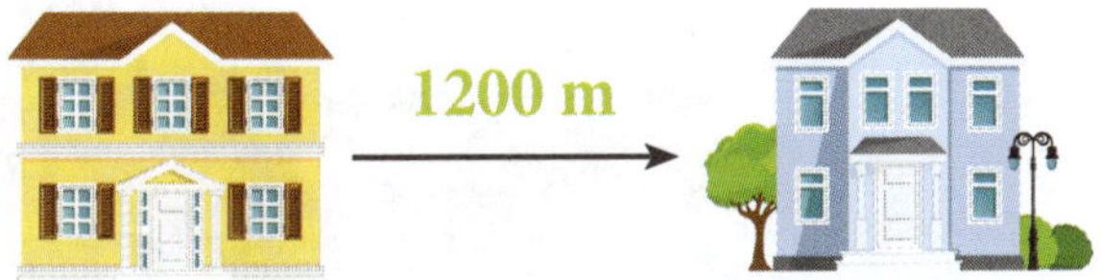

   a. 1200 m b. 1000 m
   c. 2000 m d. 2400 m

5. When 450 is added to a 3-digt number, we get a 4-digit number. When 420 is subtracted from a 4-digit number, we get 650. Find the numbers.

   a. 600, 1000 b. 602, 1070 c. 620, 1070 d. 660, 1170

6. The ones, tens and hundreds digits of the answer are the same. Fill in the missing digits to show the subtraction.

	H	T	O
	8	7	8
−			

   a. 434 b. 333 c. 444
   d. 111

7. If ✿ × △ × ★ = 60, ✿ × △ = 12 and ✿ × ★ = 15, then △ =?

   a. 2 b. 4 c. 6 d. 8

8. If ☀ ÷ ★ = ☾, then ★ × ☾ = _____ and ☀ ÷ ☾ = _____.

   a. ☀, ☀ b. ☀, ☾ c. ★, ☾ d. ☀, ★

6 Fractions

Learning Objectives

- To understand the concept of fractions
- To recognize fraction of a region and a collection
- To find fractions of the given collection
- To learn about the different types of fractions
- To solve word problems on fractions

Let's Get Started

21 CS Critical Thinking, Communication

HQ Understanding Values in Relationships

Juby and her elder brother, John, were alone at home. Juby was feeling hungry and wanted to eat a sandwich. John checked the refrigerator and found there were only two slices of bread, one slice of cheese and a few vegetables. So, they decided to share the sandwich.

This is the sandwich that John made.

Help John and Juby to divide the sandwich equally among themselves. Mark with a line on it to show how they can do so.

Is there only one way to divide this sandwich into two equal pieces? Write yes or no.

____

If no, then what could be the other possible way to do so? Illustrate.

____

FRACTIONS

In the previous section, we could divide a whole sandwich into two pieces in the following ways.

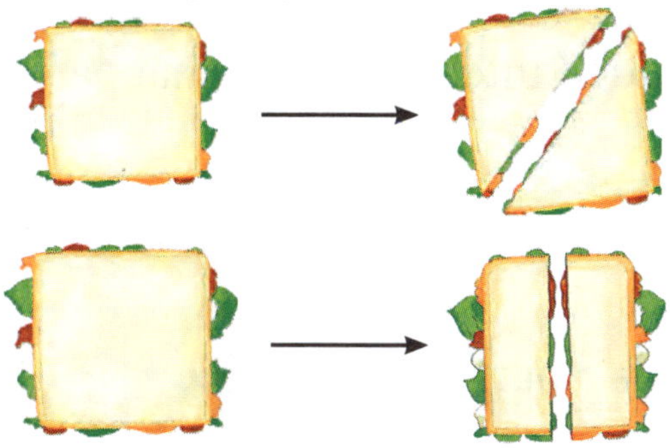

Each of these pieces is of the **same size**. So, we can say that all the pieces are **equal**.

Also, each piece is a part of the whole sandwich.

When a whole is divided into equal parts, each part is called a **fraction** of the whole.

In other words, a **fraction** shows one part of a whole that is divided into equal number of parts.

If a whole is not divided into equal parts, then the parts do not represent a fraction. Look at the following examples.

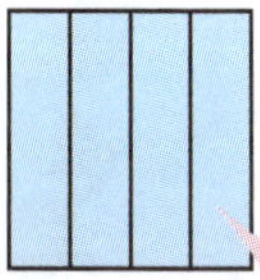

This figure is divided into 4 parts.
Each part is of the same size.
All the parts are **equal**.

These two figures are also divided into 4 parts.
Each part is not of the same size.
All the parts are **unequal** (or **not equal**).

MENTAL MATHS

Look at the given figures. Put a tick (✓) for figures with equal parts and a cross (✗) for figures with unequal parts.

1.
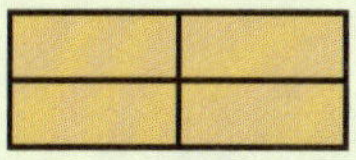

2.
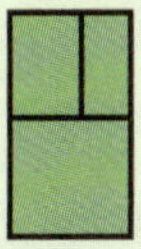

3.
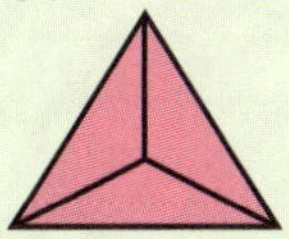

4.
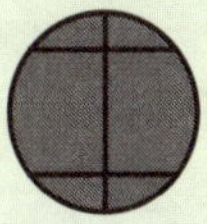

5.

6.

7.
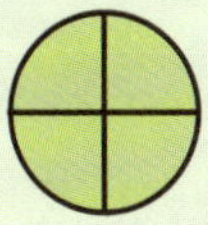

8.

9.
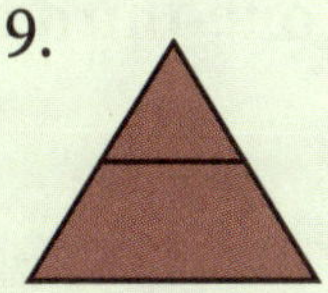

Parts of a Whole

We can consider a whole either as a region or a collection of things.

- When a figure or an object is taken as one, we call it a region.

Example:  This is one whole cake. It can be divided into different equal parts.

- When a group of things or people are being considered, we call it as a collection.

Example: On the right, it is a collection of apples.

Three apples are kept outside the basket; it represents a part of this collection.

READING AND WRITING FRACTIONS

Remember, we divided the sandwich into two equal parts.

Each equal part is called a **half** or **one-half** of the whole, which means one part out of two equal parts.

It is written as $\frac{1}{2}$. This is an example of a fraction.

In a fraction, the number written on top is called the **numerator** and the number written below is called the **denominator**.

A line separates the numerator and the denominator. This line is called the fraction bar.

That is, $\frac{1}{2}$

- **Numerator:** It shows the required number of parts.
- Fraction bar
- **Denominator:** It shows the total number of equal parts.

> **NOTE**
> Fractions are numbers that name equal parts of a whole (which could be a region or a collection).

Now, if we need to equally divide the same sandwich among three or four people, how do we do so? Let us see.

Divide into three equal parts:

Each part is equal to $\frac{1}{3}$, that is, one part out of three equal parts.

It is read as **one-third** of the whole.

Divide into four equal parts:

 or 

Each part is equal to $\frac{1}{4}$, that is, one part out of four equal parts.

It is read as **one-fourth** or **a quarter** of the whole.

NOTE

A **whole** describes an entire figure, object or thing and is equal to one.

1 whole = $\frac{2}{2}$

1 whole = $\frac{3}{3}$

1 whole = $\frac{4}{4}$

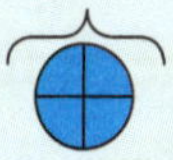

FRACTION OF A REGION

Look at the following figures or shapes. Each shape is divided into equal parts. In each shape, different number of parts are shaded or coloured.

Let us write the fractions corresponding to the parts shaded in each shape.

$$\text{Fraction} = \frac{\text{Number of parts shaded}}{\text{Total number of equal parts in the whole}}$$

Region/ shape	Number of parts shaded	Total number of equal parts	Fraction	
			Written as	Read as
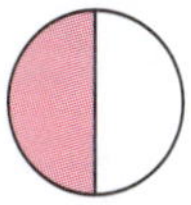	1	2	$\frac{1}{2}$	One-half
	1	3	$\frac{1}{3}$	One-third
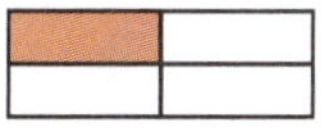	1	4	$\frac{1}{4}$	One-fourth
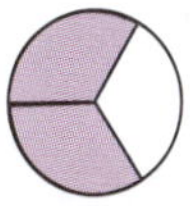	2	3	$\frac{2}{3}$	Two-thirds
	3	4	$\frac{3}{4}$	Three-fourths

More fractions:

Fraction	Read as
$\frac{1}{6}$	One-sixth
$\frac{1}{7}$	One-seventh
$\frac{1}{8}$	One-eighth
$\frac{1}{9}$	One-ninth
$\frac{1}{10}$	One-tenth
$\frac{1}{11}$	One-eleventh
$\frac{1}{12}$	One-twelfth

GO EASY!

1

One whole

$\frac{1}{2}$	$\frac{1}{2}$

1 out of 2 equal parts = $\frac{1}{2}$

$\frac{1}{4}$	$\frac{1}{4}$	$\frac{1}{4}$	$\frac{1}{4}$

2 out of 4 equal parts = $\frac{2}{4}$

$\frac{1}{8}$	$\frac{1}{8}$	$\frac{1}{8}$	$\frac{1}{8}$	$\frac{1}{8}$	$\frac{1}{8}$	$\frac{1}{8}$	$\frac{1}{8}$

4 out of 8 equal parts = $\frac{4}{8}$

COMMON ERRORS

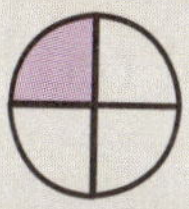

The shaded portion as a fraction:

$\frac{4}{1}$ 👎 $\frac{1}{4}$ 👍

EXERCISE 6A

1. Write the fraction for the shaded portion in each figure. One has been done for you.

a. 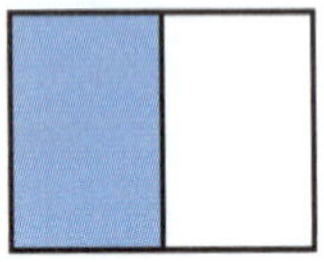

Half = $\frac{1}{2}$

b. 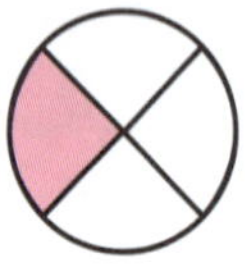

_____ = _____

c. 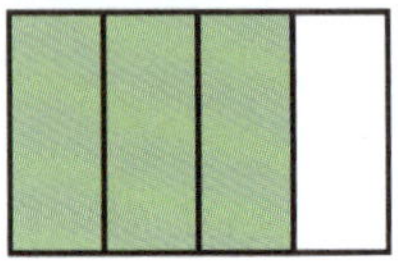

_____ = _____

d. 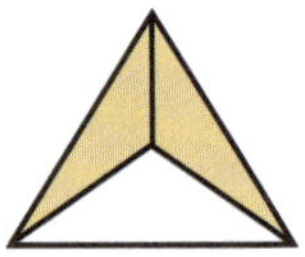

_____ = _____

2. Write the numerator and denominator for each fraction.

Fraction	$\frac{2}{5}$	$\frac{1}{6}$	$\frac{3}{7}$	$\frac{5}{9}$
Numerator				
Denominator				

3. Match the figures to the fractions they represent.

a. 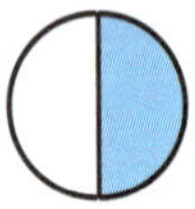
b. 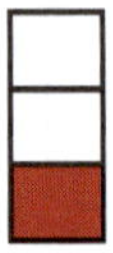
c. 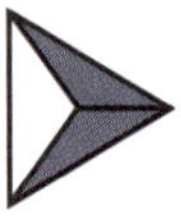
d. 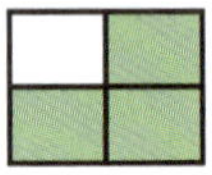
e. 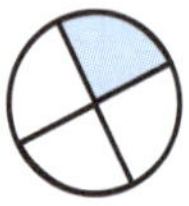

$\frac{1}{4}$ $\quad$ $\frac{2}{3}$ $\quad$ $\frac{1}{2}$ $\quad$ $\frac{1}{3}$ $\quad$ $\frac{3}{4}$

4. Colour each figure to represent the given fraction.

a. $\frac{1}{3}$ 

b. $\frac{1}{4}$ 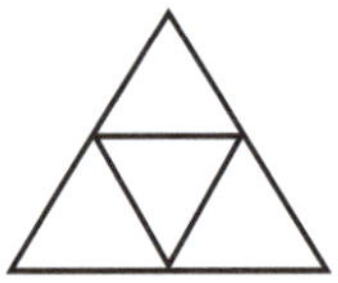

c. $\frac{1}{2}$ 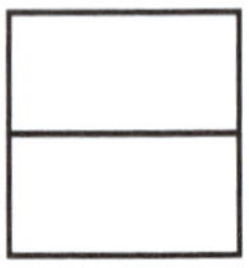

FRACTION OF A COLLECTION

This is a collection of Christmas balls. Out of 4 balls, one ball is red and three balls are blue.

So, fraction of red balls = $\dfrac{\text{Number of red balls}}{\text{Total number of balls}} = \dfrac{1}{4}$

and fraction of blue balls = $\dfrac{\text{Number of blue balls}}{\text{Total number of balls}} = \dfrac{3}{4}$

Example 1: In the given collection of 5 butterflies, write the fraction of yellow and pink butterflies.

Solution: Fraction of yellow butterflies = $\frac{2}{5}$

Fraction of pink butterflies = $\frac{3}{5}$

Example 2: There are 7 cats in the group shown here. Out of which, 3 are black cats and 4 are brown.

Solution: Fraction of black cats = $\frac{3}{7}$

Fraction of brown cats = $\frac{4}{7}$

NOTE

If we take 2 parts out of 4 equal parts, then the fraction is not called two-fourths, because 2 parts out of 4 equal parts is equal to half.

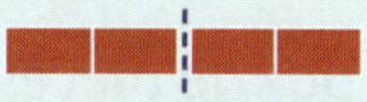 = Half = $\frac{1}{2}$

EXERCISE 6B

1. **Write the fraction for the number of red cars in the given collection.**

   Fraction of red cars =__________

2. **Colour the given collections as instructed.**

   a. $\frac{2}{3}$ of the flowers:

   b. $\frac{1}{4}$ of the leaves:

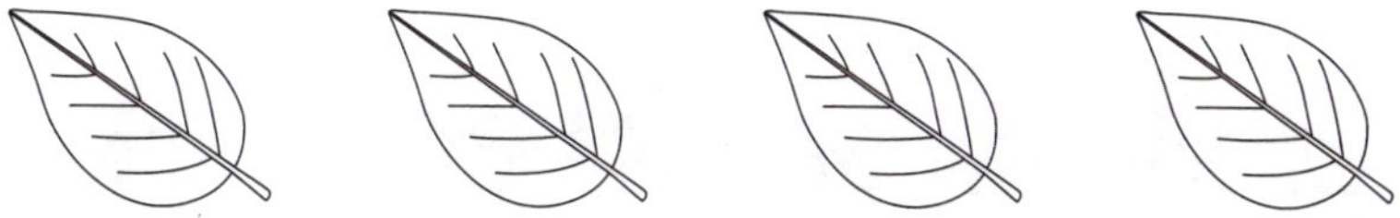

   c. $\frac{3}{5}$ of the triangles:

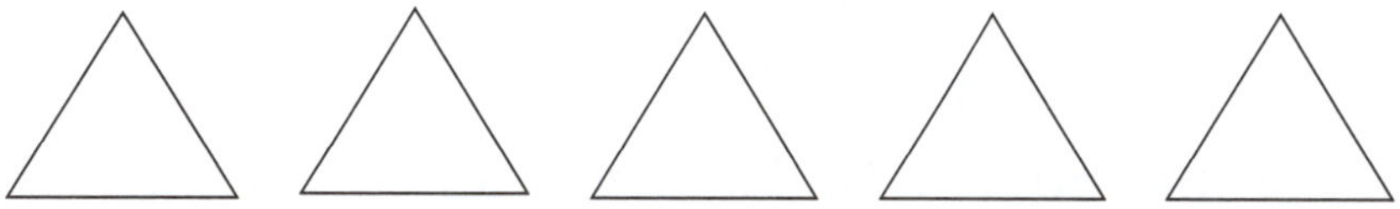

3. **Fill in the blanks with the fractions for the coloured and uncoloured parts of the following collections.**

   a. 

   Coloured: ____; uncoloured: ____

   b. 

   Coloured: ____; uncoloured: ____

c.

Coloured: ____; uncoloured: ____

d.

Coloured: ____; uncoloured: ____

MENTAL MATHS

If the red puzzle pieces represent $\frac{2}{6}$, then the total number of puzzle pieces is _______.

FINDING FRACTIONS

Finding Half

Roma bought 10 flowers from a florist. She put half of the flowers in a vase. Find the number of flowers, she put in the vase.

We know that half ($\frac{1}{2}$) is 1 part out of 2 equal parts.

So, to find half of the given collection, divide it into two equal groups.

This can be understood as follows.

Each group has 5 flowers.

Another method: To find half, we can also divide the total number of things in the collection by 2.

$\frac{1}{2}$ of 10 flowers = $\frac{1}{2} \times 10$ [first multiply 1 (numerator) by 10 and then divide the product by 2 (denominator)]

$= \frac{10}{2} = 10 \div 2$

= 5 flowers

Thus, Roma put 5 flowers in the vase.

DO YOU KNOW?

Fractions represent division.

$\frac{2}{3} = 2 \div 3$

$\frac{4}{7} = 4 \div 7$

$\frac{1}{2} = 1 \div 2$

NOTE

The word 'of' with a fraction means multiplication (×).

Finding One-Third

Nick got 9 chocolate eggs from his grandparents. He gave one-third of the eggs to his younger brother. How many chocolate eggs did Nick's brother get?

> One-third ($\frac{1}{3}$) is 1 part out of 3 equal parts.

To find one-third, we divide 9 eggs into 3 equal groups as shown.

We get 3 eggs in each group.

Also, we can divide 9 by 3.

$\frac{1}{3}$ of 9 eggs $= \frac{1}{3} \times 9 = 9 \div 3 = 3$ eggs

So, Nick's brother got 3 chocolate eggs.

Finding One-Fourth

Jeyaisha had a packet of balloons which contained 16 balloons. While blowing the balloons, one-fourth of them burst. How many balloons burst?

> One-fourth ($\frac{1}{4}$) is 1 part out of 4 equal parts.

To find one-fourth, we divide 16 balloons into 4 equal groups as shown.

So, there are 4 balloons in each group.

Also, we can divide 16 by 4.

That is, $\frac{1}{4}$ of 16 balloons $= \frac{1}{4} \times 16 = 16 \div 4 = 4$ balloons

So, 4 balloons burst.

SOLVED EXAMPLES

Example 3: Calculate $\frac{1}{3}$ of 6.

Solution: $\frac{1}{3}$ of $6 = \frac{1}{3} \times 6$ (as $1 \times 6 = 6$)

$= \frac{6}{3} = 6 \div 3 = 2$

$$3 \overline{)\,6\,} = 2, \quad 6 - 6 = 0$$

$\frac{1}{3}$ of $6 = 2$

Example 4: Solve the following.

Solution: $\frac{1}{5}$ of 10

$\frac{1}{5}$ of $10 = \frac{1}{5} \times 10$ (as $1 \times 10 = 10$)

$= \frac{10}{5} = 10 \div 5 = 2$

$$\begin{array}{r} 2 \\ 5 \overline{)\,10} \\ -\,10 \\ \hline 0 \end{array}$$

$\frac{1}{5}$ of $10 = 2$

Go Easy!

To find the fraction of a given collection, follow these:

- to find $\frac{1}{2} \longrightarrow$ divide by 2 (as **half** has 2 in the denominator)
- to find $\frac{1}{3} \longrightarrow$ divide by 3 (as **one-third** has 3 in the denominator)
- to find $\frac{1}{4} \longrightarrow$ divide by 4 (as **one-fourth** has 4 in the denominator)

Exercise 6C

1. Find the fraction of the following collections and circle it.

Fraction	Collection of objects
a. $\frac{1}{2}$ of 8	
b. $\frac{1}{4}$ of 24	
c. $\frac{1}{3}$ of 18	

2. Solve the following. One has been done for you.

a. $\frac{1}{2}$ of 8

$1 \times 8 = 8$

$8 \div 2 = 4$

$\frac{1}{2}$ of $8 = 4$

$$\begin{array}{r} 4 \\ 2 \overline{)\,8} \\ -\,8 \\ \hline 0 \end{array}$$

b. $\frac{1}{3}$ of 9

____ × ____ = ____

____ ÷ ____ = ____

____

c. $\frac{1}{4}$ of 12

____ × ____ = ____

____ ÷ ____ = ____

____

TYPES OF FRACTIONS

Unit Fractions

Fractions that have the numerator as 1 are called unit fractions.

Examples: $\frac{1}{2}$ 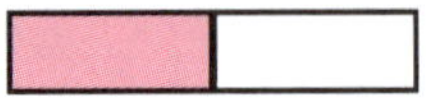 $\frac{1}{3}$ 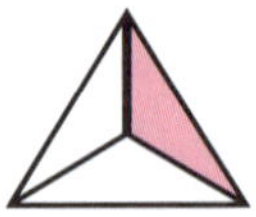 $\frac{1}{4}$ 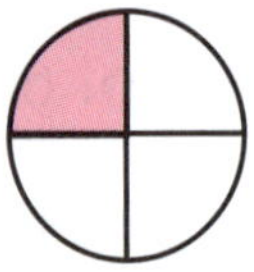

Like and Unlike Fractions

Fractions with the same denominator are called like fractions.

Examples: $\frac{1}{6}$ 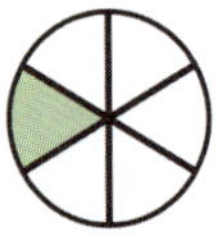 $\frac{5}{6}$ 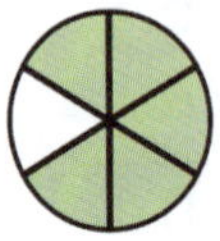 $\frac{3}{6}$ 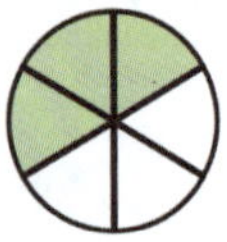

Fractions with different denominators are called unlike fractions.

Examples: $\frac{1}{3}$ 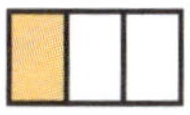 $\frac{2}{7}$ 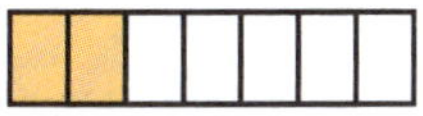 $\frac{3}{5}$ 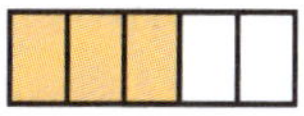

Proper and Improper Fractions

Fractions that have numerators smaller than their denominators are called proper fractions.

Examples: $\frac{1}{4}$ $\frac{6}{7}$ $\frac{3}{8}$

Fractions that have numerators greater than or equal to their denominators are called improper fractions.

Examples: $\frac{11}{6}$ $\frac{5}{2}$ $\frac{9}{8}$ $\frac{7}{7}$

WORD PROBLEMS

Let us learn to solve a few word problems on fractions.

Example 5: Jenny ordered a pizza which had 8 slices. She ate 3 slices of it. What fraction of pizza did she eat?

Solution: Number of slices in the pizza = 8

Number of slices Jenny ate = 3

Fraction of pizza ate by Jenny = $\frac{3}{8}$

Example 6: Rahul has 12 marker pens. Half of the pens are blue. How many blue marker pens does Rahul have?

Solution: Total number of marker pens = 12

Fraction of blue pens = half or $\frac{1}{2}$

Number of blue pens Rahul has = $\frac{1}{2}$ of 12 = $\frac{1}{2} \times 12 = \frac{12}{2}$ = 6 pens

Exercise 6D

1. Look at the following fractions and write them in the appropriate boxes.

$\frac{4}{5}$ $\frac{5}{3}$ $\frac{1}{2}$ $\frac{17}{15}$ $\frac{4}{12}$ $\frac{13}{9}$ $\frac{8}{9}$ $\frac{6}{4}$ $\frac{18}{15}$ $\frac{3}{5}$ $\frac{8}{10}$ $\frac{1}{7}$ $\frac{1}{34}$ $\frac{9}{10}$

Unit fractions	Like fractions	Unlike fractions	Proper fractions	Improper fractions

2. **Solve the following word problems.**

a. There are 9 ribbons in a packet. Of these, 5 ribbons are red. What fraction of ribbons are red in colour?

b. One-fifth of 20 children like to play cricket. How many children like to play cricket?

c. In a box, $\frac{2}{3}$ of the 12 chocolates are milk chocolates. Find the number of milk chocolates.

d. Mrs Naidu bought a packet of biscuits which had 16 biscuits in total. She gave $\frac{1}{4}$ of the biscuits to a street dog. How many biscuits did she give to the dog?

MATHS LAB ACTIVITY

21 CS Collaboration, Communication EL

Aim: To understand the meaning of fraction of a collection

Materials required: Jelly toys, a bag, a notebook, a pencil

Procedure: This activity can be performed in pairs.

1. Take about 30 jelly toys. Put the jelly toys in a bag.
2. From each pair, one player should put his hand in the bag and take out as many toys as he can in his turn. Both players should take turns to take out the toys.
3. Now, count the total number of toys that both players take out. That becomes the denominator of the fraction.
4. Then, count the number of toys that each player has. That becomes the numerator of each fraction.
5. In a notebook, write down the fraction of jelly toys each player has.
6. Similarly, each pair can repeat steps 2 to 4 to find more such fractions and record them in their notebooks.

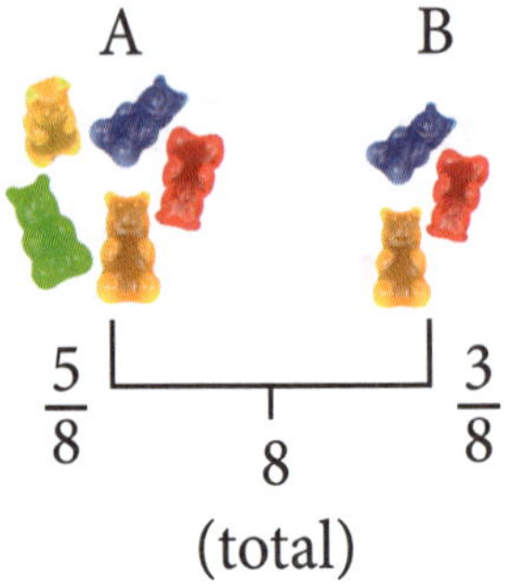

Conclusion: Each fraction formed represents the fraction of a collection.

Concept Map

Fraction
(a part of a whole)

- Consider a whole as a region
- Consider a whole as a collection of things
- Read and write fractions
- Find fractions of a region or a collection
- Types of fractions
  - Unit fractions: $\frac{1}{6}, \frac{1}{4}$
  - Like fractions: $\frac{2}{5}, \frac{1}{5}$
  - Unlike fractions: $\frac{2}{5}, \frac{1}{2}$
  - Proper fractions: $\frac{4}{5}, \frac{3}{7}$
  - Improper fractions: $\frac{8}{5}, \frac{5}{2}$
- Solve word problems

Key Concepts

- **Fraction:** When a region or a collection of things is divided into equal parts, each equal part is called a fraction.
- **Numerator:** The number which is written above the fraction bar in a fraction
- **Denominator:** The number which is written below the fraction bar in a fraction
- **Unit Fractions:** Fractions that have the numerator as 1
- **Like Fractions:** Fractions with the same denominators
- **Unlike Fractions:** Fractions with different denominators
- **Proper Fractions:** Fractions that have numerators smaller than their denominators
- **Improper Fractions:** Fractions that have numerators greater than or equal to their denominators

CHAPTER REVISION

A. Choose the correct option.

1. Which of the following fractions is read as half?

   a. $\frac{5}{7}$ b. $\frac{9}{8}$ c. $\frac{6}{5}$ d. $\frac{1}{2}$

2. Where is the numerator written in a fraction?

   a. bottom b. top c. left d. right

3. Which of the following is a unit fraction?

   a. $\frac{2}{3}$ b. $\frac{7}{9}$ c. $\frac{1}{5}$ d. $\frac{4}{7}$

4. Which of the following are like fractions?

   a. $\frac{1}{9}, \frac{2}{3}$ b. $\frac{3}{7}, \frac{5}{7}$ c. $\frac{2}{5}, \frac{1}{6}$ d. $\frac{4}{9}, \frac{4}{5}$

B.

1. Colour $\frac{1}{3}$ of each figure:

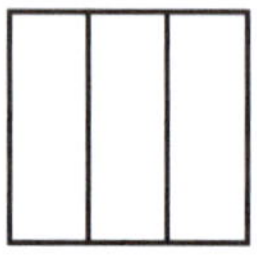

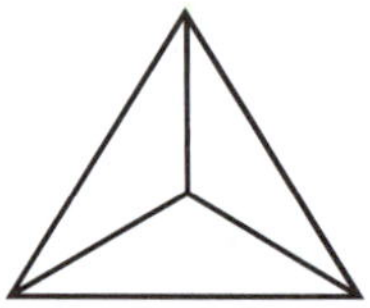

2. Colour $\frac{3}{4}$ of each figure:

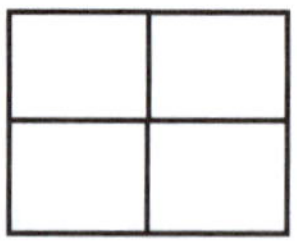
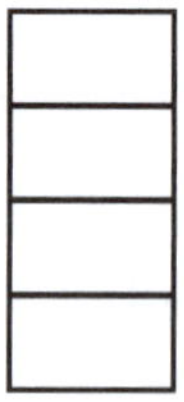
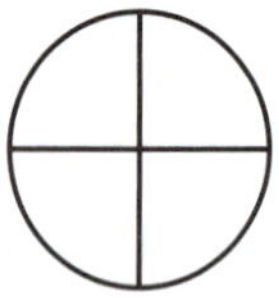

C. Write the fraction of the shaded and unshaded portion in each of the given figures.

1. 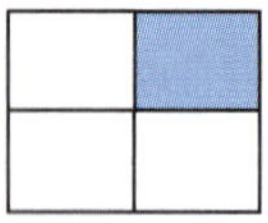

   Shaded: ________

   Unshaded: ________

2. 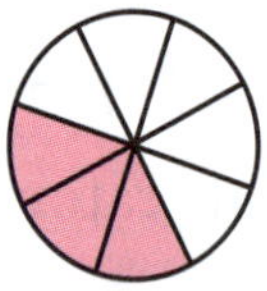

   Shaded: ________

   Unshaded: ________

3. 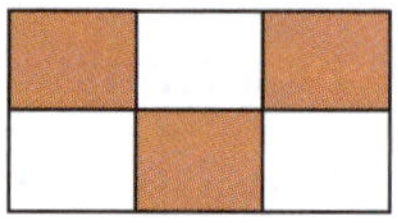

   Shaded: ________

   Unshaded: ________

D. Write the fractions for the following.

1. Half = ________
2. One-third = ________
3. Two-thirds = ________
4. Three-fourths = ________
5. Numerator: 2, denominator: 5 = ________
6. Numerator: 4, denominator: 9 = ________

E. Match the figures in column A to their fractions in column B.

A		B
1.	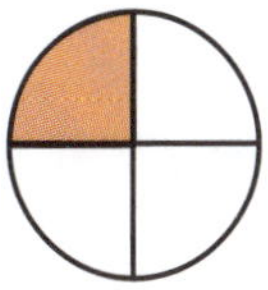	a. $\frac{5}{6}$
2.	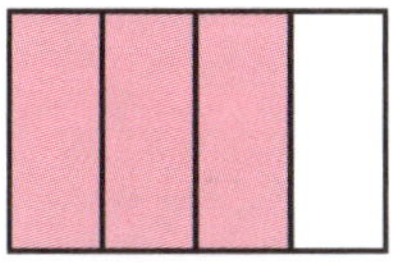	b. $\frac{1}{3}$
3.	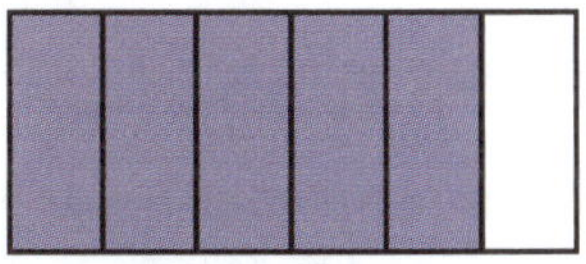	c. $\frac{1}{4}$
4.	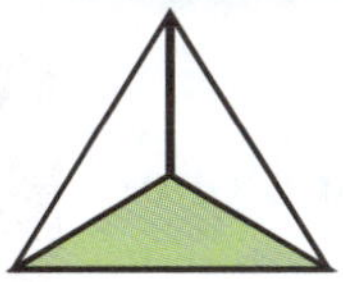	d. $\frac{3}{4}$

F. Write the fraction for the following collection and circle it.

Collection of objects	Fraction
	1. Pink caps: _____
	2. Pigeons: _____
	3. Red stars: _____

G. Solve the following.

a. $\frac{1}{2}$ of 18

b. $\frac{1}{6}$ of 24

c. Out of 18 notebooks, the teacher corrected $\frac{1}{6}$ of the notebooks. How many notebooks were corrected by the teacher?

d. Samir had 20 marbles. He gave away $\frac{1}{5}$ of the marbles to a friend. Calculate the number of marbles his friend got.

e. Mansi had 12 hair clips in her collection. She gifted 5 hair clips to her sister on her birthday. What fraction of the clips did Mansi gift?

SKILL UP!

A. 21 CS Communication, Life Skills | EL

The concept of fractions is used while cooking in the kitchen as well. Recipe of most dishes include food items that are measured in fractions. With the help of your mother, write down the recipe of a favourite dish in your notebook in the format shown alongside. Identify the food items whose amount is needed in fractions.

B. 21 CS Critical Thinking, Information Literacy | HQ Happiness My Goal

Olivia likes to read storybooks. Before going to sleep, she reads one-eighth of a book daily.

How many pages does she read if the total number of pages in the book is 80?

In how many days would Olivia be able to finish reading the book?

____

Do you like reading books? Name any two books that you have read.

____

It is said that reading is a good habit. Is it so? Share your thoughts on this.

C. 21 CS Critical Thinking | EL

Aarav ate half of a hot dog.
Poonam ate half of another hot dog.
Who ate more? Justify your answer.

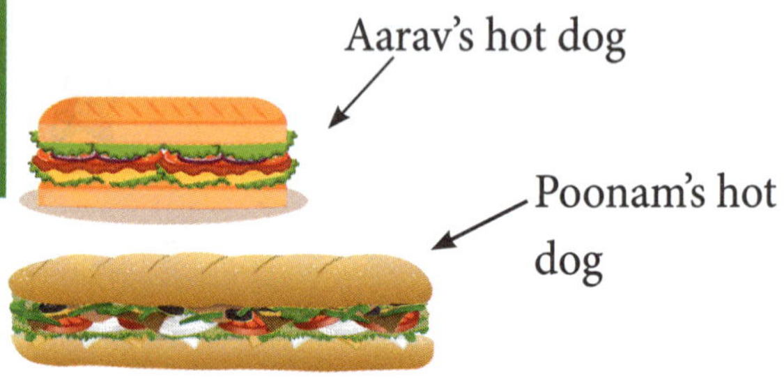

SUSTAINABLE DEVELOPMENT GOALS

Questions A and C are in line with SDG 2 Zero Hunger and SDG 3 Good Health and Well-Being, respectively. Is your favourite food a healthy food? What should Aarav and Poonam do with their leftover hot dogs?

Question B is in line with SDG 4 Quality Education.

Worksheet 6

21 CS Critical Thinking AI

Cerah owns a flower shop. She put flowers of two different colours in some vases as shown below. Colour the flowers in each vase to show the given fraction. Choose from the colours mentioned alongside the vases.

Also, write the fraction for the flowers of the other colour of flower in each vase in the space provided.

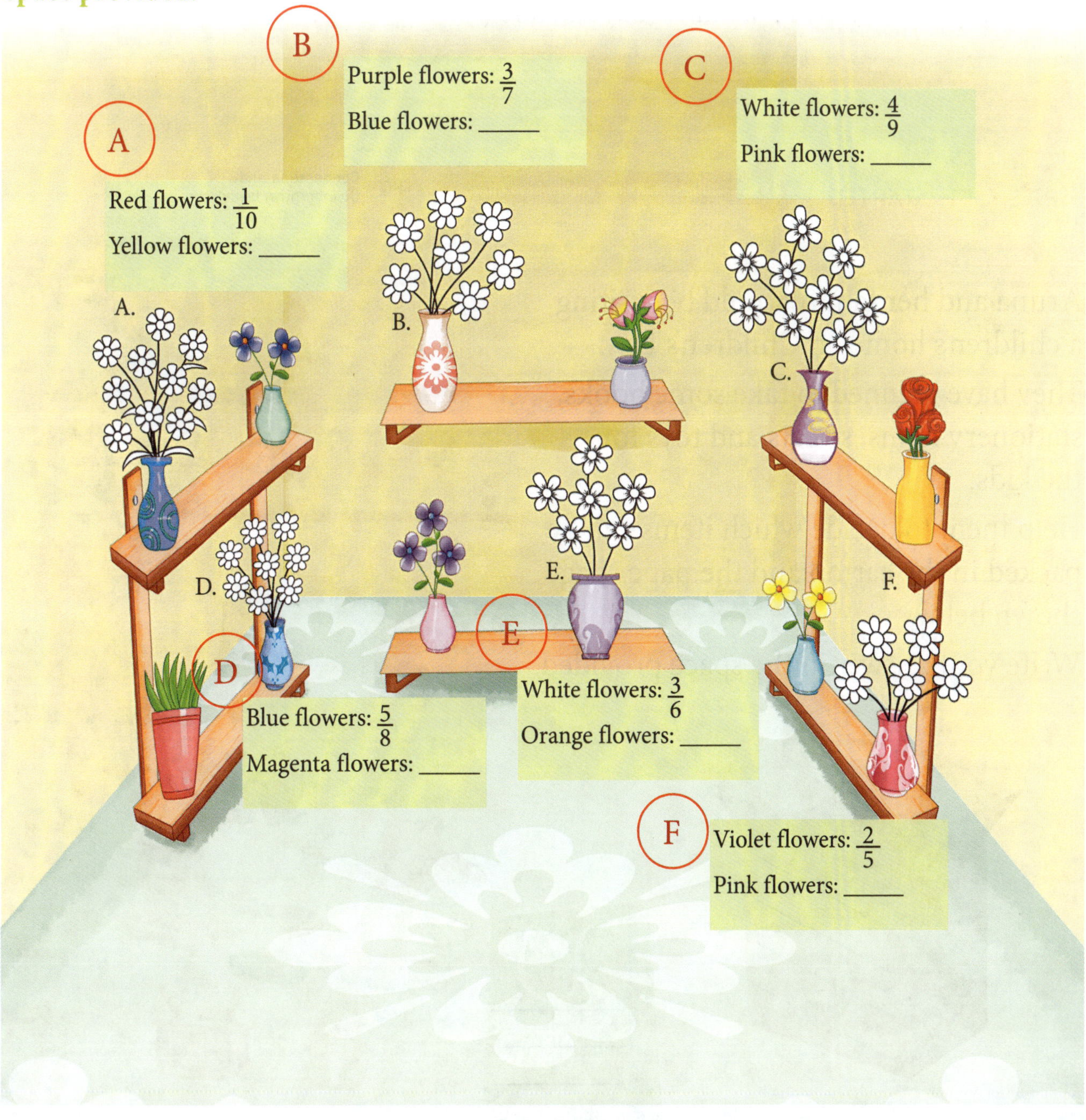

7 Measurement

Learning Objectives

- To estimate and measure length using a ruler
- To express length in centimetre (cm), metre (m) and kilometre (km)
- To express mass in milligram (mg), gram (g) and kilogram (kg)
- To express capacity in millilitre (mℓ) and litre (ℓ)

Let's Get Started

21 CS Critical Thinking, Information Literacy

HQ Cooperation and Collaborative Living

Aruna and her family would be visiting a children's home on Children's Day.

They have planned to take some books, stationery items, sweets and toys for the kids.

Help them to decide which items can be packed in the carton and the paper bag shown below.

Write your answer in the space provided.

MEASUREMENT OF LENGTH

We have learnt that in ancient times, people used non-standard units like handspan, cubit, footspan, pace, etc. to measure the lengths of various objects.

NOTE

Length is the distance from one end of an object to its other end, along its longest side.

To measure length means to find out how **long**, **tall** or **wide** an object is.

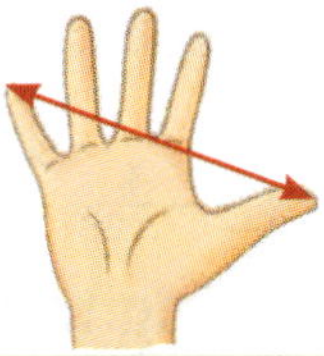
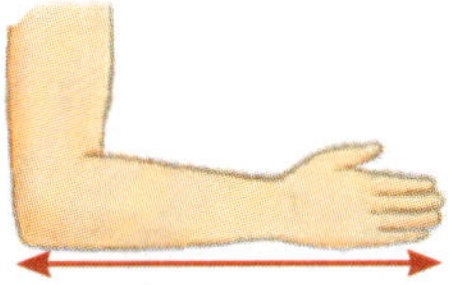
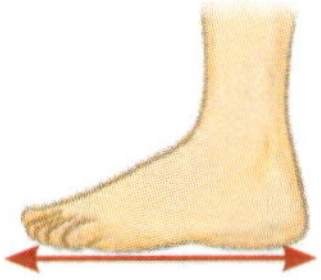
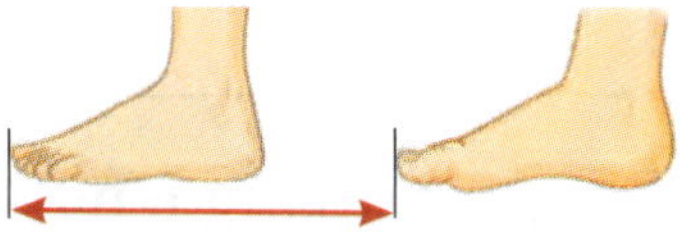

Handspan	Cubit	Footspan	Pace
With stretched fingers, the distance between tip of the little finger and the tip of the thumb.	The distance between the elbow and the tip of the middle finger.	The distance between the end of the heel and the tip of the big toe.	The distance between the front foot and the back foot when a single step is taken.

Later, it was found that measuring length using non-standard units does not give the exact or correct values. This is because the lengths of hands, arms and feet vary from person to person and are not fixed. So, the need for a fixed or standard system of measurement arose and the metric system was adopted.
Let us learn more about this.

Standard Units of Measuring Length

To get an exact measurement of length instead of estimation, we use standard units of measurement. In the metric system, to measure length, we use the following standard units.

Standard units of length	
Centimetre  About 1 cm	• The centimetre is a smaller unit of length. • It is used to measure shorter lengths. **Examples:** length of a pencil, a book, a crayon, etc. • It is written as **'cm'** in short. • The length of a centimetre is approximately the width of one's forefinger.
Metre  About 1 m	• The metre is a larger unit of length. • It is used to measure longer lengths. **Examples:** length of a piece of cloth, height of a door or wall, length of a classroom • It is written as **'m'** in short. • The length of a metre is approximately the distance between both the hands when we stretch them. • Relation between m and cm: **1 m = 100 cm**

Kilometre 	• The kilometre is a much larger unit of length. • It is used to measure very long distances. **Example:** distance between two cities, distance between an airplane flying in the sky and the ground, etc. • It is written as **'km'** in short. • A milestone by the roadside shows the distance in kilometres from that point to the next city or other places. • Relation between km and m: **1 km = 1000 m**

For measuring length, we use tools like a ruler (scale) and a measuring tape.

This is equal to 1 cm.

Ruler

Measuring tape

NOTE

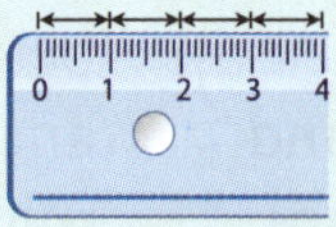

The lengths between the centimetre markings on a ruler are equal.

EXERCISE 7A

1. Write the given units of measuring length in increasing order.

centimetre kilometre metre

2. Which of the following objects are longer than 1 metre? Tick the correct answers.

a. Height of a refrigerator ☐

b. Length of a safety pin ☐

c. Length of an ant ☐

d. Length of a calculator ☐

e. Length of a bed ☐

3. Write the correct unit of measurement (cm, m or km) for each of the following.

a. Length of a pen ____

b. Length of a swimming pool ____

c. Distance from one town to another ____

d. Height of a bookshelf ____

Measuring Length Using a Ruler

Look at the following ruler. Let us measure the length of a crayon using this ruler.

- First, keep the edge of the ruler along the length of the object.
- Then, align the 0 mark of the ruler with one end of the object.

- Next, read the marking on the ruler where the other end of the object reaches.
- This reading gives the measurement of its length.

So, the length of this crayon is 6 cm.

In case a ruler is broken or the 0 mark on it is not clear, we can measure the length of the objects using a different start point.

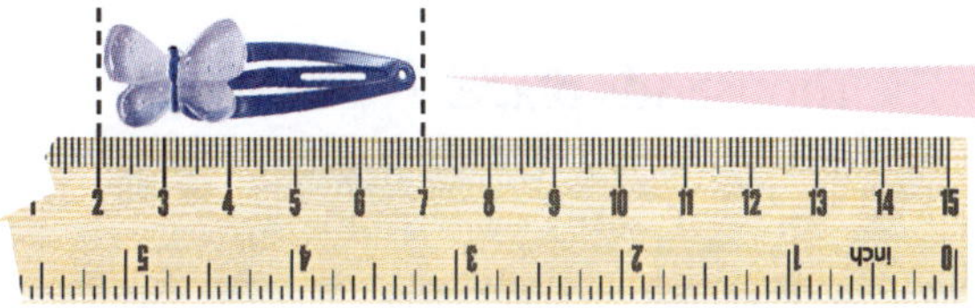

- To find the length, subtract the reading at one end from the reading at the other end.
- Here, the length of hair clip is 7 – 2 = 5 cm.

CONVERSION OF LENGTH UNITS

Metres to Centimetres

1 metre = 100 centimetres

1 m is 100 times as long as 1 cm.

To convert metres to centimetres, multiply the number of metres by 100 and change the unit to centimetre (cm).

Example 1: Convert the following to cm. a. 2 m b. 3 m 45 cm

Solution: a. 2 m = 2 × 100 = 200 cm.

b. 3 m = 3 × 100 = 3 0 0 cm

45 cm = + 4 5 cm

3 4 5 cm

So, 3 m 45 cm = 345 cm.

GO EASY!

To convert:

× 100 (as value increases)

Metre (1 m) → Centimetre (100 cm)

÷ 100 (as value decreases)

Centimetres to Metres

100 centimetres = 1 metre

To convert centimetres to metres, divide the number of centimetres by 100 and change the unit to metre.

Example 2: Convert the following to m. a. 400 cm b. 253 cm

Solution: a. 400 cm = 400 ÷ 100 = 4 m

b. 253 cm = 253 ÷ 100

= 2 m 53 cm

$$\begin{array}{r} 2 \\ 100\,\overline{)\,253} \\ -\,200 \\ \hline 53 \end{array}$$

NOTE

When we convert **cm** to **m** using the long division method, the quotient represents metres and the remainder represents centimetres.

GO EASY!

- When dividing by 100, draw a line after the hundreds place.

  The 2 on the left of the line represents metres and the 53 on the right represents centimetres.
- Similarly, when dividing by 1000, draw a line after the thousands place.

H	T	O
2	5	3

Kilometres to Metres

1 kilometre = 1000 metres

To convert kilometres to metres, multiply the number of kilometres by 1000 and change the unit to metre.

Example 3: Convert 2 km 50 m to m.

Solution:

2 km = 2 × 1000 = 2 0 0 0 m

50 m = + 5 0 m

2 0 5 0 m

So, 2 km 50 m = 2050 m.

Metres to Kilometres

1000 metres = 1 kilometre

To convert metres to kilometres, divide the number of metres by 1000 and change the unit to kilometre.

Example 4: Convert 2453 m to km.

Solution:

Th	H	T	O
2	4	5	3

2453 m = 2453 ÷ 1000

= 2 km 453 m.

So, 2453 m = 2 km 453 m.

Exercise 7B

1. **Use a ruler to measure the following.**
   a. Length of an eraser ________ b. Length of an envelope ________
   c. Length of a cell phone ________ d. Height of a glass ________
2. **Convert the following to cm.**
   a. 3 m = ________ cm b. 9 m = ________ cm
   c. 3 m 42 cm = ________ cm d. 4 m 59 cm = ________ cm
3. **Convert the following.**
   a. 300 cm = ________ m b. 469 cm = ________ m ________ cm
   c. 4 km 320 m = ________ m d. 1596 m = ________ km ________ m

MEASUREMENT OF MASS

In our previous classes, we learnt that mass can be measured using non-standard units such as stones and marbles. As such things can vary in size and shape, we use standard units for measuring mass.

Note

To measure the amount of mass means to find out how **heavy** or **light** an object is.

Standard Units of Measuring Mass

In the metric system, to measure mass, we use the following standard units.

Standard units of mass	
Milligram 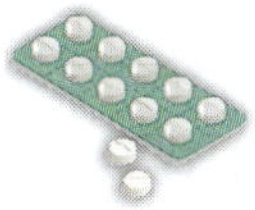 A medicine tablet weighs about 20 mg.	• The milligram is a very small unit of mass. • It is used to weigh very small or light objects. **Examples:** very small jewellery items, medicines, some food items, etc. • It is written as '**mg**' in short.
Gram  A 5-rupee coin weighs about 6 g.	• The gram is a small unit of mass. • It is used to weigh light objects. **Examples:** a binder clip, currency coins, a teaspoon of sugar, a packet of powdered spices, etc. • It is written as '**g**' in short. • Relation between g and mg: **1 g = 1000 mg**
Kilogram  8 or 9 tomatoes weigh about 1 kg.	• The kilogram is a larger unit of mass. • It is used to weigh heavier objects. **Examples:** a luggage bag, a watermelon, 8 or 9 tomatoes, etc. • It is written as '**kg**' in short. • Relation between kg and g: **1 kg = 1000 g**

We use a **simple balance** or a **weighing scale** to weigh an object. A simple balance has two pans. When we put objects on both the pans of the balance, the pan with the heavier object goes down, while the other pan with the lighter object goes up.

In the image given alongside, the pineapple is heavier than the guava.

Same mass

If the objects kept on both the pans are of equal mass, the pans balance. Here in the image shown, the book has the same mass as the chalk box.

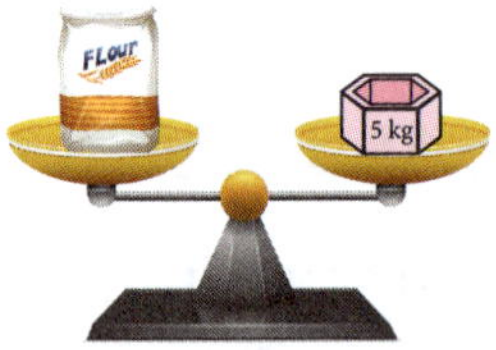

The packet of flour weighs 5 kg.

Some standard weights used for measurement of mass are shown below.

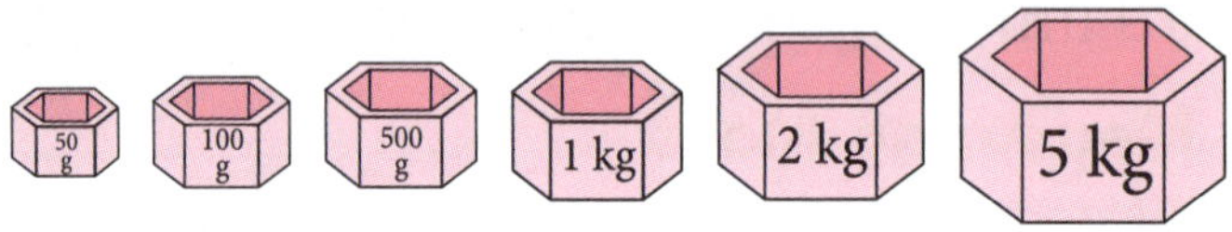

CONVERSION OF MASS UNITS

Kilograms to Grams

1 kilogram = 1000 grams

To convert kilograms to grams, multiply the number of kilograms by 1000 and change the unit to gram.

Example 5: Convert 3 kg 245 g to g.

Solution: 3 kg = 3 × 1000 = 3 0 0 0 g

245 g = + 2 4 5 g

$$\begin{array}{r} 3\,0\,0\,0\text{ g} \\ +\;\;2\,4\,5\text{ g} \\ \hline 3\,2\,4\,5\text{ g} \end{array}$$

So, 3 kg 245 g = 3245 g.

Grams to Kilograms

1000 grams = 1 kilogram

To convert grams to kilograms, divide the number of grams by 1000 and change the unit from gram to kilogram.

Example 6: Convert 3249 g to kg and g.

Solution:

3249 g = 3249 ÷ 1000 = 3 | 249

= 3 kg 249 g

So, 3249 g = 3 kg 249 g.

EXERCISE 7C

1. **Write the appropriate unit of measurement (mg, g, kg) for the given objects.**

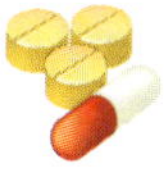

a. ________ b. ________ c. ________ d. ________ e. ________

2. **How much does each object weigh? Write in the space provided.**

a. ________ b. ________ c. ________

3. **Convert the following to g.**

a. 5 kg b. 8 kg c. 1 kg 375 g d. 7 kg 130 g

4. **Convert the following to kg and g.**

a. 5000 g b. 7342 g c. 3581 g d. 2467 g

MEASUREMENT OF CAPACITY

At home, we often use a glass to measure the amount of water needed while cooking. A glass is a non-standard unit for measurement. Examples of other containers used in everyday life as non-standard units are as follows:

- 2 cups of water
- 1 spoonful of medicine
- 1 bowl of soup
- 3 bottles of juice

Look at the following containers. Let us compare their capacities.

All the milk from the bottle completely fills two mugs.

All the milk from the bottle completely fills three glasses.

DO YOU KNOW?

Capacity is the total amount of liquid a container can hold.

Volume is the amount of liquid present in a container.

So, capacity of the bottle = capacity of 2 mugs = capacity of 3 glasses.

The sizes of cups, mugs, spoons, bowls, glasses and bottles vary and are not fixed. Thus, like length and mass, we use standard units for capacity as well.

Standard Units of Measuring Capacity

In the metric system, we use the following standard units to measure capacity.

Standard units of capacity	
Millilitre  About 1 mℓ	• The millilitre is a smaller unit of capacity. • It is used to measure smaller amounts of liquid. **Examples:** a dropper, a feeding bottle, a glass of water, a bottle of liquid medicine, etc. • It is written as '**mℓ**' in short.
Litre  About 20 ℓ	• The litre is a larger unit of capacity. • It is used to measure larger amounts of liquid. **Examples:** a bucket of water, a water tank, a cold drink bottle, etc. • It is written as 'ℓ' in short. • Relation between ℓ and mℓ: **1 ℓ = 1000 mℓ**

Measuring cups and measuring cylinders are used to determine the amount of liquid a container can hold.

The purple bottle is filled with water.

The water is emptied into a measuring cup.

So, the capacity of the bottle is 500 mℓ.

Measuring cup

Measuring cylinder

CONVERSION OF CAPACITY UNITS

Litres to Millilitres

1 litre = 1000 millilitres

To convert litres to millilitres, multiply the number of litres by 1000.

Example 7: Convert 5 ℓ 306 mℓ to mℓ.

Solution: 5 ℓ = 5 × 1000 = 5 0 0 0 mℓ

306 mℓ = + 3 0 6 mℓ

5 3 0 6 mℓ

So, 5 ℓ 306 mℓ = 5306 mℓ.

Millilitres to Litres

1000 millilitres = 1 litre

To convert millilitres to litres, divide the number of millilitres by 1000.

Example 8: Convert 6792 mℓ to ℓ and mℓ.

Solution:

6792 ÷ 1000 = 6 | 792 = 6 ℓ 792 mℓ

So, 6792 mℓ = 6 ℓ 792 mℓ.

COMMON ERRORS

Convert 5 ℓ 26 mℓ to mℓ.

5 ℓ 26 mℓ = 526 mℓ

5 ℓ = 5 × 1000 = 5000 mℓ

26 mℓ = + 26 mℓ

So, 5 ℓ 26 mℓ = 5026 mℓ

Exercise 7D

1. Tick the measurement you think is correct.

a. 
500 ℓ / 500 mℓ

b. 
1 ℓ / 1 mℓ

c. 

30 ℓ / 30 mℓ

d. 
5 mℓ / 5 ℓ

e. 
100 mℓ / 100 ℓ

2. Convert the following to mℓ.
   a. 2 ℓ b. 5 ℓ c. 3 ℓ 20 mℓ d. 4 ℓ 780 mℓ
3. Convert the following to ℓ and mℓ.
   a. 3000 mℓ b. 7000 mℓ c. 5278 mℓ d. 9346 mℓ

WORD PROBLEMS

Example 9: The distance between the school and Osaka's home is 2 km 350 m. What is the distance in metres?

Solution:

$$\begin{array}{rr} 2\text{ km} = 2 \times 1000 = & 2\,0\,0\,0\text{ m} \\ 350\text{ m} = & +\quad 3\,5\,0\text{ m} \\ \hline & 2\,3\,5\,0\text{ m} \\ \hline \end{array}$$

Thus, the distance is 2350 metres.

Example 10: Chanchal's fish tank can hold 9945 millilitres of water. How much would that be in litres and millilitres?

Solution: 9945 mℓ = 9945 ÷ 1000
= 9 | 945 = 9 ℓ 945 mℓ

Thus, the fish tank can hold 9 litres 945 millilitres of water.

Exercise 7E

1. Pooja bought 7 m of cloth from the market. Find the length of the cloth in centimetres.
2. Anil's height is 249 cm. What is his height in metres and centimetres?
3. Rihaan's younger sister weighs about 7485 g. How much will she weigh in kilograms and grams?
4. The capacity of a juice container is 2 litres 370 millilitres. Calculate the capacity in millilitres.

Maths Lab Activity

21 CS Critical Thinking, Collaboration EL

Aim: To understand the concept of capacity using different containers

Materials required: A jug, plastic bottles, bowls and water

Procedure:

1. Take three different containers: a jug, bowls and plastic bottles.
2. Take the jug and fill it completely with water. Fill this water into the bowls. Count the number of bowls needed to empty all the water from the jug.

3. Again, fill the jug completely with water. Now, fill this water into the bottles. Count the number of bottles needed to empty all the water from the jug.

4. What do you observe?

Observation: The number of bowls needed is more than the number of bottles needed to empty all the water from the jug. This is because the bottle has more (higher) capacity than the bowl.

Conclusion: Different containers have different capacities.

Concept Map

Measurement

- **Length** → Standard units: m, cm, km → *relation* → 1 m = 100 cm; 1 km = 1000 m
- **Mass** → Standard units: mg, g, kg → *relation* → 1 g = 1000 mg; 1 kg = 1000 g
- **Capacity** → Standard units: mℓ, ℓ → *relation* → 1 ℓ = 1000 mℓ

Key Concepts

- **Centimetre:** A smaller unit of length, written as cm
- **Metre:** A larger unit of length, written as m
- **Kilometre:** A much larger unit of length, written as km
- **Milligram:** A very small unit of mass, written as mg
- **Gram:** A small unit of mass, written as g
- **Kilogram:** A larger unit of mass, written as kg
- **Millilitre:** A smaller unit of capacity, written as mℓ
- **Litre:** A larger unit of capacity, written as ℓ

A. Circle the unit of measurement you would use to measure the following.

1. Length of a pencil box

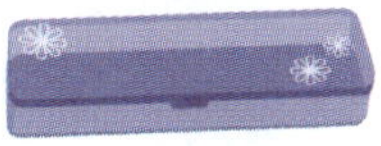

cm m km

2. Height of a wall

cm m km

3. Mass of a baby

g mg kg

B. Fill in the blanks using the correct words.

mass
millilitres
kilometres
length
litres

1. Darisa has two pieces of fabric. The total ________ of the two pieces of fabric is 5 m 92 cm.
2. Ajmal is weighing his luggage. The total ________ of his luggage is 55 kilograms.
3. Nathan wants to know how much water his tank can hold. He measures its capacity to be 9 ________ 500 ________.
4. Cathy has to travel several ________ by train to visit her grandparents.

C. Match the following.

Column A	Column B
1. 5 m	a. 12 m
2. 1200 cm	b. 2035 g
3. 2 kg 35 g	c. 500 cm
4. 6000 mℓ	d. 7298 mℓ
5. 7 ℓ 298 mℓ	e. 6 ℓ

D. Convert the following to m and cm.

1. 200 cm = ______ m ______ cm
2. 759 cm = ______ m ______ cm

E. Convert the following to g.

1. 5 kg 68 g = ______ g
2. 2 kg 375 g = ______ g

F. Convert the following to ℓ and mℓ.

1. 1745 mℓ = ___ ℓ ____ mℓ
2. 6087 mℓ = ___ ℓ ____ mℓ

G. Solve the following.

1. Nidhi gave 2 metres of cloth to the tailor to stitch a shirt. How many centimetres is that?
2. Mohan walked 3 km 200 m in the morning. Find the distance in metres.
3. Sudha bought 5 kg of apples. How many grams is that?
4. The capacity of a fish bowl is 1500 mℓ. What is the capacity in litres?
5. Sunny drank 2 litres of milk in 4 days. How many millilitres is that?

SKILL UP!

A. 21 CS Critical Thinking, Information Literacy EL

A regular bottle of water normally has a capacity of 1 litre.

It is equal to ______ mℓ.

Pour the water from the bottle into glasses.

How many glasses does it fill?

How many glasses are equal to 1 litre? ______.

Work in pairs and try the same activity with the same bottle of water and a teacup. Do not let a drop of water to go waste while doing this activity.

B. 21 CS Critical Thinking, Life Skills CC Integration with Science

6 CLEAN WATER AND SANITATION

Radha's mother gave her a 1-litre bottle of water to drink the whole day. Radha drank only 200 mℓ of water from it. Did Radha drink enough water?

It is suggested that children must drink at least 1 litre of water every day. Do you think it is important to drink sufficient amount of water every day? Why?

C. 21 CS Critical Thinking, Life Skills

If you need to buy 1 kg of apples and 1 kg of chips, which would be a bigger packet? Why?

Do you think we will need more feathers or bricks to collect 1 kg of each? Explain with reasons.

SUSTAINABLE DEVELOPMENT GOALS

Questions A and B are in line with SDG 6 Clean Water and Sanitation. Many people may have sufficient clean water. However, many others do not have it.

WORKSHEET 7

21 CS Critical Thinking, Information Literacy | EL | HQ Knowing My Needs

Nick and Tanvi are at the supermarket with their mothers for grocery shopping. Take a look at the things they see in the market and answer the questions that follow.

1. Nick's height is 132 cm and Tanvi's height is 1 m 28 cm. Who is taller and by how much?
2. Whose length is more: the air conditioner or the monitor on the wall? Which unit of measurement would you use to measure their lengths?
3. Tanvi's mother bought 3 kg 250 g of fruits, while Nick's mother bought 3 kg 750 g of fruits. Who bought more fruits? Write the mass in grams.
4. Tanvi took 1 litre carton of orange juice from the beverages section. Nick took 2 tetrapacks of 500 mℓ of guava juice. Who do you think has more quantity of juice and why?
5. Looking at a butter pack, Nick said the quantity of butter is measured in grams. Tanvi disagreed and said it is measured in millilitres. Who do you think is right? Justify your answer.

8 Time

Learning Objectives

- To read and write time to half past, quarter past, quarter to and 5-minute correctness
- To learn relation between various time units and estimate time
- To read a calendar and prepare a timeline

Let's Get Started

21 CS Communication, Life Skills HQ Happiness My Goal

Tarun and Tanvi are classmates. During their vacation, they visited two different places. Given below are two pictures clicked by them during their stay. Identify the season in each picture and write its name in the space provided.

__________________ __________________

Which is your favourite season?

____

What do you like to do the most in this season?

____

READING TIME ON A CLOCK

We know that a clock tells us the exact time of the day. It has two hands: the minute hand and the hour hand.

The minute hand moves faster than the hour hand. In one hour, the minute hand goes around the clock once, while the hour hand moves from one number to the next.

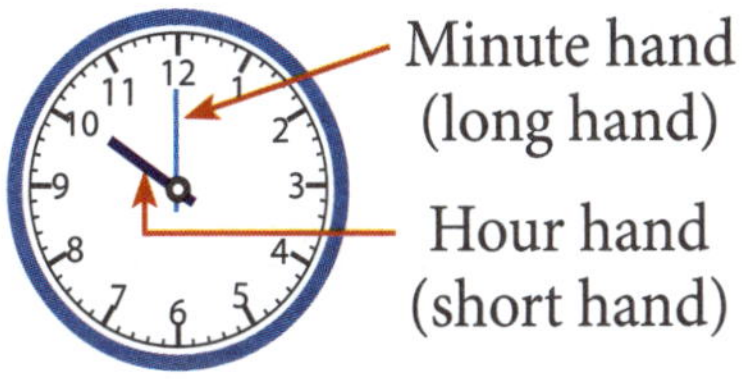

In this clock, the minute hand is at 12 and the hour hand is at 10.
So, the time is 10 o'clock or 10:00.

Half Past the Hour

Look at the face of a clock closely. There are 5 equal divisions between two numbers and each division represents 1 minute. This means, when the minute hand moves from one number to the next, it takes 5 minutes (or 5 minutes have passed). So, when the minute hand reaches 6 starting from 12, it has moved 30 minutes since it left 12.

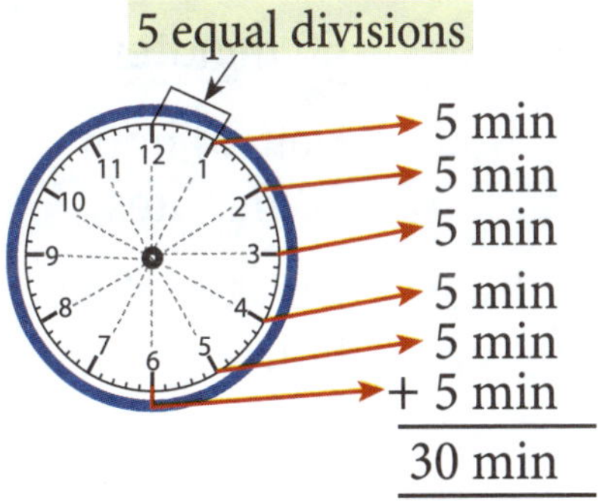

60 minutes = 1 hour
30 minutes = half an hour

For the minute hand at 6, read the time as **30 minutes past** or **half past** the hour. In this clock, the minute hand is at 6 and the hour hand is between 12 and 1. So, the time is 30 minutes past 12 or half past 12.

30 minutes past 12 or 12:30 or half past 12

NOTE

In a clock, the minute hand is longer than the hour hand. That is why the minute hand is also known as the long hand and the hour hand is known as the short hand.

Quarter Past the Hour

When the minute hand reaches 3 starting from 12, it has moved 15 minutes since it left 12.

For the minute hand at 3, read the time as **15 minutes past** or **quarter past** the hour.

Here, the minute hand is at 3 and the hour hand is between 12 and 1. So, the time is 15 minutes past 12 or quarter past 12.

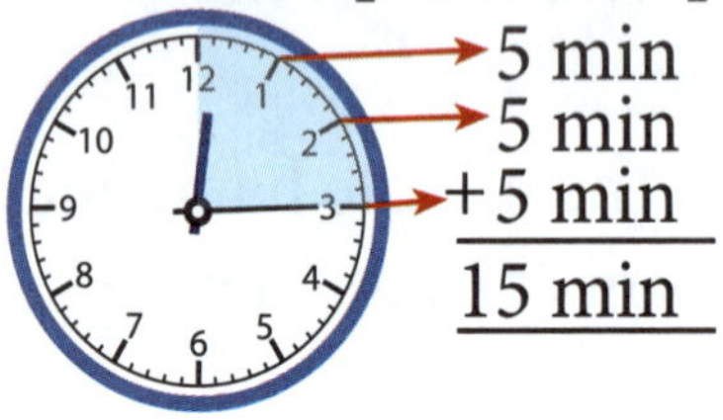

15 minutes past 12 or
12:15 or quarter past 12

Quarter to the Hour

When the minute hand reaches 9 starting from 12, it has moved 45 minutes since it left 12.

For the minute hand at 9, read the time as **45 minutes past**. It is also read as **15 minutes to** or **quarter to** the hour. The reason is the minute hand will take another 15 minutes (a quarter) to reach 12, and hence, to the next hour.

In the given clock, the minute hand is at 9 and the hour hand is between 12 and 1. So, the time is 15 minutes to 1 or quarter to 1.

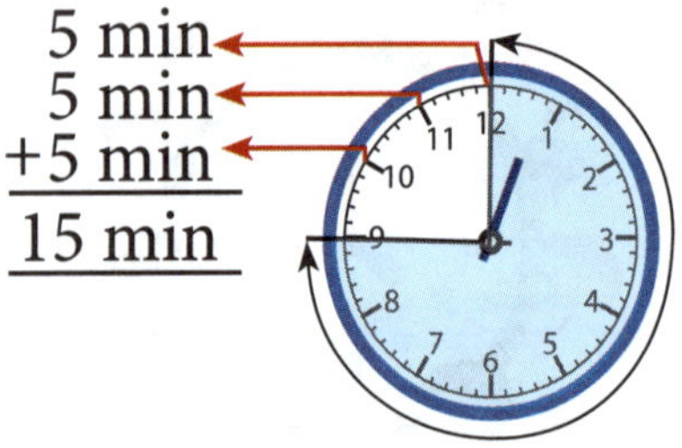

45 minutes past 12 or
12:45 or 15 minutes to 1 or
quarter to 1

NOTE

1 hour = 60 minutes

$\frac{1}{2}$ hour = Half an hour
= 30 minutes

$\frac{1}{4}$ hour = Quarter of an hour
= 15 minutes

EXERCISE 8A

1. Write the time shown by the following clocks in both the ways.

a. 

______ or ______

b. 

______ or ______

c. 

______ or ______

d. 

______ or ______

2. **Draw hands in each clock according to the given time.**

a. 

5:00 or
5 o'clock

b. 

3:30 or
Half past 3

c. 

10:15 or
Quarter past 10

d. 

7:45 or
Quarter to 8

READING TIME TO 5-MINUTE CORRECTNESS

We have learnt that when the minute hand moves from one number to the next, the time taken is 5 minutes. Knowing the table of 5 or counting by fives makes it easier to read the time.

9:00 9:05 9:10 9:15 9:20 9:25

9:30 9:35 9:40 9:45 9:50 9:55 10:00

SOLVED EXAMPLES

Example 1: Calculate the time taken by the minute hand to move from:

a. 4 to 8

Solution:

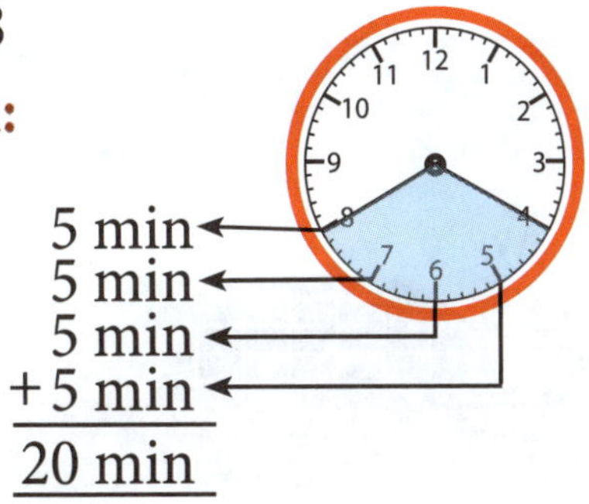

So, the minute hand takes 20 minutes to move from 4 to 8.

b. 12 to 2

Solution:

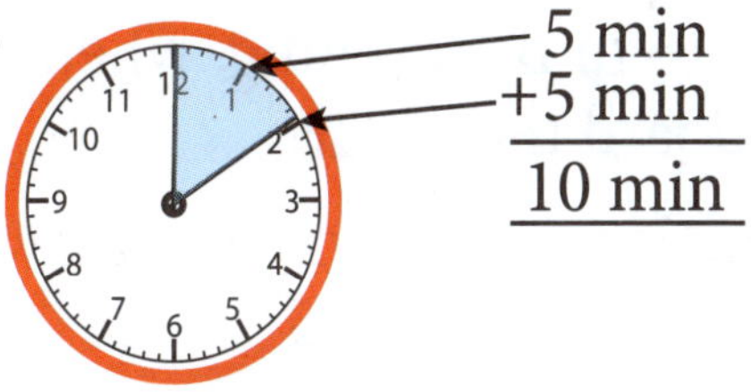

So, the minute hand takes 10 minutes to move from 12 to 2.

TELLING TIME TO THE NEXT HOUR

We can represent time in two ways:

- Number of minutes past the hour.
- Number of minutes to the next hour.

7 o'clock or
7:00

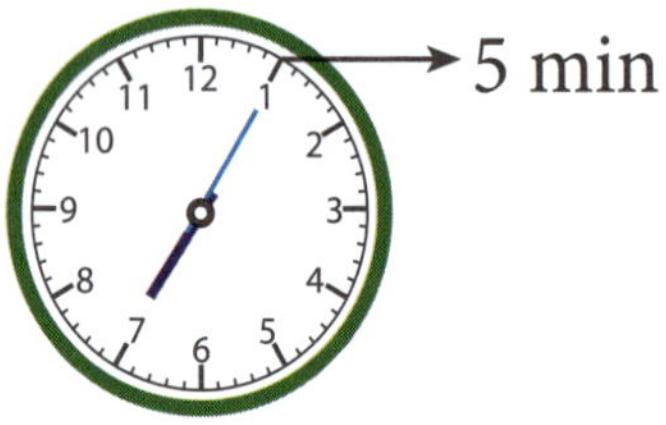

5 minutes past 7 or
7:05

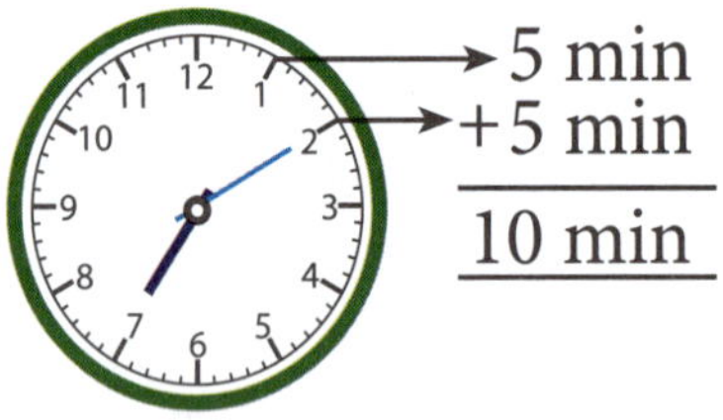

10 minutes past 7 or
7:10

40 minutes past 7 or
7:40 or 20 minutes to 8

45 minutes past 7 or
7:45 or quarter to 8

TELLING THE TIME BEFORE AND AFTER

When the time is 3:15, it indicates 15 minutes past 3. Here, 3 represents the number of hours and 15 represents the number of minutes.

Example 2: Sakshi reached a park at 4 o'clock and left from there after one hour. At what time did Sakshi leave the park?

Solution: Sakshi reached the park at: 4:00

Time after 1 hour: 4:00 + 1 hour = 5:00

So, Sakshi left the park at 5 o'clock.

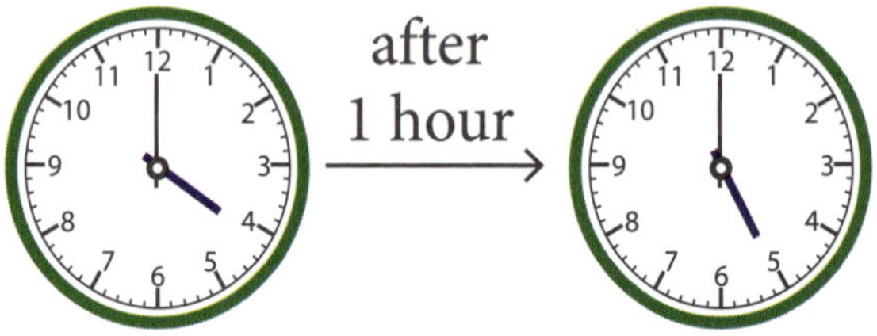

4:00 5:00

Example 3: Manav boarded the flight 3 hours ago from Pune. If he reached Delhi at 7:15 in the evening, when did he board the flight?

Solution: Time when Manav reached Delhi: 7:15

Time 3 hours ago: 7:15 – 3 hours
= 4:15

So, Manav boarded the flight from Pune at 4:15.

Exercise 8B

1. How many minutes does the minute hand take to move from 12 to each of the following numbers?

   a. 2 b. 3 c. 7 d. 10 e. 11

2. Write the time for the following clocks in two ways.

   a. 

   ______ or ______

   b. 

   ______ or ______

   c. 

   ______ or ______

3. Draw the hands of each clock according to the given time.

   a. 

   11:00 or
   11 o'clock

   b. 

   2:25 or
   25 minutes past 2

   c. 

   9:55 or
   55 minutes past 9

4. Answer the following.

   a. Farha went to her friend's house at 6:00 and left after 2 hours. When did she leave her friend's house?

   b. The movie began at 3:30 and was 3 hours long. At what time did the movie get over?

RELATION BETWEEN TIME UNITS

We know that the minute hand takes one hour to complete one full round of the clock. In that time, the minute hand has passed 60 minutes. So,

1 hour = 60 minutes

The hour hand takes one hour to move from one number to the next.
To complete one round of the clock, it takes 12 hours.

In one day, the hour hand takes two rounds of the clock. So, we can say a day is equal to 24 hours.

1 day = 24 hours

Another unit used to measure time is the second. A second is shorter than a minute. One minute is equal to 60 seconds. That is,

1 minute = 60 seconds

ESTIMATING TIME

A minute is a shorter period of time. An hour is a longer period of time.

It takes about a minute to drink a glass of juice. It takes about 5 minutes to make a cup of tea.

It takes about 1 hour to get ready for school. It takes about 4 hours to travel from New Delhi to Chandigarh by train.

CALENDAR

A calendar is a page or series of pages showing the days, weeks and months of a particular year. Look at the calendar for the year 2022.

2022

JANUARY

SUN	MON	TUE	WED	THU	FRI	SAT
						1
2	3	4	5	6	7	8
9	10	11	12	13	14	15
16	17	18	19	20	21	22
23	24	25	26	27	28	29
30	31					

FEBRUARY

SUN	MON	TUE	WED	THU	FRI	SAT
		1	2	3	4	5
6	7	8	9	10	11	12
13	14	15	16	17	18	19
20	21	21	22	24	25	26
27	28					

MARCH

SUN	MON	TUE	WED	THU	FRI	SAT
		1	2	3	4	5
6	7	8	9	10	11	12
13	14	15	16	17	18	19
20	21	21	22	24	25	26
27	28	29	30	31		

APRIL

SUN	MON	TUE	WED	THU	FRI	SAT
					1	2
3	4	5	6	7	8	9
10	11	12	13	14	15	16
17	18	19	20	21	22	23
24	25	26	27	28	29	30

MAY

SUN	MON	TUE	WED	THU	FRI	SAT
1	2	3	4	5	6	7
8	9	10	11	12	13	14
15	16	17	18	19	20	21
22	23	24	25	26	27	28
29	30	31				

JUNE

SUN	MON	TUE	WED	THU	FRI	SAT
			1	2	3	4
5	6	7	8	9	10	11
12	13	14	15	16	17	18
19	20	21	22	23	24	25
26	27	28	29	30		

JULY

SUN	MON	TUE	WED	THU	FRI	SAT
					1	2
3	4	5	6	7	8	9
10	11	12	13	14	15	16
17	18	19	20	21	22	23
24	25	26	27	28	29	30
31						

AUGUST

SUN	MON	TUE	WED	THU	FRI	SAT
	1	2	3	4	5	6
7	8	9	10	11	12	13
14	15	16	17	18	19	20
21	22	23	24	25	26	27
28	29	30	31			

SEPTEMBER

SUN	MON	TUE	WED	THU	FRI	SAT
				1	2	3
4	5	6	7	8	9	10
11	12	13	14	15	16	17
18	19	20	21	22	23	24
25	26	27	28	29	30	

OCTOBER

SUN	MON	TUE	WED	THU	FRI	SAT
						1
2	3	4	5	6	7	8
9	10	11	12	13	14	15
16	17	18	19	20	21	22
23	24	25	26	27	28	29
30	31					

NOVEMBER

SUN	MON	TUE	WED	THU	FRI	SAT
		1	2	3	4	5
6	7	8	9	10	11	12
13	14	15	16	17	18	19
20	21	21	22	24	25	26
27	28	29	30			

DECEMBER

SUN	MON	TUE	WED	THU	FRI	SAT
				1	2	3
4	5	6	7	8	9	10
11	12	13	14	15	16	17
18	19	20	21	22	23	24
25	26	27	28	29	30	31

- There are about 52 weeks and 1 day in a year.
- There are 7 days in a week, which are Monday, Tuesday, Wednesday, Thursday, Friday, Saturday and Sunday.
- There are 12 months in a year. The months have either 30 or 31 days, except for February, which has 28 or 29 days. February has 29 days once in 4 years, that is, in a leap year.
- A normal year has 365 days. A leap year has 366 days and it comes every four years.
- Each month has about 4 weeks and a few days.
- To write a **date**, we need the day, month and year. A date is generally written in the format date/month/year. For example, 15 February 2022 or 15/02/2022 or 15/02/22 or 15.02.2022 or 15.02.22.

Do you know?

Why are there 366 days in a leap year?

The Earth takes 365 and a quarter days to revolve around the Sun. A normal year has only 365 days.

The quarter days add up to 1 day in four years.

$$\left(\frac{1}{4}+\frac{1}{4}+\frac{1}{4}+\frac{1}{4}\right) = 1$$

This 1 day is added to February in the leap year. So, a leap year has 366 days.

Example 4: Debbie and her family have planned a road trip after three months. If this is the month of March, then in which month will they go for the trip?

Solution: Three months after March will be June (April ⟶ May ⟶ **June**).

So, they will go for the road trip in June.

TIMELINE

A **timeline** is a list of events arranged in the order as they happened or according to the time of their occurrence. Timelines can be written either vertically or horizontally.

Example 5: Given below are some events in Ruby's life.

A. Ruby celebrated her third birthday in 2012.
B. Ruby joined Class 1 in 2015.
C. Ruby was born in 2009.
D. Ruby went for her school trip in 2017.
E. Ruby turned 1-year-old in 2010.

Create a timeline for all the events given above from Ruby's life.

NOTE

1 year = 12 months
1 year = 52 weeks and one day
1 year = 365 days
1 leap year = 366 days
1 month = 4 weeks + a few days
1 month = 31/30/28/29 days
1 week = 7 days
1 fortnight = 14 days or 2 weeks
1 day = 24 hours
1 hour = 60 minutes
1 minute = 60 seconds

Solution: First, write the events in the correct order as they happened.

1. C - Ruby was born in 2009.
2. E - Ruby turned 1-year-old in 2010.
3. A - Ruby celebrated her third birthday in 2012.
4. B - Ruby joined Class 1 in 2015.
5. D - Ruby went for her school trip in 2017.

This can be represented on a timeline vertically or horizontally as shown below.

Vertical timeline

2009 — Ruby was born.
2010 — Ruby turned 1-year-old.
2012 — Ruby celebrated her third birthday.
2015 — Ruby joined Class 1.
2017 — Ruby went for her school trip.

Horizontal timeline

C	E	A	B	D
2009	2010	2012	2015	2017

PUZZLE!

I left the house at 5 o'clock. I walked for the next 10 minutes. Then, I took a rickshaw and travelled for 5 minutes. I stopped to buy a gift for my friend, which took 15 minutes. I walked again for 10 minutes and reached my friend's house.
What time did I reach my friend's house?

EXERCISE 8C

1. Given is the calendar of 2022. Look at it and answer the questions that follow.

2022

JANUARY

SUN	MON	TUE	WED	THU	FRI	SAT
						1
2	3	4	5	6	7	8
9	10	11	12	13	14	15
16	17	18	19	20	21	22
23	24	25	26	27	28	29
30	31					

FEBRUARY

SUN	MON	TUE	WED	THU	FRI	SAT
		1	2	3	4	5
6	7	8	9	10	11	12
13	14	15	16	17	18	19
20	21	21	22	24	25	26
27	28					

MARCH

SUN	MON	TUE	WED	THU	FRI	SAT
		1	2	3	4	5
6	7	8	9	10	11	12
13	14	15	16	17	18	19
20	21	21	22	24	25	26
27	28	29	30	31		

APRIL

SUN	MON	TUE	WED	THU	FRI	SAT
					1	2
3	4	5	6	7	8	9
10	11	12	13	14	15	16
17	18	19	20	21	22	23
24	25	26	27	28	29	30

MAY

SUN	MON	TUE	WED	THU	FRI	SAT
1	2	3	4	5	6	7
8	9	10	11	12	13	14
15	16	17	18	19	20	21
22	23	24	25	26	27	28
29	30	31				

JUNE

SUN	MON	TUE	WED	THU	FRI	SAT
			1	2	3	4
5	6	7	8	9	10	11
12	13	14	15	16	17	18
19	20	21	22	23	24	25
26	27	28	29	30		

JULY

SUN	MON	TUE	WED	THU	FRI	SAT
					1	2
3	4	5	6	7	8	9
10	11	12	13	14	15	16
17	18	19	20	21	22	23
24	25	26	27	28	29	30
31						

AUGUST

SUN	MON	TUE	WED	THU	FRI	SAT
	1	2	3	4	5	6
7	8	9	10	11	12	13
14	15	16	17	18	19	20
21	22	23	24	25	26	27
28	29	30	31			

SEPTEMBER

SUN	MON	TUE	WED	THU	FRI	SAT
				1	2	3
4	5	6	7	8	9	10
11	12	13	14	15	16	17
18	19	20	21	22	23	24
25	26	27	28	29	30	

OCTOBER

SUN	MON	TUE	WED	THU	FRI	SAT
						1
2	3	4	5	6	7	8
9	10	11	12	13	14	15
16	17	18	19	20	21	22
23	24	25	26	27	28	29
30	31					

NOVEMBER

SUN	MON	TUE	WED	THU	FRI	SAT
		1	2	3	4	5
6	7	8	9	10	11	12
13	14	15	16	17	18	19
20	21	21	22	24	25	26
27	28	29	30			

DECEMBER

SUN	MON	TUE	WED	THU	FRI	SAT
				1	2	3
4	5	6	7	8	9	10
11	12	13	14	15	16	17
18	19	20	21	22	23	24
25	26	27	28	29	30	31

a. What is the date today? __________

b. What is the day today? __________

c. What will be the date tomorrow? __________

d. What will be the day tomorrow? __________

e. How many full weeks are there in March 2022? __________

f. How many full weeks are there in December 2022? __________

2. Fill in the blanks.

a. 1 week = __________ days
b. 1 year = __________ months

c. 1 year = __________ weeks
d. 1 year = __________ days

e. 1 leap year = __________ days

3. Write the number of days in the following months.

a. January ______
b. March ______
c. June ______

d. July ______
e. August ______
f. November ______

4. Given below are some events from Madhav's life that happened in the year 2019.

a. Madhav visited Mumbai in October 2019 during Dussehra holidays.

b. He completed Class 2 in March 2019.

c. His Christmas holidays began in December 2019.

d. Madhav went for a school picnic in September 2019.

e. His next year's classes began in April 2019.

Write the above events in the correct order as they happened.

Also, create a horizontal and a vertical timeline in your notebook.

Go Easy!

Shortcut to remember the number of days in each month:

Start with your forefinger's knuckle:

1st knuckle: January–31 days

Groove: February–28 or 29 days

2nd knuckle: March–31 days

Groove: April–30 days

3rd knuckle: May–31 days

Groove: June–30 days

4th knuckle: July–31 days

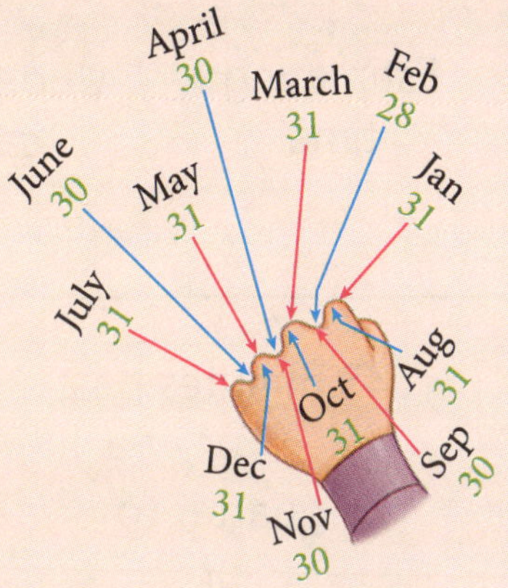

Return to your forefinger's knuckle:

1st knuckle: August–31 days

Groove: September–30 days

2nd knuckle: October–31 days

Groove: November–30 days

3rd knuckle: December–31 days

Maths Lab Activity

21 CS Creativity and Innovation EL AI

Aim: To practice telling time using a paper plate clock

Materials required: Paper plates (preferably white in colour), a marker pen or crayons, a dark-coloured paper or card, scissors, thumb/split pins, glue, a ruler and a pencil

Procedure:

1. Take two paper plates. Using a ruler and a pencil, divide the edges of one plate into 12 equal sections.
2. Now, using scissors, cut the edges of the plate along the 12 equally divided sections, up to a length of 3 cm each.
3. Next, take the second paper plate and paste the first plate on it using glue. Do not paste together the edges or outer rim of both the plates.
4. Write the numbers from 1 to 12 around the rim of the top plate, leaving even spaces between the numbers. Try to write the numbers 12, 3, 6 and 9 first.
5. Write the minutes on the rim of the second plate below the lift-up flaps (cut edges of the first plate), as shown here.
6. With the dark-coloured paper or card, cut out two strips of equal width for the hands of the clock. One strip should be longer than the other.
7. Make a small hole in the centre of the plate to fix the hands and use the split pins to secure. Your paper plate clock is ready.

Activities to be conducted: Move the hands of the clock to a specific time and let the students read the clock and tell what time it is.

Or, call out different times and ask the students to show the given time on their clocks.

Concept Map

- **Time**
  - Reading time
    - Half past or 30 minutes past the hour
    - Quarter past or 15 minutes past the hour
    - 45 minutes past or quarter to or 15 minutes to the hour
    - To 5-minute correctness
    - To the nearest hour
  - Telling the time before and after
  - Estimating time
  - Understanding calendar
  - Understanding timeline

Key Concepts

- **Half Past:** To read the time at 30 minutes past the hour
- **Quarter Past:** To read the time at 15 minutes past the hour
- **Quarter To:** To read the time at 15 minutes to the hour
- **Estimating Time:** Understanding the time taken for a particular activity
- **Calendar:** A page or a series of pages showing the days, weeks and months of a particular year
- **Timeline:** A list of events arranged in the order as they happened

A. Choose the correct option.

1. 

a. 7:30 b. 7:45
c. 7:15 d. 7:10

2. 

a. Half past ten b. Quarter past ten
c. Ten o'clock d. Five minutes past ten

3. 

a. Quarter past two b. Half past two
c. Quarter to three d. Two o'clock

4. 

a. 7:15 b. 7:30
c. 7:05 d. 7:20

B. Match the clock in first row to the time in second row.

1. 
2. 
3. 
4. 

a. 4:30 or 30 minutes past 4
b. 10:00 or 10 o'clock
c. 7:50 or 10 minutes to 8
d. 1:55 or 55 minutes past 1

C. Draw the hands of each clock to show the given time.

1. 

11:10
or
10 minutes past 11

2. 

2:15
or
Quarter past 2

3. 

9:35
or
35 minutes past 9

D. Tick the correct answer for the time taken to do the following activities.

1. Wearing our shoes	a. 3 minutes	b. 30 minutes
2. Driving to the movie hall	a. 2 minutes	b. 2 hours
3. Sleeping at night	a. 8 minutes	b. 8 hours
4. Doing homework	a. 1 minute	b. 1 hour

E. Write T for True and F for False.

1. In the calendar for 2022, 1 week has 9 days. ☐
2. September 2022 has 4 Sundays. ☐
3. 2022 is a leap year. ☐
4. There are 7 months which have 31 days. ☐
5. New Year's day falls on Monday in 2022. ☐

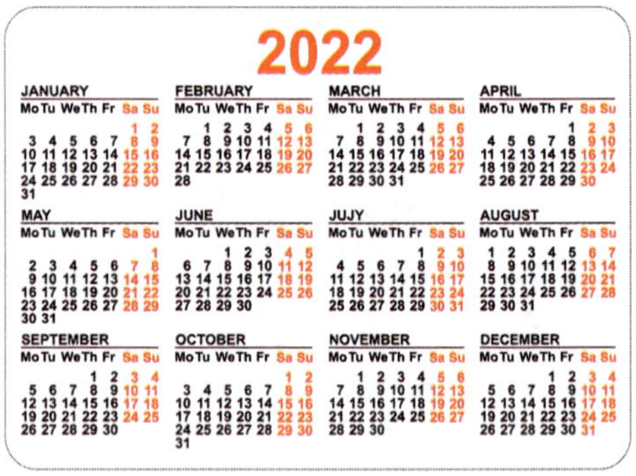

F. Answer the following.

1. How many minutes does the minute hand take to move from 12 to 8?

2. Jimmy's class began at 10:40 in the morning and got over after 3 hours. At what time did Jimmy's class get over?
3. Samaira takes music classes which get over at 5:45. If the class lasts for 2 hours, when does the class begin?
4. Prashant started his journey to his hometown in Assam on 22 October. If it takes 4 days to reach there, on which date will he reach his hometown? If he starts his return journey on 10 November, then on which date will he reach his current place of residence?
5. The following are a few important incidents from Mr Khan's life:

   a. Went on a holiday to London in 2017.

   b. Graduated from college in 2000.

   c. Was born in 1980.

   d. Got married in 2009.

   e. Got his first job in 2002.

   f. Received the best student award in 1997.

   Sequence the above events in the correct order.

☐ ☐ ☐ ☐ ☐ ☐

Also, create a horizontal and a vertical timeline.

SKILL UP!

A. 21 CS Information Literacy | EL | HQ Why Education

Find out the timings of all the classes and activities at school. Also, find out the time for the break and the time when the school gets over. Make your own time table accordingly.

B. 21 CS Information Literacy | EL | AI

Make a birthday timeline of the students in your class. Prepare a card for each month by noting down the names of students whose birthdays fall in that month. Decorate the cards by colouring and drawing designs. Then, arrange the cards in sequential order and paste them on a string or wool thread to hang it in the classroom.

C. 21 CS Critical Thinking, Life Skills | HQ Why Education

The school starts at 8 o'clock in the morning every day.

Jessy reaches the school 5 minutes before 8:00 and Romik reaches the school at 8:15 every day.

Who reaches the school at a better time?

Do you think Romik reaches school on time? Does he reach early or late, and by how much time?

Do you reach your school on time daily? Is it important to be on time? Why?

D. 21 CS Critical Thinking, Information Literacy

Write down your date of birth. Work out your age in years, months and days. Based on the calculation, how old are you now?

SUSTAINABLE DEVELOPMENT GOALS

Questions A and C are in line with SDG 4 Quality Education. Why do you think we need to go to school? Why do you think we have a time table? You may go to school every day. However, there are many children who cannot afford to go to school. What can you do for children who cannot go to school?

Worksheet 8

21 CS Communication, Information Literacy EL AI

This is Amal's birth certificate. A birth certificate is an official document issued to record the birth of a child.

Form No. XXX

Government of National Capital Territory of Delhi

BIRTH CERTIFICATE

This is to certify that the following information has been taken from the original record of Central Zone office which is in the register for South Delhi Municipal Corporation of Delhi.

Name:	AMAL TANDON
Gender:	MALE
Date of Birth:	12/09/2011
Place of Birth:	STAR HOSPITAL, NEW DELHI
Date of Registration:	25/09/2011
Registration No.:	MCDOLIR-0016
Name of Mother:	ARUNA TANDON
Name of Father:	JITENDRA TANDON
Present Address:	A-4, 2nd FLOOR, S.S. COLONY, NEW DELHI-02
Permanent Address:	SAME AS ABOVE

01/12/2011
Date of issue

Sub-Registrar/Registrar of Births/Deaths
Seal and Address of Issuing Authority

Answer the questions based on this certificate.

1. How old will Amal be on 12 September 2025? ________
2. As per the certificate, Amal was born on 12 ________ of the year ________.
3. How many years old is Amal now? ________
4. After how many months of his birth was the certificate issued? ________
5. On which date will he be 9 years old? Write it in numbers.

____

Do you have a birth certificate? Find out from your parents. Draw one for yourself in your notebook and fill in the required details, as shown above.

9 Money

Learning Objectives

- To learn to convert rupees to paise and paise to rupees
- To add, subtract, multiply and divide money
- To solve word problems on money
- To learn to make and interpret bills and rate charts

Let's Get Started

21 CS Communication, Information Literacy HQ Knowing My Needs

The Jolly Toy Store has a sale.
Nip and his father are at the toy store.

Nip saw these toys on sale.
He bought his favourite two toys. His father paid a total of ₹75 to the shopkeeper.

a. Can you guess which toys Nip bought from the store?

Toy 1 = ☐ Toy 2 = ☐

b. How did you arrive at the answer? Explain.

____

____

____

RECALL MONEY

We know that we need money to buy food, clothes, medicines, etc. Every country has its own currency which consists of notes and coins. In India, the currency used is called 'rupee' and 'paisa'. The symbol for rupee is ₹ and the symbol for paisa is **p**.

> **NOTE**
> The plural of rupee is rupees and the plural of paisa is paise.

Look at some of the notes and coins used in India.

Notes

₹5

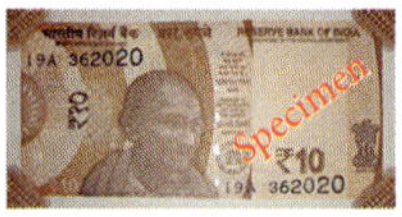

₹10

₹20

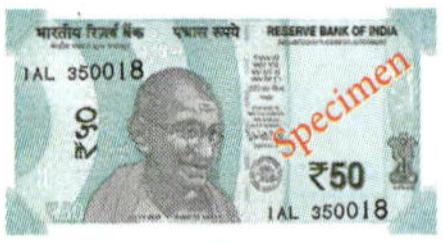

₹50

₹100

₹200

₹500

₹2000

Coins

₹1

₹2

₹5

₹10

> **DO YOU KNOW?**
> Different countries have a different name and symbol for their currencies. For example:
> - The USA uses the dollar ($).
> - England uses the pound (£).
> - Japan uses the yen (¥).

Some of the coins and notes given below are not in circulation these days.

25 paise

50 paise

₹1

₹2

We also had coins of 1 paisa, 2 paise, 3 paise, 5 paise, 10 paise and 20 paise in India, which are no longer in use.

Counting of Money

When we write rupees and paise together, we put a dot in between.

₹ 10 . 25

- The number on the left of the dot shows rupees.
- This dot separates the rupees and paise.
- The number on the right of the dot shows paise.

We read ₹10.25 as ten rupees twenty-five paise.

₹5.75 as five rupees seventy-five paise.

> **NOTE**
> When there is no paise, we write two zeros after the dot in place of paise.
> For example, 50 rupees = ₹50.00.

Now, count and tell how much amount is this.

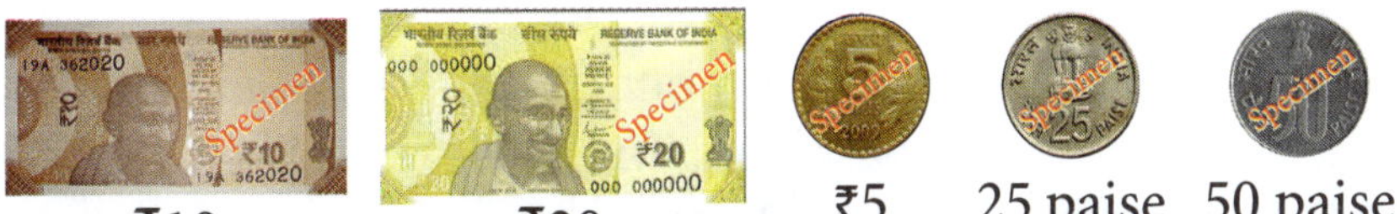

₹10 ₹20 ₹5 25 paise 50 paise

Whenever we have different amounts to count, it is always easier to start counting from the greatest amount. Arrange in the decreasing order and then count.

₹20 ₹10 ₹5 50 paise 25 paise

20 ⟶ 30 ⟶ 35 ⟶ 35.50 ⟶ 35.75 = ₹35.75

CONVERSION OF MONEY

Rupees to Paise

We know that

₹1 = 100 p (100 paise make a rupee.)

To convert rupees to paise, we multiply by 100.

Example 1: Convert ₹3 to paise.

Solution: ₹3 = 3 × 100 = 300 paise

So, ₹3 = 300 paise

Example 2: Convert ₹17.35 to paise.

Solution: ₹17 = 17 × 100 = 1 7 0 0 paise

35 p = + 3 5 paise

1 7 3 5 paise

So, ₹17.35 = 1735 paise.

Paise to Rupees

100 p = ₹1

To convert paise to rupees, we divide by 100.

Example 3: Convert 725 paise to rupees.

Solution: To convert 725 paise to rupees, divide by 100.

Leave two digits from the right and put the dot.

725 ÷ 100 = 7.25

So, 725 paise = ₹7.25.

NOTE

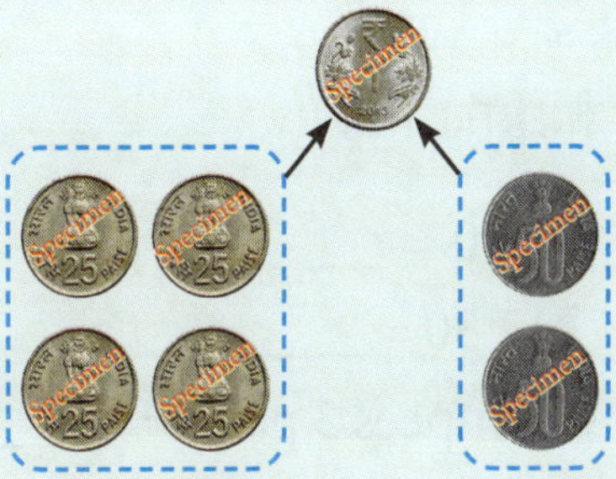

4 coins of 25 paise make ₹1. 2 coins of 50 paise make ₹1.

COMMON ERRORS

Convert 5 rupees 80 paise to paise.

5080 paise (wrong) 580 paise (correct)

GO EASY!

A shorter method for converting rupees and paise to paise is to just remove the point.

Examples: ₹3.75 = 375 p

₹17.35 = 1735 p

Example 4: Convert 5 paise to rupees.

Solution: Keep the last two digits from the right for paise and put the dot.

$5 \div 100 = 0.05$

So, 5 paise = ₹0.05.

Example 5: Convert 2 rupees 45 paise to rupees.

Solution:

2 rupees =		2	0	0	paise
45 paise =	+		4	5	paise
		2	4	5	paise

Put the dot two places from the right.

245 paise = ₹2.45

So, 2 rupees 45 paise = ₹2.45.

Note

Remember that there are always 2 digits for paise because 100 has 2 zeros.

So, 5 paise = ₹0.05.

Similarly, 8 paise = ₹0.08

10 paise = ₹0.10

Common Errors

Convert 7 paise to rupees.

₹7 ✗ ₹ 0.07 ✓

Mental Maths

1. ₹2.50 = ________ p
2. ₹6.05 = ________ p
3. ₹17.30 = ________ p
4. 3 rupees 15 paise = ₹________
5. 89 rupees 3 paise = ₹________
6. 129 rupees 8 paise = ₹________

Exercise 9A

1. Count and write the total amount shown.

a. 

₹10 ₹50 ₹5 25 paise ____________

b. 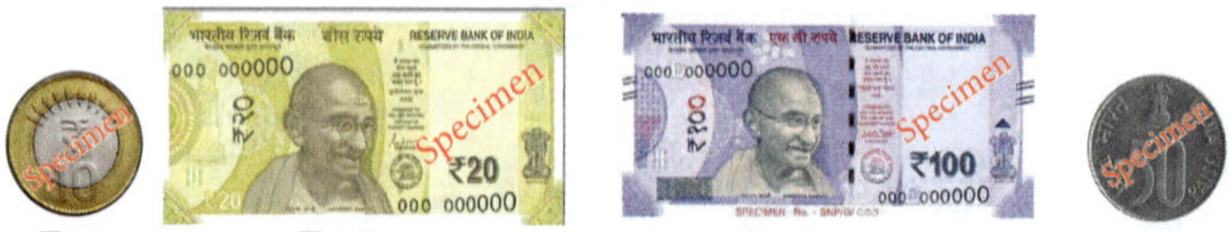

₹10 ₹20 ₹100 50 paise ____________

2. Convert the following to paise.

a. ₹6 b. ₹23 c. ₹13.50 d. 52 rupees 7 paise

3. Convert the following to rupees.

a. 430 paise b. 1305 paise c. 82 rupees 50 paise d. 19 rupees 2 paise

ADDITION AND SUBTRACTION OF MONEY

We add rupees and paise in the same way as we add numbers. Let us learn by solving the following examples.

> **NOTE**
> After adding or subtracting, remember to place the dot just before two places from the right.

SOLVED EXAMPLES

Example 6: Add the following.

a. ₹1000 + ₹200 + ₹5 b. ₹15.75 + ₹2.50 c. ₹149 + ₹63.05 + 13 p

Solution:

a.

	₹
	1 0 0 0
	2 0 0
+	5
	1 2 0 5

Answer: ₹1205

b.

	₹	p
	1	
	1 5 .	7 5
+	2 .	5 0
	1 8 .	2 5

Answer: ₹18.25

c.

	₹	p
	1 1	
	1 4 9 .	0 0
	6 3 .	0 5
+	0 .	1 3
	2 1 2 .	1 8

Answer: ₹212.18

Example 7: Subtract the following.

a. ₹695 – ₹174 b. ₹18.49 from ₹92.35

Solution:

a.

	₹
	6 9 5
–	1 7 4
	5 2 1

Answer: ₹521

b.

	₹	p
	11	12
	8 ~~1~~	~~2~~ 15
	~~9~~ ~~2~~ .	~~3~~ ~~5~~
–	1 8 .	4 9
	7 3 .	8 6

Answer: ₹73.86

> **NOTE**
> 1. First, align the dots and then add or subtract the numbers.
> 2. If there is no paise, write 00 after the dot.

Example 8: Hiyang and his sister went to a stationery shop. They bought a packet of erasers for ₹10, a notebook for ₹12.50 and 5 pencils for ₹8.25. Find the total amount spent by them.

If Hiyang gave a 50-rupee note to the shopkeeper, how much amount was returned to him?

Solution:

		₹	p
		1	
Cost of erasers =		1 0 .	0 0
Cost of notebook =		1 2 .	5 0
Cost of pencils =	+	8 .	2 5
Total amount spent		3 0 .	7 5

		₹	p
		9	9
		4 10 .	10 10
Money given =		~~5~~ ~~0~~ .	~~0~~ ~~0~~
Total amount spent =	–	3 0 .	7 5
Amount returned		1 9 .	2 5

So, the shopkeeper returned ₹19.25 to Hiyang.

MULTIPLICATION AND DIVISION OF MONEY

Example 9: Sajida went to a jewellery store to buy bracelets for her cousins. She bought six bracelets. If the cost of one bracelet is ₹21.50, how much did she pay?

Solution:

Cost of 1 bracelet = ₹21.50

Cost of 4 bracelets = ₹21.50 × 6

$$\begin{array}{r} ₹\ \ \ \text{p} \\ {}^{3} \\ 21.50 \\ \times \quad 6 \\ \hline 129.00 \\ \hline \end{array}$$

So, Sajida paid ₹129 for six bracelets.

Example 10: Rubin has ₹144 in his piggy bank. He gave all the money to two of his best friends. How much did each friend get if the money was distributed equally?

Solution:

Total money Rubin had = ₹144

Number of friends who got the money = 2

Amount each friend got = ₹144 ÷ 2

$$\begin{array}{r} 72 \\ 2\overline{)144} \\ -14\downarrow \\ \hline 04 \\ -\ \ 4 \\ \hline 0 \end{array}$$

So, each friend got ₹72.

EXERCISE 9B

1. **Solve the following.**

a. $\begin{array}{r} ₹\ \ \ \text{p} \\ 5.46 \\ +\ 28.95 \\ \hline \\ \hline \end{array}$

b. $\begin{array}{r} ₹\ \ \ \text{p} \\ 192.38 \\ +\ \ 45.09 \\ \hline \\ \hline \end{array}$

c. $\begin{array}{r} ₹\ \ \ \text{p} \\ 45.29 \\ -\ 13.18 \\ \hline \\ \hline \end{array}$

d. $\begin{array}{r} ₹\ \ \ \text{p} \\ 350.41 \\ -\ \ 76.89 \\ \hline \\ \hline \end{array}$

e. $\begin{array}{r} ₹ \\ 36 \\ \times\ \ 6 \\ \hline \\ \hline \end{array}$

f. $\begin{array}{r} ₹\ \ \ \text{p} \\ 18.25 \\ \times\ \ \ \ 9 \\ \hline \\ \hline \end{array}$

g. ₹252 ÷ 6 = ____

h. ₹49 ÷ 7 = ____

2. **Answer the following.**

a. In the school fair, Jerry bought balloons for ₹15, a toy for ₹55.50 and ate a burger for ₹22.50. Find the total amount spent by him.

b. If 1 sweet costs ₹12, then what will be the cost of 6 sweets?

c. Six friends bought six necklaces from a shop. In total, they paid ₹750 to the shopkeeper. If all of them paid equal amounts, how much did each pay?

BILLS AND RATE CHARTS

Have you noticed that whenever we buy things from any shop, the shopkeeper gives a piece of paper or document called the **bill**. A bill shows the details of how much we are paying for each item bought from a shop. It also tells us the total amount we have to pay for the items bought.

> **Do you know?**
> The following countries use the name rupee (Rs) to represent their currency.
> Sri Lanka Nepal
> Pakistan Mauritius
> Seychelles

A **rate chart** helps us to make the bill. It gives the cost of each item that is on sale.

For example, if 1 cupcake costs ₹15, then 3 cupcakes would cost ₹45 (₹15 × 3). We **multiply** the cost of one item with the number of the items bought.

ITEM NAME	PRICE LIST
Tea	₹8.00
Green Tea	₹14.50
Jasmine Tea	₹16.50
Coffee	₹12.00
Cold Coffee	₹18.00
Cookies and Cream	₹10.00

Look at the following examples.

Example 11: Rajat goes to a stationery shop to buy the given items: a box of pencil colours, 2 pens, 2 pencil boxes and an eraser. The shopkeeper made the following bill for him.

Excel Stationery Shop			
Item	**Quantity**	**Rate per item**	**Amount**
Box of pencil colours	1	₹20	₹20
Pens	2	₹5	₹10
Pencil boxes	2	₹10	₹20
Eraser	1	₹2	₹2
		Total	₹52

₹5 × 2 = ₹10

₹10 × 2 = ₹20

So, the total amount that Rajat has to pay is ₹52.

Example 12: Samvridha bought the following items for her birthday party. Look at the bill she got and identify if there are any mistakes.

Jolly's Store			
Item	**Quantity**	**Rate per item**	**Amount**
Balloons	20	₹2	₹40
Streamers	20	₹4	₹70
Candles	15	₹2	₹30
Banners	5	₹3	₹5
		Total	₹185

Corrected bill:

Jolly's Store			
Item	**Quantity**	**Rate per item**	**Amount**
Balloons	20	₹2	₹40
Streamers	20	₹4	**₹80**
Candles	15	₹2	₹30
Banners	5	₹3	**₹15**
		Total	**₹165**

NOTE

We should always ensure to check our bill before paying any amount to the shopkeeper.

EXERCISE 9C

1. Unni owns a bakery shop. He is preparing a bill for the things bought by a customer at his shop. Help him to complete the bill by filling in the missing amounts.

Sweet Bakers			
Item	**Quantity**	**Rate per item**	**Amount**
Pastries	9	₹25	₹225
Cupcakes	8	₹12	______
Doughnuts	15	______	₹150
Cookies	15	______	₹15
		Total	______

2. Mrs Llama bought the following school uniform for her children from a garment shop. Look at the bill carefully. Identify and circle the errors and correct them as well.

Pearls Garments			
Item	**Quantity**	**Rate per item**	**Amount**
Shirts	3	₹150	₹350
Trousers	2	₹225	₹450
Tunics	1	₹110	₹220
		Total	₹1020

MATHS LAB ACTIVITY

21 CS Creativity and Innovation, Collaboration EL AI

Aim: To develop skills of handling money

Materials required: Chart papers, a ruler, pencils, sheets of white paper, scissors, crayons

Procedure: This is a group activity.

1. Form four teams to play this game. Give paper sheets and a chart paper to each team.
2. Making play notes: Ask each team to divide the paper sheets into rectangles (these need not be of same size) using a ruler and a pencil. Cut out the rectangles.
3. Draw a circle (with any image or rupee symbol inside the circle) in the centre of each rectangle, on both sides (front and back). Write the value of each note inside the circle on both sides. Notes can be coloured using crayons.
4. Make 20 notes of each of these values: ₹1, ₹2, ₹5, ₹10, ₹20, ₹50 and ₹100.
5. Now, using these play notes/money, each team is required to make all the possible combinations of notes for the amount called out by the teacher.
6. The teams can record their observations in a table (as shown below) on the given chart paper. For instance, for ₹100, a few combinations are:

S.No.	₹1	₹2	₹5	₹10	₹20	₹50	₹100	Total
1.						2		₹50 + ₹50 = **₹100**
2.			4	4	2			₹5 + ₹5 + ₹5 + 5 + ₹10 + ₹10 + ₹10 + ₹10 + ₹20 + ₹20 = **₹100**

7. The team which comes up first with the maximum number of combinations for the given amount wins each round.

Concept Map

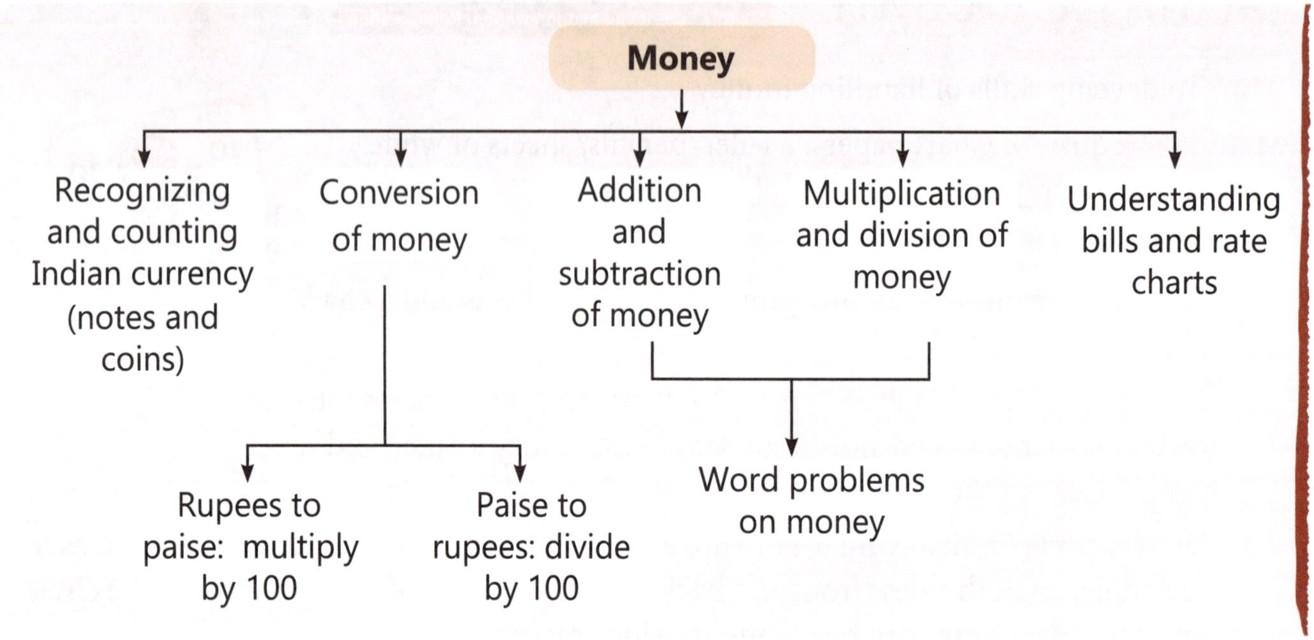

Key Concepts

- **Currency:** The money used in a country, consisting of notes and coins
- In India, the currency used is called 'rupee' (₹) and 'paisa' (p). ₹1 = 100 p
- **Conversion of Money:** To convert rupees to paise, multiply by 100, and to convert paise to rupees, divide by 100
- **Bill:** Gives details of each item bought from a shop and the total amount we need to pay
- **Rate Chart:** Tells us the cost of each item that is on sale

CHAPTER REVISION

A. Convert the following to paise.

1. ₹3 2. ₹17 3. 6 rupees 70 paise 4. ₹19.89

B. Convert the following to rupees.

1. 20 paise 2. 1900 paise 3. 3 rupees 47 paise 4. 18 rupees 8 paise

C. Match the following.

1. 

2. 

3. 

4. 

a. 

b. 

c. 

d. 

D. Answer the following.

1. Shreya spent ₹349 on a doll and ₹58 on a toy. What is the total amount of money that Shreya spent?
2. Judy wants to buy a dress for ₹565. She has only ₹420 with her. How much more money does she need?
3. Shalini bought a pen for ₹35. How much will 8 such pens cost her?
4. ₹560 is distributed among 5 people. How much will each person get?
5. Farzana bought shoes for ₹130, socks for ₹45.50 and a belt for ₹101.25. She gave the shopkeeper two ₹200 notes. How much money should the shopkeeper return to her?

E. Charu went to a mall with her mother for shopping. A few items and their cost are given. Based on this, complete the given bill.

Star Mall			
Item	**Quantity**	**Rate per item**	**Amount**
Skirt	2		
Frock	1		
Top	1		
Pair of bellies	1		
		Total	

What is the total amount that Charu's mother should pay?

SKILL UP!

A. 21 CS Creativity and Innovation, Communication | EL | AI

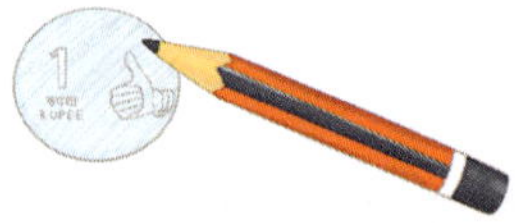

Make a greeting card by coin tracing. You will need a scrapbook paper, sheets of white paper, a variety of coins, crayons or colour pencils and scissors.

On a sheet of paper, lay out a few coins and cover these coins with another sheet of paper. Then, start tracing the coins by rubbing over them with crayons or colour pencils on the sheet. You will get coin impressions as shown here.

Using scissors, cut out each coin's impression (you can take an adult's help). With these cut-outs, decorate the greeting card (made of scrapbook paper) with a pattern or design of your choice. To make the card, fold the scrapbook paper in half. A few designs are given here for reference.

B. 21 CS Critical Thinking, Life Skills | HQ Harmony in Relationships

Sonal and her four friends were out in the park. Sonal wanted to have ice cream. One ice cream was for ₹20. Her friends did not have money, so Sonal bought 5 ice creams. How much should Sonal pay for all the ice creams?

Do you think Sonal did the right thing?

Would you share or buy things for your friends if they do not have the money to do so?

C. 21 CS Critical Thinking, Life Skills | EL

You went to a gift shop and bought items worth ₹576. How can you pay the shopkeeper using the least number of currency notes and coins? Write down the number of each currency you would give to the shopkeeper in the space provided.

SUSTAINABLE DEVELOPMENT GOALS

Questions B and C are in line with SDG 1 No Poverty. Many people in the world do not have enough money to buy food or clothes. Things, such as ice creams and gifts, are not useful at all to some people. They would rather buy other food.

Worksheet 9

21 CS Information Literacy, Life Skills | HQ How Similar Are We

Given is the rate chart of the food items available at 'Titbits and More' cafeteria. Bhaswati and her three friends are having a get-together party at the cafeteria. Read the rate chart and answer the given questions.

Snacks

Pizza	₹70
Pasta	₹50
Sandwich	₹25
Burger	₹30
Chowmein	₹55
Patty	₹20

Desserts

Pastry	₹30
Ice cream	₹20
Brownie	₹25

Drinks

Shake	₹38
Cold coffee	₹35
Juice	₹44

1. Hameed spends ₹80 on 1 snack and 1 dessert. Which two items did he possibly buy? ____________________
2. Rita had ₹90. She ordered a snack and has ₹35 left with her. She wants to order a drink. Which drink can she order?
   ____
3. Jaya ordered pasta and a pastry. How much did she spend?
   ____
4. Bhaswati paid ₹100 for 1 snack, 1 dessert and 1 drink. She was returned ₹22 as change. How much did she spend?
   ____
5. Find the total amount spent by them at the cafeteria.
   ____

Reasoning Worksheet 2

1. What fraction of the image given alongside is shaded?

   a. $\frac{5}{16}$ b. $\frac{4}{10}$ c. $\frac{4}{16}$ d. $\frac{5}{10}$

2. What fraction of the following letters cannot be drawn using only curved lines?

   D O F S B R C L U

   a. $\frac{5}{9}$ b. $\frac{4}{9}$ c. $\frac{3}{9}$ d. $\frac{6}{9}$

3. Which of the following does not belong to this group?

   a. centimetre b. kilometre c. litre d. metre

4. In the given image, find the height of the cupboard if the height of the lamp is 65 cm.

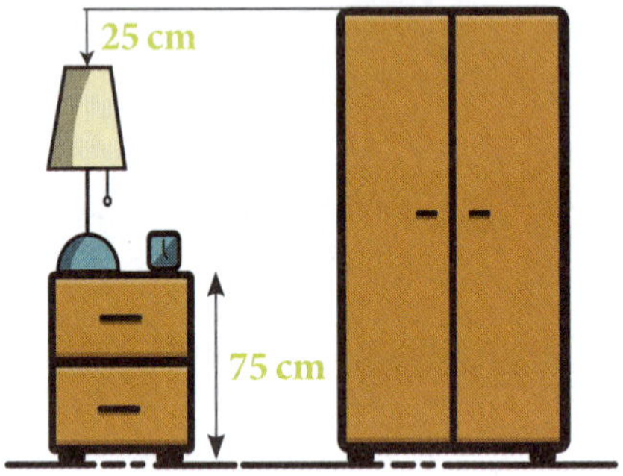

   a. 165 cm b. 160 cm
   c. 155 cm d. 170 cm

5. Three pencils cost the same as two erasers. Four erasers cost the same as one pen. Pencils are more expensive than pens. If the first two statements are true, the third statement is

   a. True b. False c. Not sure

6. Look at the given figures and identify the lightest ball.

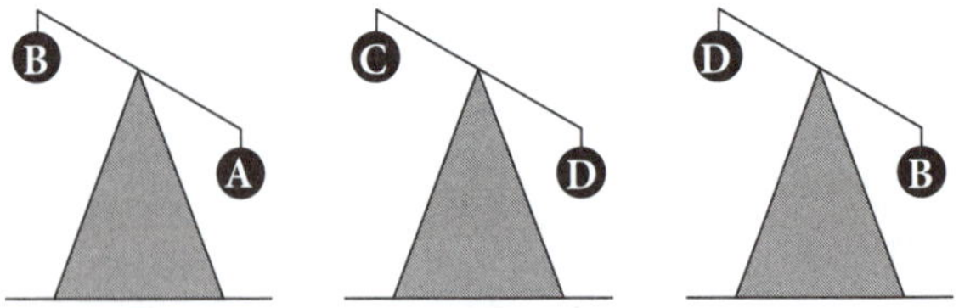

   a. A b. B
   c. C d. D

7. If the day before yesterday was Monday, then the day after tomorrow will be ________.

   a. Tuesday b. Thursday c. Wednesday d. Friday

10 Geometry

Learning Objectives

- To learn more on flat shapes and solid shapes
- To understand the concept of open and closed figures
- To understand the concept of point, line and line segment
- To learn about symmetry

Let's Get Started

21 CS Information Literacy AI

Colour the picture according to the colour codes given below.

FLAT SHAPES

We learnt about flat shapes in Class 2. Let us recall what we had learnt.

Shapes are made of straight lines and curved lines. These lines are called **sides** or **edges**. The points where two sides or edges meet are called **corners**. Flat shapes are also called **plane shapes** or **two-dimensional (2-D) shapes**. They can be drawn on any plane surface.

This is Aanya's room. Let us identify the flat shapes we can see in her room.

The **mirror** on the wall is in the shape of an **oval**.

An oval has 1 curved side and no corners.

The **painting** on the wall is in the shape of a **rectangle**.

A rectangle has 4 sides and 4 corners. Opposite sides are of equal length.

The **sail** of the toy boat is in the shape of a **triangle.**

A triangle has 3 sides and 3 corners.

The **clock** has the shape of a **circle**.

A circle has 1 curved side and no corners.

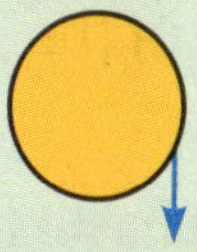

The **tiles** on the floor have the shape of a **square**.

A square has 4 sides and 4 corners. All sides are of equal length.

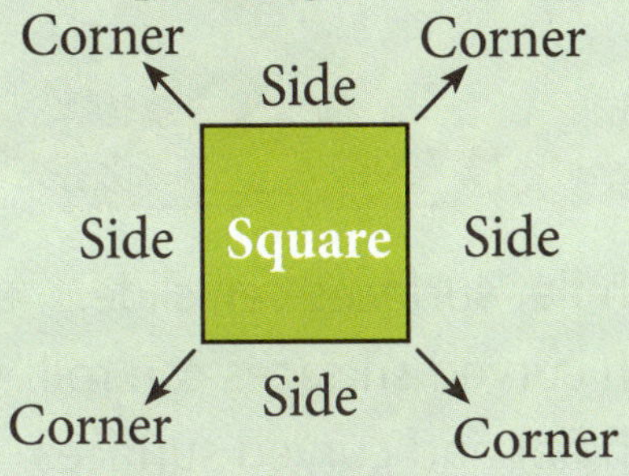

MENTAL MATHS

Write the name of one more thing in this room which looks like the following:

Rectangle: ____________

Square: ____________

Triangle: ____________

Circle: ____________

Oval: ____________

SOLID SHAPES

We see many solid shapes or objects around us. Solid shapes are flat shapes that have height. They are also called **three-dimensional (3-D) shapes**.

Each solid shape occupies space and has surface that we can see and feel. The surfaces can be flat (plane) or curved.

Each flat surface of a solid shape is called a **face**. The line where two adjacent faces meet is called a **side** or an **edge**.

The point where two or more sides or edges meet is called a **vertex**. The plural of vertex is vertices.

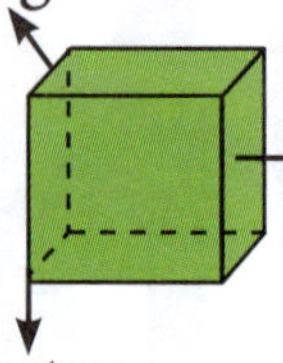

This is Dhairya's room. Look at the solid shapes we can see in his room and learn more about them.

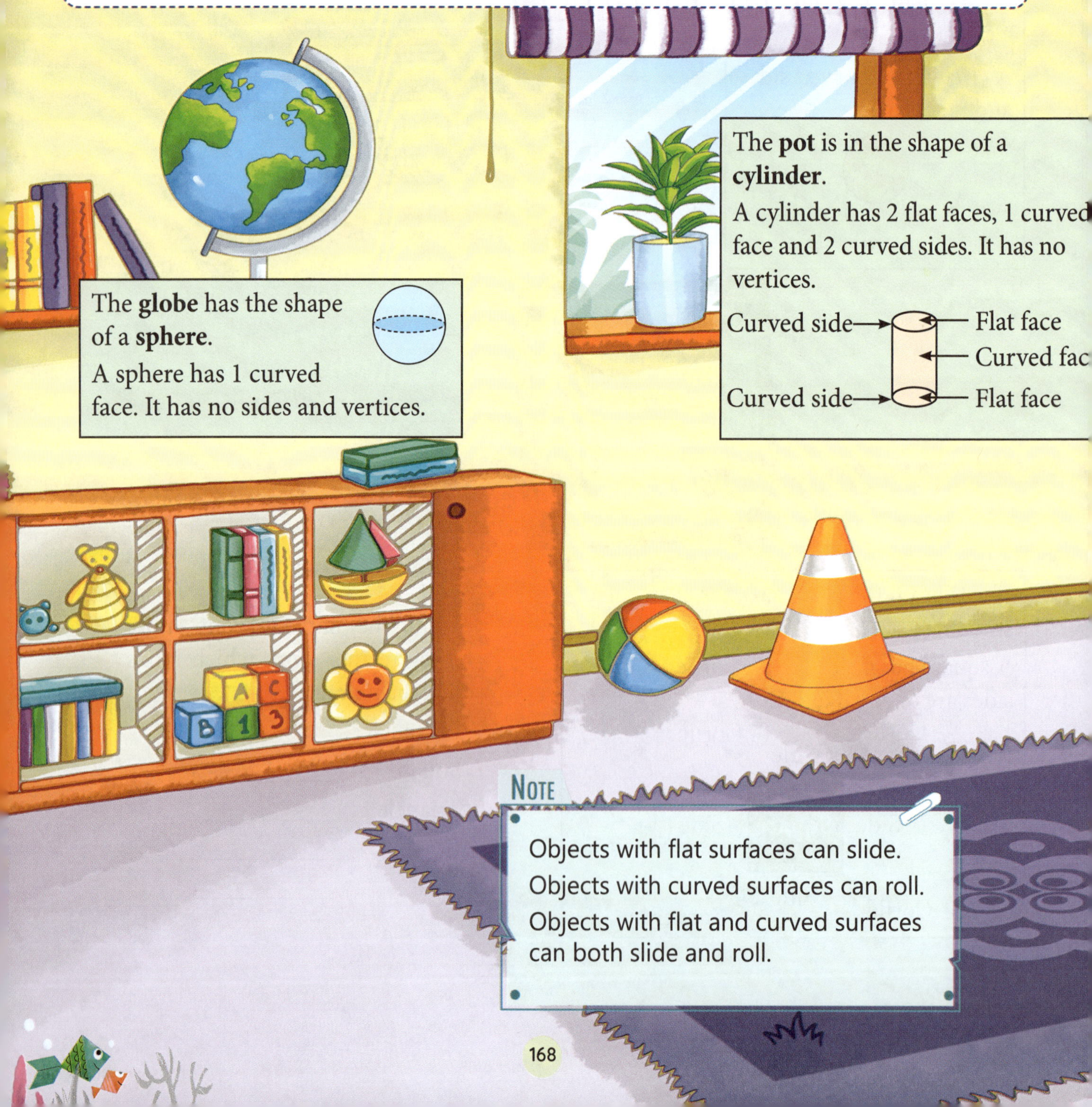

The **globe** has the shape of a **sphere**.

A sphere has 1 curved face. It has no sides and vertices.

The **pot** is in the shape of a **cylinder**.

A cylinder has 2 flat faces, 1 curved face and 2 curved sides. It has no vertices.

Curved side → Flat face

Curved fac

Curved side → Flat face

NOTE

Objects with flat surfaces can slide.

Objects with curved surfaces can roll.

Objects with flat and curved surfaces can both slide and roll.

The **lampshade** is in the shape of a **cone**.

A cone has 1 flat face, 1 curved face and 1 curved side. It has 1 vertex (apex).

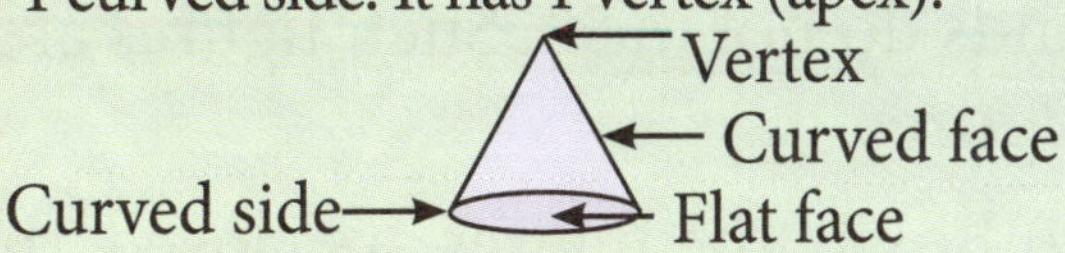

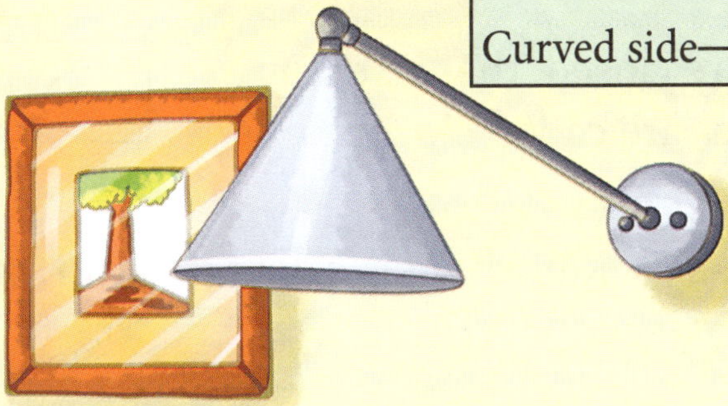

The **divan bed** has the shape of a **cuboid**.

A cuboid has 6 flat faces, 12 straight sides and 8 vertices.

Opposite sides are of equal length.

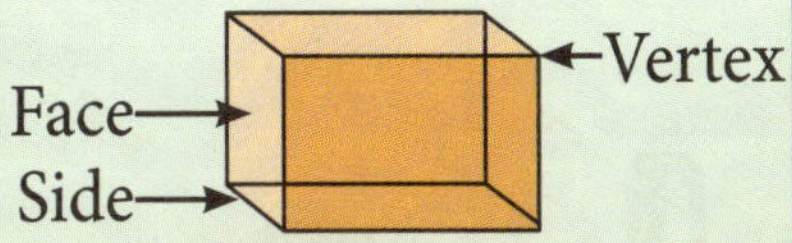

MENTAL MATHS

Write the name of one more thing in this room which looks like the following:

Cuboid: ____________

Cube: ____________

Cone: ____________

Cylinder: ____________

Sphere: ____________

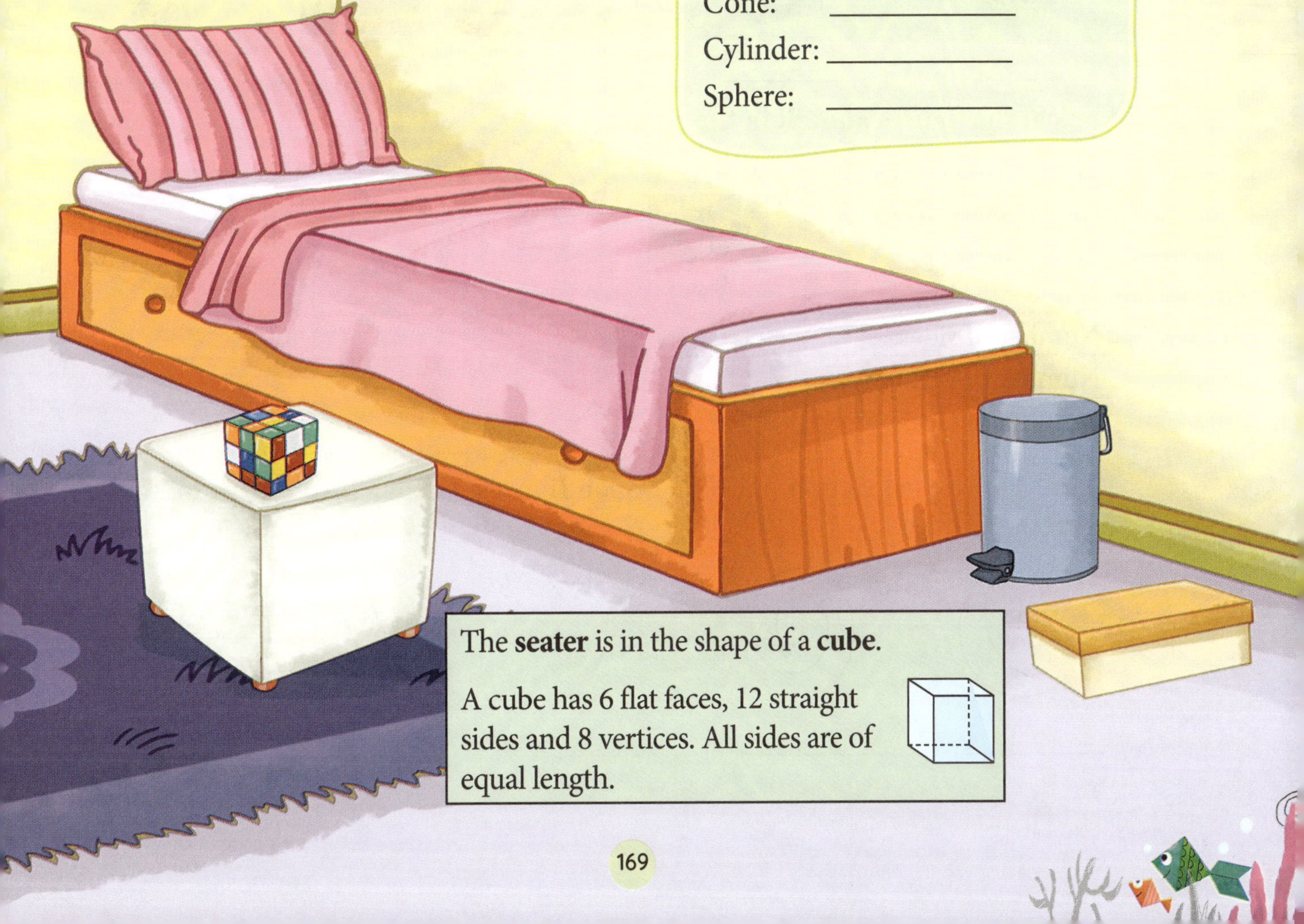

The **seater** is in the shape of a **cube**.

A cube has 6 flat faces, 12 straight sides and 8 vertices. All sides are of equal length.

OPEN AND CLOSED FIGURES

Look at the given figures.

In Box A, the figures are open, that is, their ends do not meet. Such figures are called **open figures**.

In Box B, the figures are closed, that is, their ends meet. Such figures are called **closed figures**.

Box A

Box B

Closed figures enclose a region which is called its **interior**.

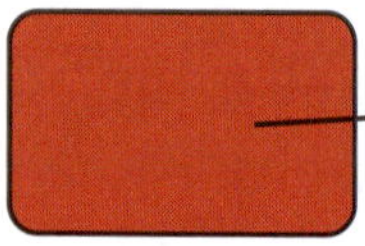

EXERCISE 10A

1. Look at the given objects and write the name of the solid shape each of these represent.

a.  ________

b.  ________

c.  ________

d.  ________

e. 

____

2. Look at the figures and fill in the blanks.

Shape	a. 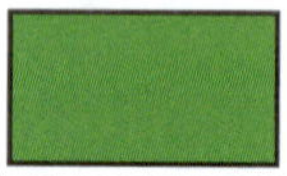	b. 	c. 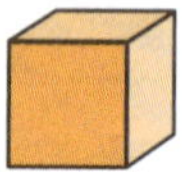	d. 
Name				
Number of sides				
Number of vertices				
Number of faces				

3. Write C for closed figures and O for open figures. Colour the interior of closed figures.

a.  ________

b. 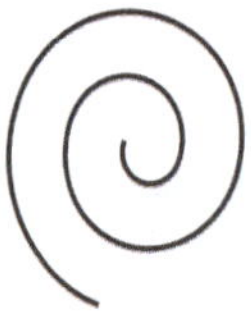 ________

c.  ________

d. 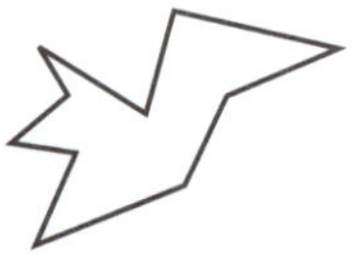 ________

e. 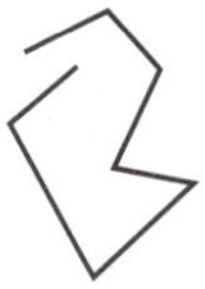 ________

TERMS RELATED TO GEOMETRY

Point: A point is represented by a dot. It is named with a capital letter.

B, O and X are 3 points. They are named as point B, point O and point X.

Line: A line is a collection of points. It extends in both directions.

AB, PQ and YZ are lines. They are written as $\overleftrightarrow{AB}$, $\overleftrightarrow{PQ}$ and $\overleftrightarrow{YZ}$.

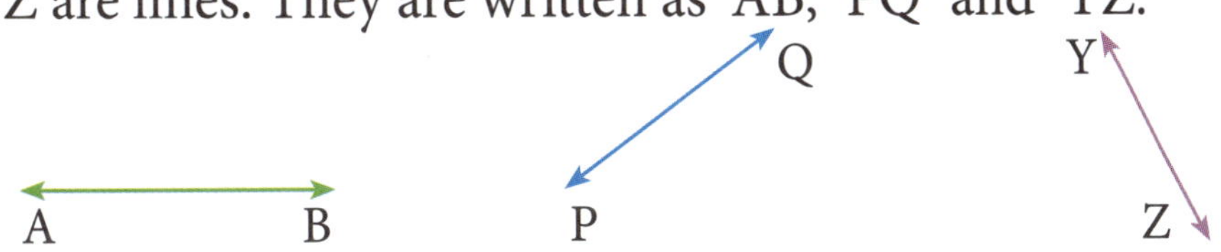

Line Segment: A line segment is a part of a line. It cannot extend in any direction. It has two end points. CD is a line segment and is written as $\overline{CD}$.

Ray: A ray has one end point and extends endlessly in the other direction, like the Sun's rays. AB is a ray and is written as $\overrightarrow{AB}$.

A is the end point and the ray extends endlessly towards B.

Curve: A curve is a collection of points which do not follow a straight path. AB is a curve.

DOT GRID

A dot grid is a set of evenly spaced dots where we can create vertical, horizontal and diagonal lines as well as curves by joining the dots. A dot grid looks like the image given alongside.

Make vertical line segments

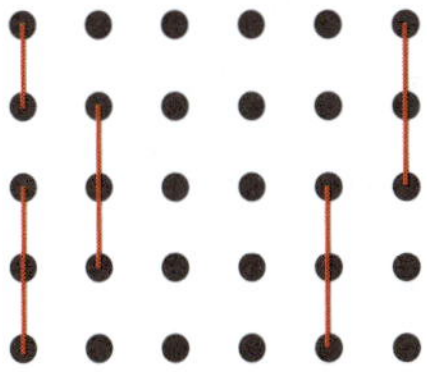

Make horizontal line segments

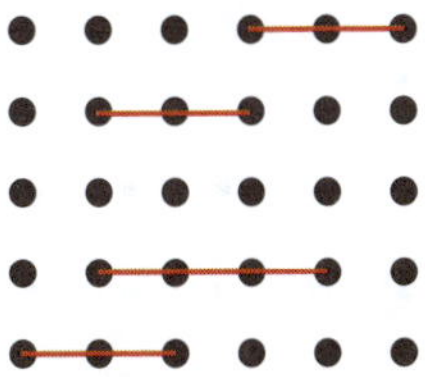

Make diagonal lines

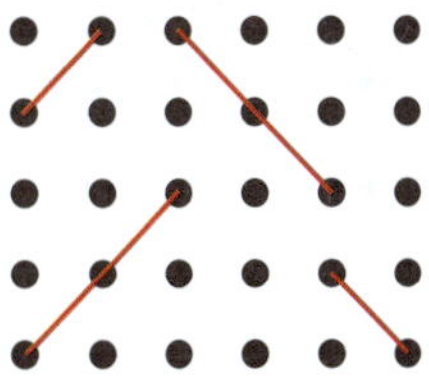

Make curves

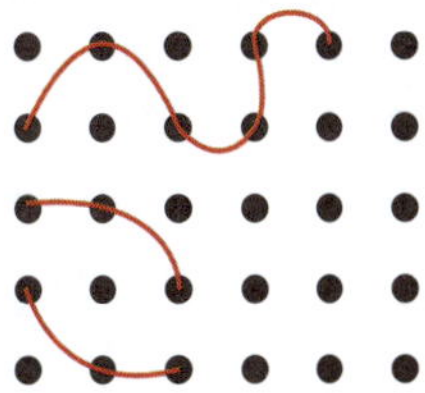

TANGRAM SHAPES

Tangram is a Chinese geometrical puzzle, which contains a square cut into seven pieces.

These pieces can be arranged in different ways to make various shapes and figures.

EXERCISE 10B

1. Write the names of the following.

a. 

____

b. 

____

c. 

____

d. 

____

e. 

____

f. 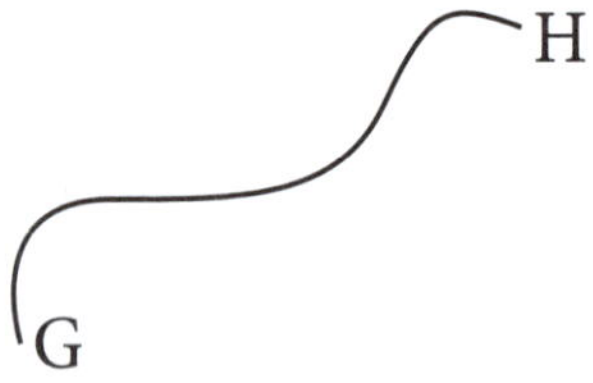

____

2. Draw the following on the given dot grid.

a. Diagonal line
b. Rectangle
c. Curve
d. Triangle

3. Look at the tangram shapes and identify the object shown in each.

a. 

____

b. 

____

c. 

____

d. 

____

SYMMETRY

Observe the images given below. What do you see?

The dotted line divides each given image into two equal parts or mirror halves. Such figures are called **symmetrical figures**. If any object, shape or figure has mirror halves, then it is said to be symmetrical. A straight line that divides a figure into two equal halves is called the **line of symmetry**.

Take a piece of paper and draw the following shapes on it. Then, cut out each shape, fold it along the dotted line (i.e., line of symmetry) as shown and observe.

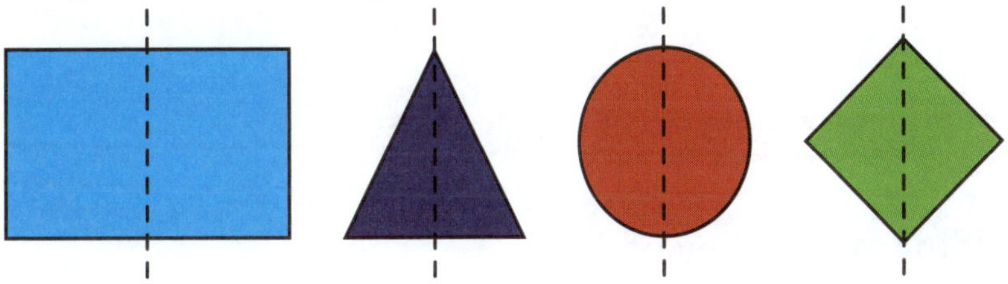

Note

Line of symmetry can be vertical, horizontal or diagonal.

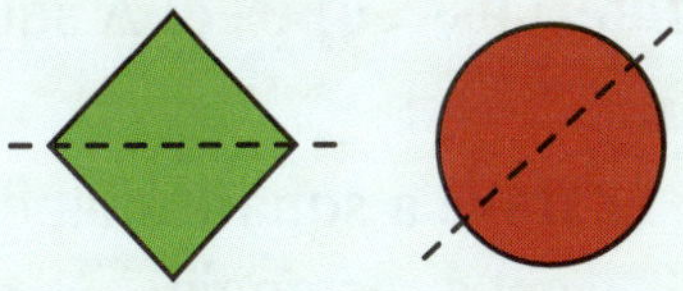

When we fold the shapes along the line of symmetry, one half of the shape falls exactly on the other half and looks like the following images.

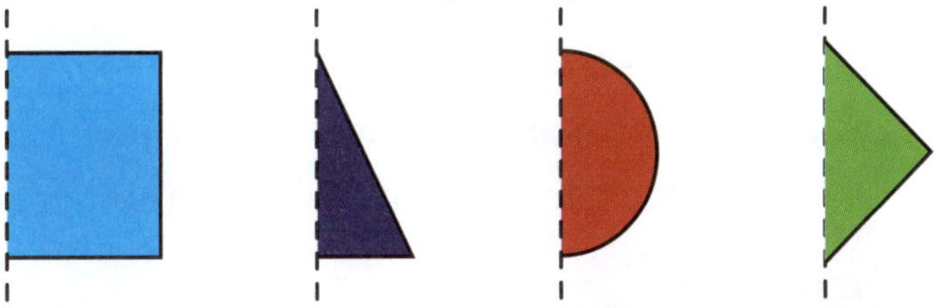

Do you know?

Human bodies are also symmetrical. When we draw a vertical line down the center of a body, the left and right sides are almost mirror images of each other.

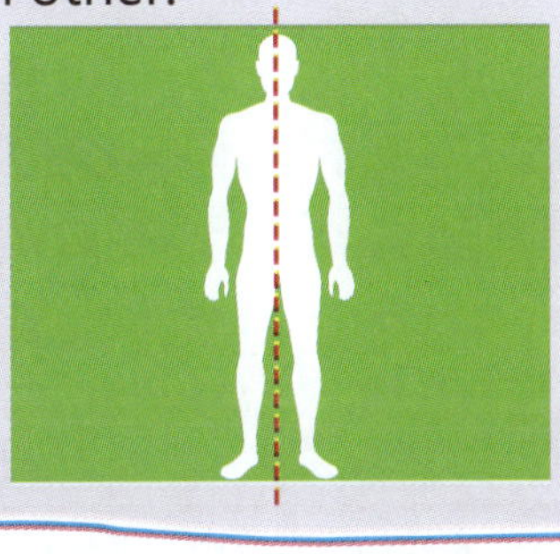

Common Errors

Draw the line of symmetry.

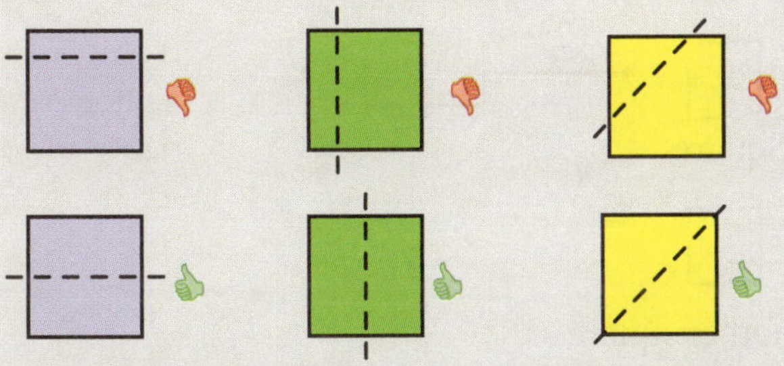

EXERCISE 10C

1. Is the dotted line in the following pictures the line of symmetry? Write Yes or No.

a. 

____

b. 

____

c. 

____

2. Draw the missing other halves of the given shapes and colour them.

a. 

b. 

c. 

MATHS LAB ACTIVITY

21 CS Creativity and Innovation EL AI

Aim: To create different shapes by folding and cutting paper

Materials required: A square-shaped piece of paper, scissors

Procedure:

1. Take a square-shaped piece of paper. Fold it in half horizontally, as shown. You will get a rectangle.
2. Now, again fold it in half vertically. It becomes a square.
3. Next, cut the square diagonally with a pair of scissors, as shown. It becomes a triangle.
4. Then, unfold the paper which is triangular in shape and you will get another square.

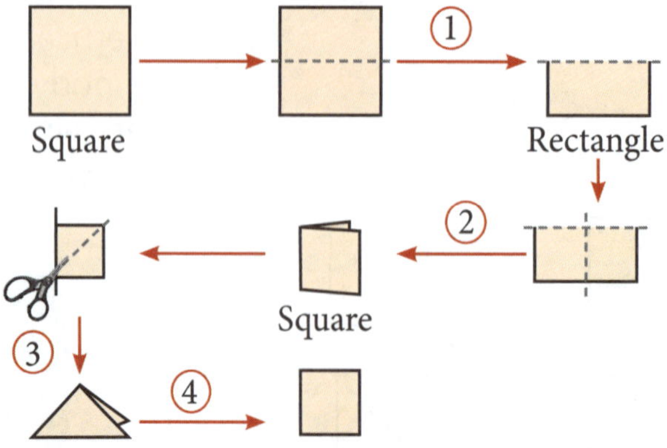

Concept Map

Geometry

- Flat (2-D) shapes have sides and corners
  - Square
  - Rectangle
  - Triangle
  - Circle
  - Oval
- Solid (3-D) shapes have edges, vertices and faces
  - Cuboid
  - Cube
  - Cone
  - Cylinder
  - Sphere
- Terms related to geometry:
  - Point
  - Line
  - Line segment
  - Ray
  - Curve

  Dot grid for making lines and curves
- Tangram shapes made of geometrical Chinese puzzle pieces
- Symmetry Figures or shapes that have mirror halves when divided by a line of symmetry

Key Concepts

- **Flat Shapes:** Shapes that do not have height, also called plane or 2-D shapes
- **Solid Shapes:** Flat shapes that have height, also called 3-D shapes
- **Vertices:** The point where two or more sides meet
- **Edges:** The line where the adjacent sides of a solid shape meet
- **Curved face:** A curved surface in a solid shape
- **Point:** Represented by a dot
- **Line:** A collection of points which follows a certain path and extends in both directions
- **Line Segment:** A part of a line that has two end points
- **Ray:** It has one end point and extends only in the other direction
- **Curve:** A collection of points which do not follow a straight path
- **Line of Symmetry:** A line that divides a shape into two equal parts or mirror halves

CHAPTER REVISION

A. Choose the correct option.

1. Which of the following is a flat shape?
   a. Cube b. Cone c. Triangle d. Cylinder
2. Which one of the following shapes has no sides and vertices?
   a. Square b. Sphere c. Triangle d. Cylinder
3. Which one of these has two end points?
   a. Curve b. Line c. Ray d. Line segment
4. How many pieces are there in a Tangram puzzle?
   a. 7 b. 6 c. 2 d. 9
5. How many mirror halves does a symmetrical figure have?
   a. One b. Two c. Three d. Four

B. Match the shapes in column A with their properties in column B.

A	B
1. 	a. 3 sides, 3 vertices
2. 	b. 6 faces, 8 vertices, 12 edges
3. 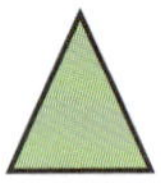	c. No vertices, 1 curved side
4. 	d. 1 curved face, 1 flat face, 1 curved side, 1 vertex

C. Fill in the blanks.

1. A ____________ has six square faces.
2. An oval is a ____________ dimensional figure.
3. When we give height to a circle, it becomes a ____________.
4. A ____________ does not follow a straight path.
5. A line segment ____________ extend in any direction.

D. Tick the shapes which are symmetrical. Also, draw the line of symmetry.

1. 
2. 
3. 
4. 

SKILL UP!

A. 21 CS Creativity and Innovation EL AI

9 INDUSTRY, INNOVATION AND INFRASTRUCTURE

Take a cardboard piece and cut different shapes from it. Join the cut pieces together to make a model of a house.
(Hint: See the image of house given here.)

Name the different kinds of shapes you used to make the house. Why do we need a house?

B. 21 CS Creativity and Innovation, Life Skills EL AI

11 SUSTAINABLE CITIES AND COMMUNITIES

Would you like to design a car? Using different shapes, design a car of your choice. Take hint from the image given alongside.

Can we use any other shape other than the circle to make the wheels of a car? Give reasons for your answer.

C. 21 CS Critical Thinking

Find the two identical objects in each row.

1. a.  b.  c.  d. 

2. a.  b.  c.  d. 

SUSTAINABLE DEVELOPMENT GOALS

Questions A and B are in line with SDG 9 Industry, Innovation and Infrastructure and SDG 11 Sustainable Cities and Communities, respectively. With good creative design and innovation, villages and cities can become better without harming the environment.

WORKSHEET 10

21 CS Creativity and Innovation, Life Skills EL AI

A. Ruhi made a table cloth by sewing together patches of different shapes. Help her to finish it by colouring the shapes according to the key given. Draw the line of symmetry on this pattern.

B. Complete the picture by drawing the other half of the puppy. Also colour it.

11 Patterns

Learning Objectives

- To identify, extend and create patterns with shapes and objects
- To identify and extend different number patterns
- To recognize and extend the given growing or reducing patterns
- To recognize different tiling and non-tiling patterns

Let's Get Started

21 CS Creativity and Innovation, Life Skills | EL | AI | HQ Happiness My Goal

There is a rangoli making competition at school. Two friends, Rihana and Tina, are participating in the competition.

Look at the rangoli designs they have made. Help them to finish their rangolis by colouring the designs shown here.

PATTERNS

Patterns are all around us—in nature, at home, in our surroundings and so on. Look at a few examples from everyday life.

Patterns carved on the ceiling

Patterns carved on wooden blocks

Pattern on wings of a butterfly

Pattern in a flower

We have learnt that a pattern is a series or sequence of repeating units.
A **repeating unit** is the part that is being repeated in a logical way in a given pattern. It could be a set of lines, shapes, colours, numbers, letters, objects, etc. Such a pattern is called a **repeating pattern**.

Patterns are mostly formed when shapes, designs, numbers or objects are arranged according to a specific rule.

Patterns with Shapes

Some examples of patterns formed with shapes are shown below.

This is the repeating unit.

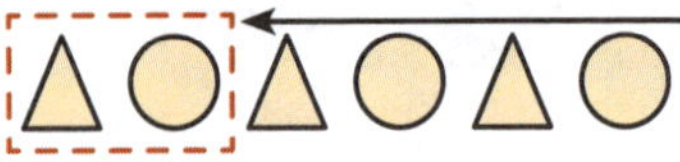
This is the repeating unit.
In this pattern, there is a change in shape.

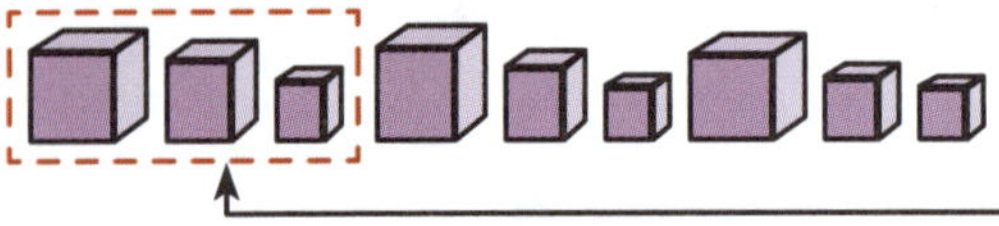
This is the repeating unit.
In this pattern, there is a change in size.

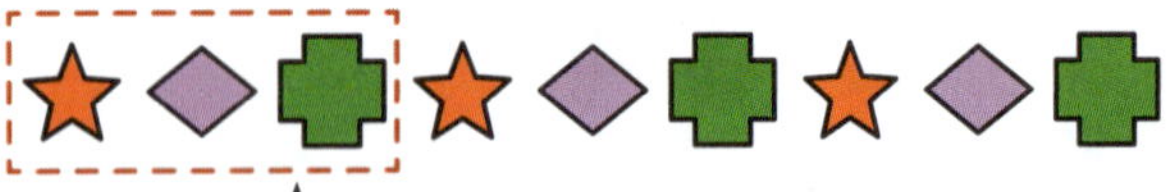
This is the repeating unit.
In this pattern, there is a change in colour as well as shape.

Patterns with Objects

Let us observe the following patterns and identify the repeating unit.

Repeating unit

EXERCISE 11A

1. Look at the patterns and complete them by colouring.

a. 

b. 

2. What comes next in the given patterns? Circle the correct picture.

a.  ______

b.  ______

3. Fill in the missing objects to complete each pattern. Circle the repeating units.

a. 

b. 

MENTAL MATHS

Identify whether the following are patterns or not. Write 'Yes' or 'No' in the space provided.

1. 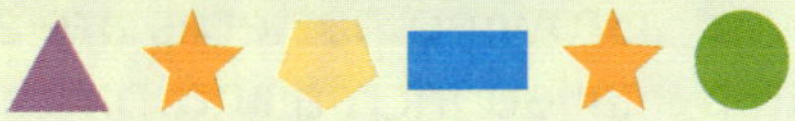 ☐

2. 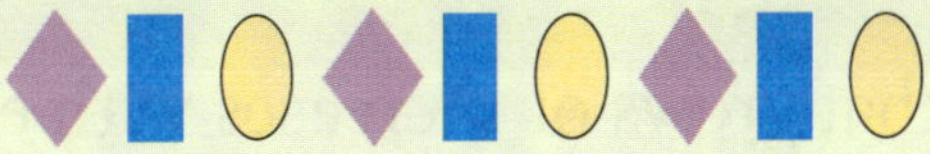 ☐

3.  ☐

4. 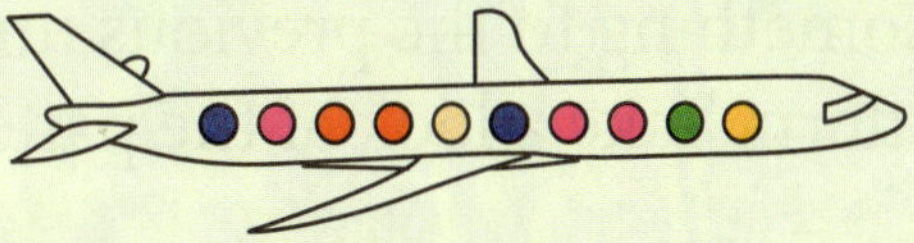 ☐

Patterns with Numbers

Look at the following number patterns and their rules.

$1 \xrightarrow{+1} 2 \xrightarrow{+1} 3 \xrightarrow{+1} 4 \xrightarrow{+1} 5 \xrightarrow{+1} 6$ — **Rule:** 1 is being added every time.

$1 \xrightarrow[+2]{} 3 \xrightarrow[+2]{} 5 \xrightarrow[+2]{} 7 \xrightarrow[+2]{} 9 \xrightarrow[+2]{} 11$ — (Odd numbers)

Rule: 2 is being added every time.

$2 \xrightarrow{+2} 4 \xrightarrow{+2} 6 \xrightarrow{+2} 8 \xrightarrow{+2} 10 \xrightarrow{+2} 12$ — (Even numbers)

10 9 8 7 6 5 — **Rule:** 1 is being subtracted every time.

1 2 4 8 16 — **Rule:** Being multiplied by 2

10 20 30 40 50 — **Rule:** 10 is being added every time.

3000 300 30 3 — **Rule:** The number is being divided by 10 every time.

MORE PATTERNS

Study the following patterns and find out the rule by which they are extending.

Rule: Here, the pattern is extending by turning the shapes. There is a change in the position of triangle in each step, that is, the triangle is moving to the next side of the square in a clockwise direction.

Rule: The arrow is turning or changing direction in a clockwise manner.

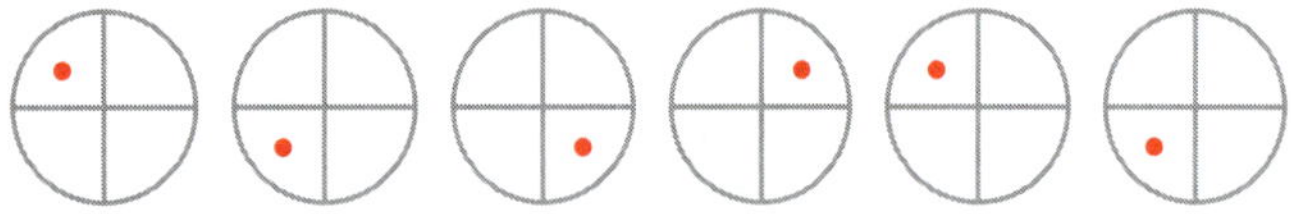

Rule: The red dot is moving to the next part of the circle or changing position in an anti-clockwise manner.

What comes next in the given pattern?

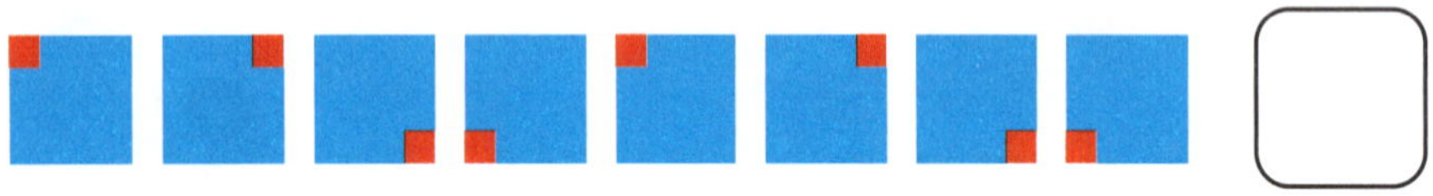

Growing Patterns

A pattern that grows or increases with every next unit by adding something to the previous unit is called a growing pattern. Take a look at the patterns shown here.

NOTE

Growing patterns are also called increasing patterns.

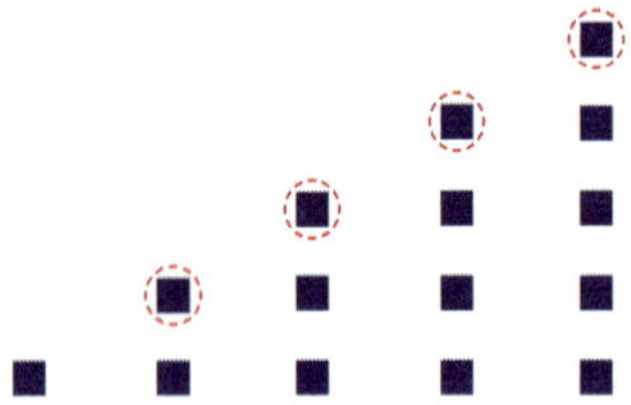

Rule: In this pattern, the figure increases in size with the addition of a square (■) to the next unit each time.

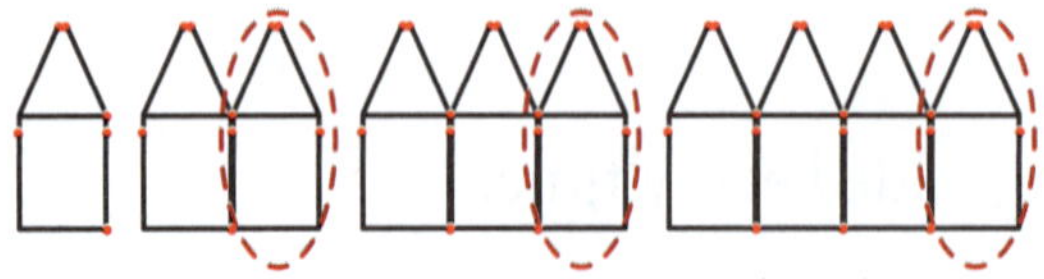

Rule: In this pattern, the house shape (⌂) is added to the next unit each time.

1 4 7 10 13 16

Rule: Here, the number 3 is added each time to the next unit (number) in the pattern.

Reducing Patterns

A pattern that reduces or decreases with every next unit by subtracting or removing something from the previous unit is called a reducing pattern. Observe the patterns given below.

> **NOTE**
> Reducing patterns are also called decreasing or shrinking patterns.

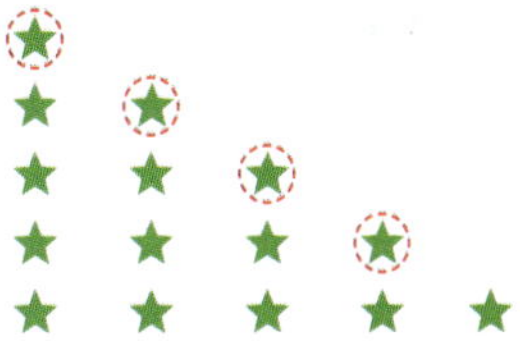

Rule: In this pattern, the figure decreases in size with the removal of a star (★) from the next unit each time.

Rule: In this pattern, one petal of the flower (●) is removed from the next unit each time.

25 20 15 10 5

Rule: Here, the number 5 is subtracted each time from the next unit (number) in the pattern.

EXERCISE 11B

Study the given patterns carefully and draw the image that should come next.

1.  ____________________

2. 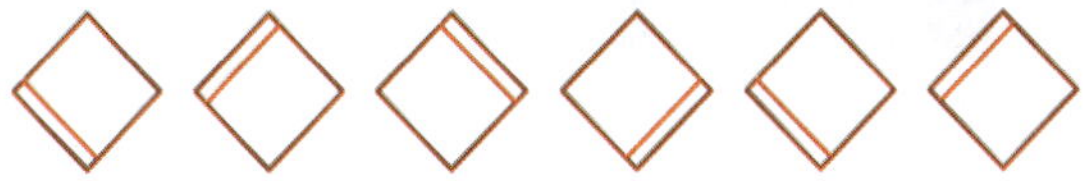 ____________________

3.  ____________________

4.  ____________________

5.  ____________________

TILING PATTERNS

At home, in a park or on footpaths, we all might have seen walls, floors or pavements covered with tiles, without leaving gaps between the tiles. This way of covering a surface or an area with tiles of the same shape and size is called **tiling.**

Tiling	Non-tiling
Each shape fits into each other without leaving gaps.	Shapes that do not fit into each other completely and leave gaps in between.
Examples:  Repeating units: 	**Examples:** 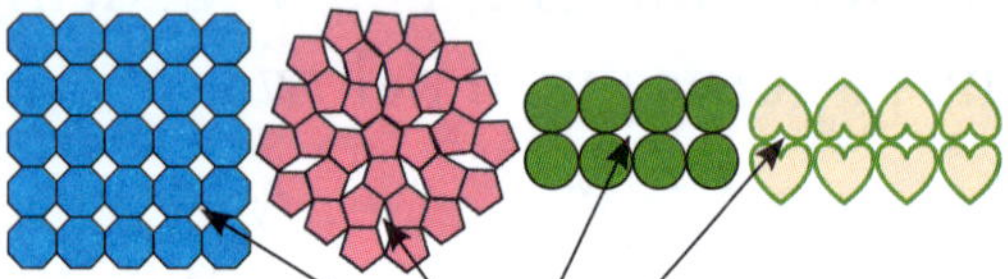
Tiling is also known as **tessellation**.	Non-tiling shapes cannot be used for tiling.

The patterns formed by repeating a shape again and again without overlaps or leaving any gaps are called **tiling patterns.**

EXERCISE 11C

1. Tick (✓) the tiling patterns.

a. 

b. 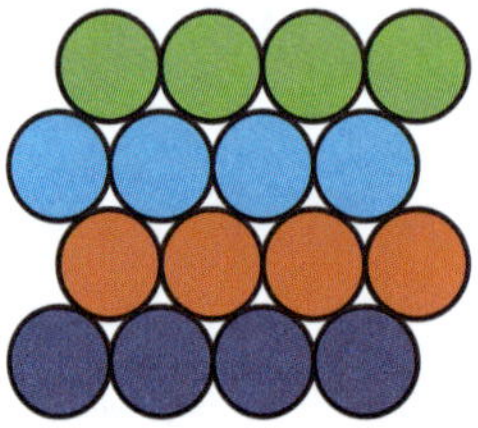

c. 

d. 

2. Observe the tiling patterns and complete them by colouring.

a. 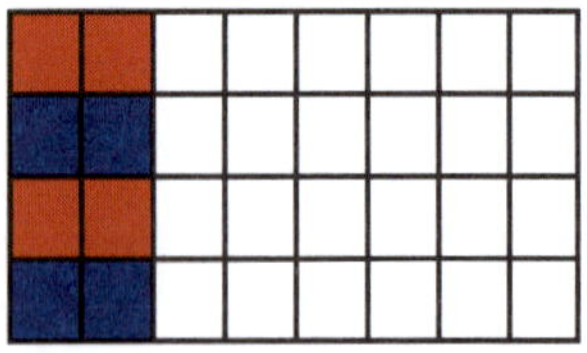

b. 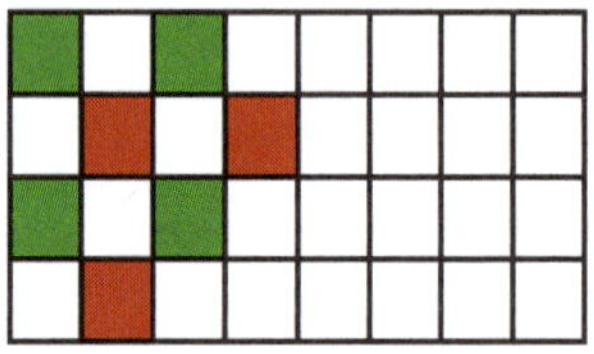

c. 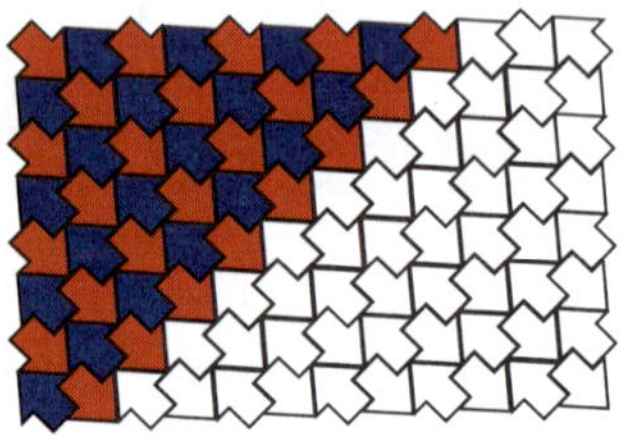

PUZZLE!

Observe the pattern. What does not fit?

1. 

2. 

3. 

4. 

Maths Lab Activity

21 CS Critical Thinking EL AI

Aim: To understand making patterns with shapes, numbers and letters

Materials required: Playing cards (three sets)

Procedure: There are 4 kinds of shapes used in playing cards.

We can use playing cards to create patterns with shapes, letters and numbers as given below.

1. 

Pattern formed by all the shapes with letter A.

2. 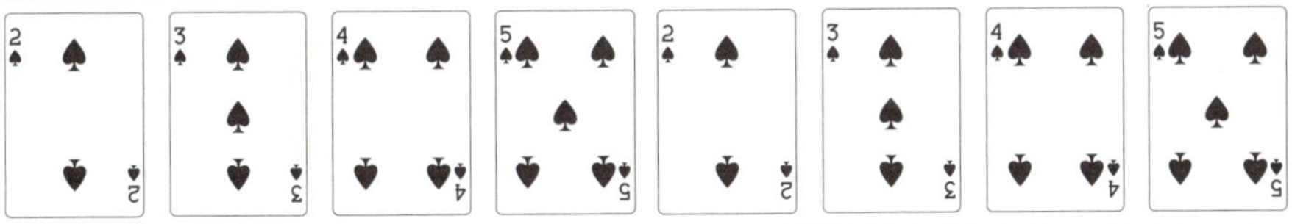

Pattern formed using one shape and numbers from 2 to 5.

3. 

Pattern formed using one shape and numbers from 6 to 8.

Make more patterns on your own.

Concept Map

Patterns

- Patterns with shapes
- Patterns with objects
- Patterns with numbers
- Growing patterns
- Reducing patterns
- Tiling patterns

Key Concepts

- **Patterns with Shapes:** Patterns formed by repeated shapes
- **Patterns with Objects:** Patterns formed by repeated objects
- **Patterns with Numbers:** Patterns formed by numbers following certain rules
- **Growing Patterns:** Patterns that increase in size with every step
- **Reducing Patterns:** Patterns that reduce in size with every step
- **Tessellation:** Patterns in which each shape fits into each other without leaving gaps

A. Observe the pattern and complete it.

1.  ______________________

2. 1 4 7 10 13 ______ ______ ______ ______

3. 15 14 13 12 11 ______ ______ ______ ______

4. 90 80 70 60 ______ ______ ______ ______

5.  ______ ______ ______ ______

6.  ______ ______ ______ ______

7.  ______ ______ ______ ______

8.  ______ ______ ______ ______

B. Choose the correct answer to complete the pattern.

1.  ______ | 

2.  ______ | 

3.  ______  | 

4.  ______  | 

C. Identify the repeating unit in the given tiling patterns and complete them by colouring.

1. 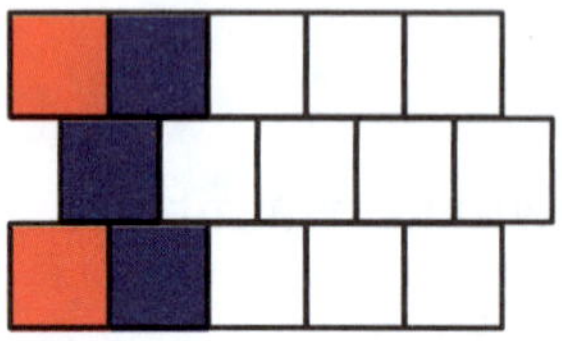

Repeating unit:

2. 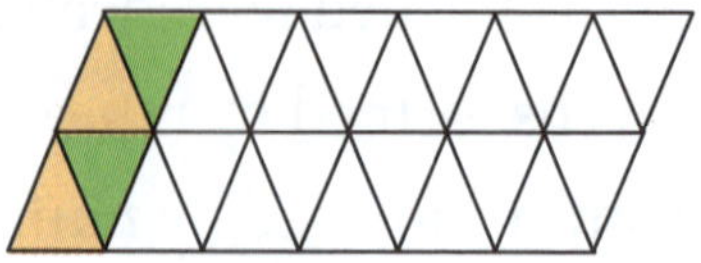

Repeating unit:

3. 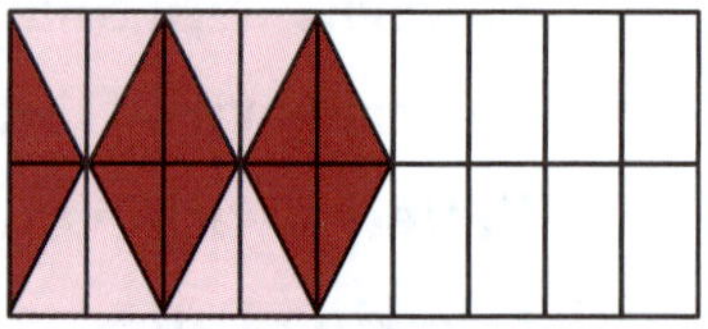

Repeating unit:

SKILL UP!

A. 21 CS Creativity and Innovation, Technology Literacy EL AI

8 DECENT WORK AND ECONOMIC GROWTH

What would you like to be when you grow up? There are many artists and designers who create beautiful designs using patterns. To make patterns, they use different designs, shapes, etc. The following are a few designs that are used.

With the help of the Internet, find out more such designs and their names.

On a chart paper, create your own patterns using these designs and present it to your class.

B. 21 CS Creativity and Innovation, Life Skills EL AI

Class 3 children got together and started making patterns with building blocks. They took blocks in red and yellow and made the following pattern.

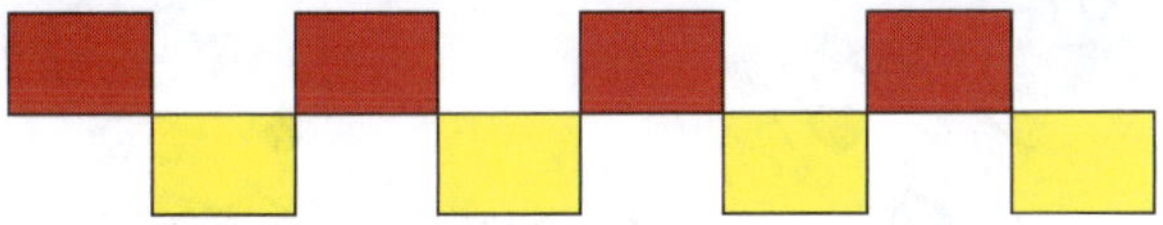

One little boy in the class wanted to add green blocks to the pattern. The other children did not let him. Should the little boy be allowed to add green blocks?

Can you show how different patterns can be made if green blocks are added?

C. 21 CS Critical Thinking

Look at the pattern given below. Study and understand it and then find the missing number.

1	3
2	

5	7
2	

9	11
2	

13	?
2	

SUSTAINABLE DEVELOPMENT GOALS

Question A is in line with SDG 8 Decent Work and Economic Growth. Developing any skill that could lead to a job is important. If you have the skill, you can even create decent jobs in the future.

Worksheet 11

21 CS Critical Thinking, Information Literacy

Anjali and her friends were playing a treasure hunt game. Anjali found the following note written in a secret language (containing shapes, patterns, etc.) with a clue to the next level. With the help of the secret codes, try to decode the note and read the clue.

A Secret Message

Decode to find the clue.

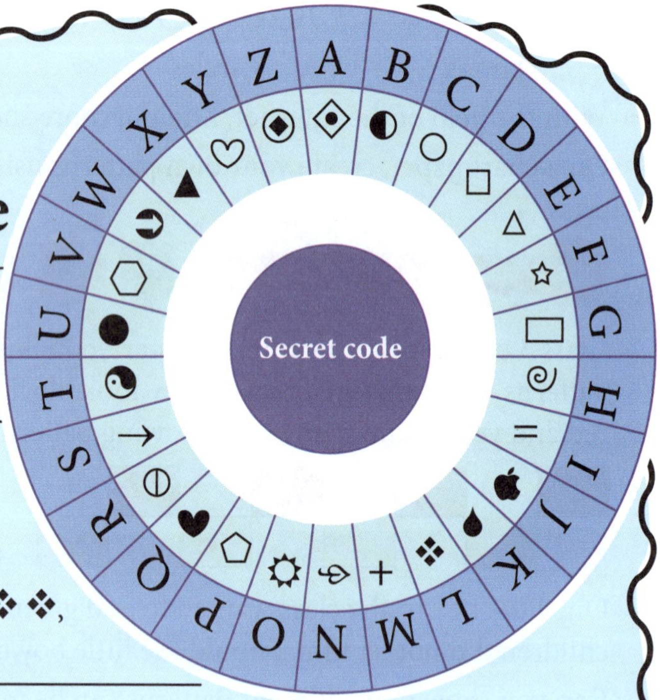

☯ = + △ ☯☼ ○ ◎ = ❖ ❖,

☯ = + △ ☯☼ ☯ ◎ = ꩜ 💧;

☆ ☼ ⦶ ♡ ☼ ● ⦶ ꩜ △ ▲ ☯ ○ ❖ ● △,

⬠ ❖ △ ◈ → △ □ ☼ ◎ △ ⦶ △

☆ ☼ ⦶ ◈ ○ ☼ ☼ ❖, ○ ☼ ☼ ❖ □ ⦶ = ꩜ 💧

12 Data Handling

Learning Objectives

- To collect and record data using tally marks
- To represent data using pictographs and bar graphs
- To draw conclusions from the collected data

Let's Get Started

21 CS Critical Thinking AI

Anjali has a collection of stickers with her. She wanted to organize them and paste them in her stickers' album. How do you think she can do so?

a. How many different types of stickers does she have in her collection? One has been done for you.

Fruits____

b. What is the total number of stickers in her collection?

____

We need to collect data for various purposes. After collecting data, it is organized and presented in various ways. This helps us to understand the data easily and find different results from it.

Let us now learn a few ways of representing data.

PICTOGRAPHS

A pictograph uses pictures or symbols to show data and provide information. It has a title which tells what the pictograph represents. Using pictorial representations, a pictograph helps in comparing information to draw some conclusions.

Look at the following example.

 stands for 1 doughnut,  = 2 doughnuts,

 = 3 doughnuts,  = ½ doughnut

> **NOTE**
>
> The following steps are together called **data handling**:
>
> 1. Collect data
> 2. Organize the data
> 3. Represent the data
> 4. Interpret the data
> 5. Draw conclusions or find useful results from it.

At times, a symbol or picture represents more than one item. Look at the following example.

 stands for 2 flowers,  = 4 flowers,

 = 6 flowers,  = 1 flower

Example: The following pictograph shows the number of seashells collected by five friends during their vacation in Goa.

Look at the pictograph and answer the given questions.

Number of seashells collected	
Sonali	
Kashish	
Tejas	
Saksham	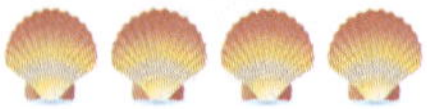
Hailey	

Each  represents 3 shells.

1. What is the title of the given pictograph? Number of seashells collected
2. How many seashells are equal to ? 3 shells
3. Find the number of shells collected by each friend.

   Sonali: $2 \times 3 = 6$ Kashish: $1 \times 3 = 3$ Tejas: $3 \times 3 = 9$

   Saksham: $4 \times 3 = 12$ Hailey: $3 \times 3 = 9$
4. How many shells were collected in all? 39
5. Who collected the maximum number of shells? Saksham

EXERCISE 12A

1. Ramu sells fruits at the market. The following pictograph shows his sales for Sunday. Look at the graph and answer the given questions.

Fruits sold on Sunday	
Fruit	Number of fruits
Apple	
Orange	
Mango	
Pear	
Watermelon	

Each fruit represents 5 pieces of that fruit.

a. How many apples did he sell in total? ____________________

b. Which fruit was sold the most? ____________________

c. Which fruit was sold the least? ____________________

d. How many kinds of fruits did Ramu sell on Sunday? ____________________

e. How many fruits were sold in all? ____________________

2. The pictograph below shows the favourite sports of the students of Class 3.

Favourite sport	
Sport	Number of students
Cricket	
Hockey	
Football	
Tennis	

Each  represents 4 students.

Study the pictograph and answer the following questions.

a. How many students enjoy tennis?_______________

b. How many students enjoy football?_______________

c. Which is the favourite sport of the most number of students? ___________

d. Which is the favourite sport of the least number of students?___________

e. How many more students enjoy cricket than football?____________

RECORDING DATA USING TALLY MARKS

Tally marks are a form of numeral used for counting the number of observations. They are a quick way of recording data or information.

Tally marks are written in groups of five. The first four numbers are shown using vertical lines. For the fifth number, a slanting line is drawn across the first four lines.

For numbers > 5, continue making straight marks.
Remember to draw every fifth mark across the previous 4 marks.

Number	Tally marks	Number	Tally marks	Number	Tally marks
1	|	6	𝍸 |	11	𝍸 𝍸 |
2	||	7	𝍸 ||	12	
3	|||	8	𝍸 |||	13	
4	||||	9	𝍸 ||||	14	
5	𝍸	10	𝍸 𝍸	15	

Try to complete the remaining column of this table.

Let us learn how to record data using tally marks in the following example.

Do you know?
Tally marks are also known as **hash marks**.
In countries like China and Brazil, different symbols are used to draw tally marks.
China: 一 丅 下 止 正
Brazil: 

Example: The art teacher of Class 3 gave a picture of a flower to each student. She asked them to colour the flower of their choice. The following tally chart shows the colour choice of students.

Colour used	Tally marks	Number of students
Blue	|||	3
Red	~~||||~~ |||	8
Pink	~~||||~~ ~~||||~~ |	11
Purple	~~||||~~ |||	8

We can represent the same information in a pictograph as shown below.

Colour used	Number of students
Blue	
Red	
Pink	
Purple	

Each  stands for 2 students.

Study the given pictograph and answer the questions.

1. How many students coloured the flower blue? 3 students
2. What is the total number of students in the class? 30 students
3. Which colour was used by the most number of students? Pink
4. Which two colours were used by the same number of students? Red and Purple
5. How many more students used red to colour the flower than blue? 5 students

EXERCISE 12B

1. **The following tally chart shows the number of storybooks read by Manav in five weeks during his summer vacation.**

   Study the chart and answer the following questions.

   a. How many books did Manav read in the following weeks?

      Week 1 __________

      Week 2 __________

      Week 3 __________

      Week 4 __________

      Week 5 __________

   b. In which week did he read the most number of books? __________

   c. In which week did he read the least number of books? __________

   d. How many books did Manav read altogether during his vacation? __________

   e. Which are the weeks in which Manav read the same number of storybooks? __________

<table>
<tr><th>Week</th><th>Number of storybooks read</th></tr>
<tr><td>Week 1</td><td>|||</td></tr>
<tr><td>Week 2</td><td>𝍸</td></tr>
<tr><td>Week 3</td><td>|</td></tr>
<tr><td>Week 4</td><td>||||</td></tr>
<tr><td>Week 5</td><td>|||</td></tr>
</table>

2. **Mr. Osaka owns a pet shop. Look at the data he recorded for his pets for one of the days. Fill in the last column of the table to show the given data using tally marks.**

<table>
<tr><th colspan="3">Osaka Pet Shop</th></tr>
<tr><th>Pet</th><th>Number of pets</th><th>Tally marks</th></tr>
<tr><td> Cat</td><td>15</td><td></td></tr>
<tr><td> Rabbit</td><td>8</td><td></td></tr>
<tr><td> Fish</td><td>20</td><td></td></tr>
<tr><td> Dog</td><td>12</td><td></td></tr>
<tr><td> Bird</td><td>9</td><td></td></tr>
</table>

BAR GRAPHS

A bar graph is a way of presenting data using bars. Let us consider an example.

Example: The following list shows the favourite flower of some students.

Flower	Rose 	Jasmine 	Tulip 	Marigold 
Number of students	7	4	5	3

We can show the above information in a bar graph as follows.

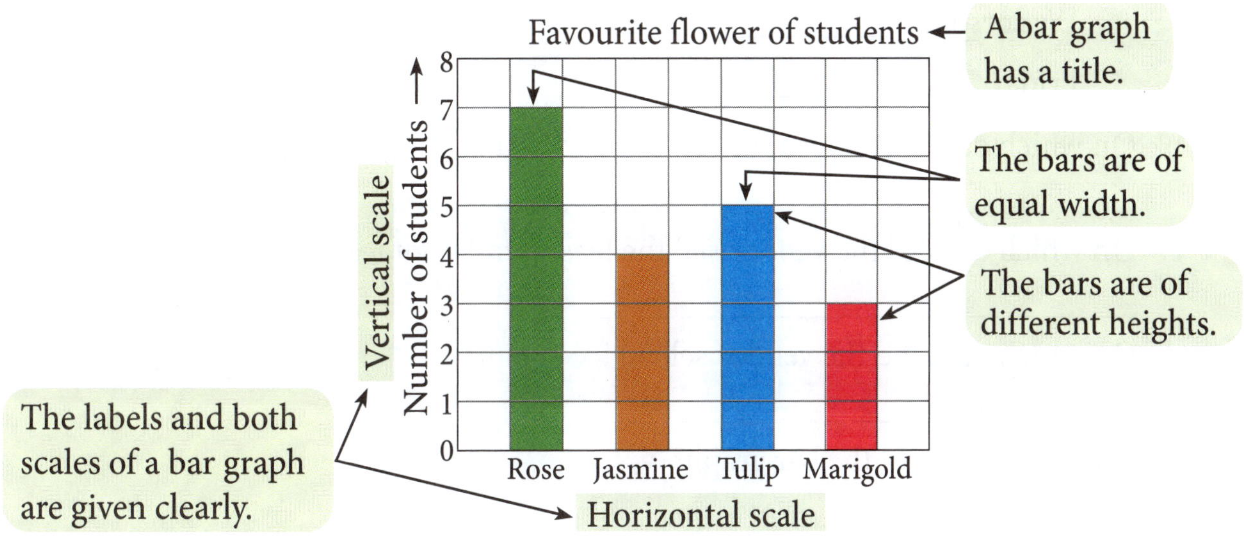

Answer these questions using the above bar graph.

a. What does the tallest bar show?

<u>It shows that rose is the favourite flower of 7 students. In other words, rose is liked by the most number of students.</u>

b. Which flower is liked by the least number of students? <u>Marigold</u>

c. How many students like tulip flower? <u>5 students</u>

d. Jasmine and marigold flowers are the favourites of the same number of students. True/False <u>False</u>

e. What is the title of the bar graph? <u>Favourite flower of students</u>

EXERCISE 12C

1. **The bar graph shows the number of ice creams sold by a vendor from Monday to Friday. Answer the following questions based on the bar graph.**

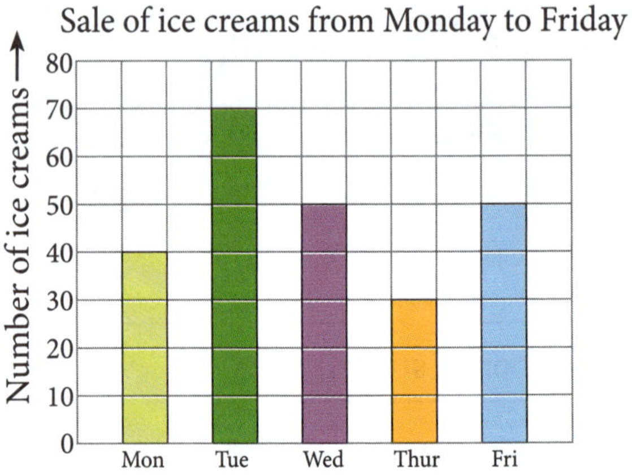

   a. How many ice creams did the vendor sell on the following days?

      Monday ________

      Tuesday ________

      Wednesday ________

      Friday ________

   b. On which day did the vendor sell the maximum number of ice creams?

      ____

   c. On which day did the vendor sell the least number of ice creams?

      ____

   d. On which days did the vendor sell 50 ice creams?

      ____

   e. What is the title of the bar graph?

      ____

2. **The following bar graph shows the transport used by the teachers and students of a particular school. Study the bar graph and answer the given questions.**

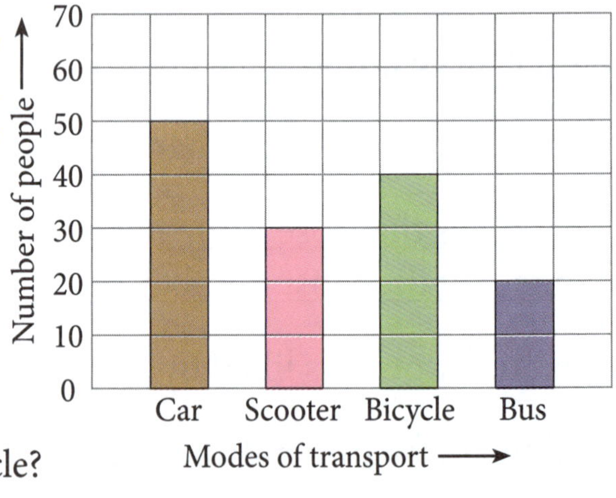

   a. How many people come by car?

      ____

   b. How many people come by bicycle?

      ____

   c. Do more people ride a scooter or a bicycle?

      ____

   d. Which mode of transport is used by the least number of people?

      ____

   e. Give a suitable title to the bar graph.

      ____

MATHS LAB ACTIVITY

21 CS Information Literacy, Communication EL

Aim: To make a pictograph of the number of family members among your friends' circle

Materials required: Chart paper, notebook, coloured counters and sketch pen

Procedure:

1. Ask each friend in your friend circle the number of members they have in their family. Record this data in a notebook.
2. Then, on a chart paper, draw a table based on the data collected; place coloured counters against each name to represent the number of members in each friend's family.

The collected data presented using pictures or symbols (in this case, counters) is called a **pictograph**.

Based on this data, you can figure out whether your friends live in a nuclear family or an extended/large family.

Name of friend	Number of family members
Friend 1	● ● ● ●
Friend 2	● ● ● ● ●
Friend 3	● ● ●

CONCEPT MAP

Data handling

↓

To collect and organize data

↓

To record data using tally marks

↓

To represent data

Pictograph | Bar graph

↓

To interpret data and draw a conclusion

KEY CONCEPTS

- **Data:** A collection of information
- **Pictograph:** A way of presenting data using pictures and symbols
- **Tally Marks:** A way of counting and recording the number of observations
- **Bar Graph:** A way of presenting data using bars

A. Fill in the blanks.

1. If  = 4 toffees, then

 = ________ toffees    = ________ toffees

 = ________ toffees    = ________ toffees

2. If | = 1, then

|| = ________ ||| = ________   𝍸 | = ________

𝍸 || = ________   𝍸 = ________   𝍸 𝍸 𝍸 = ________

B. Four friends wanted to buy a birthday gift for their common friend. The following pictograph shows how much pocket money they saved in their piggy banks. Answer the following questions based on the pictograph.

Name of child	Amount of money
Hazel	
Nick	
Dulqar	
Jyoti	

Each  represents 4 rupees.

1. Give a suitable title to the pictograph. ________________
2. How much money did Hazel save in her piggy bank? ________________
3. Who saved the maximum amount of money? ________________
4. Who saved the least amount of money? ________________
5. What is the total amount of money they have? ________________
6. If the gift costs ₹100, do they have enough money to buy it? If not, how much more money would they need to buy the gift? ________________

C. **Represent the data given in question B on a tally chart in the following table. Also, calculate and write the amount of money in figures in the second column.**

Name of child	Amount of money saved	Tally chart
Hazel		
Nick		
Dulqar		
Jyoti		

D. **The following bar graph shows the number of different flavours of pastry sold by 'Cakes and Bakes' bakery shop on a Saturday. Read the graph and answer the questions that follow.**

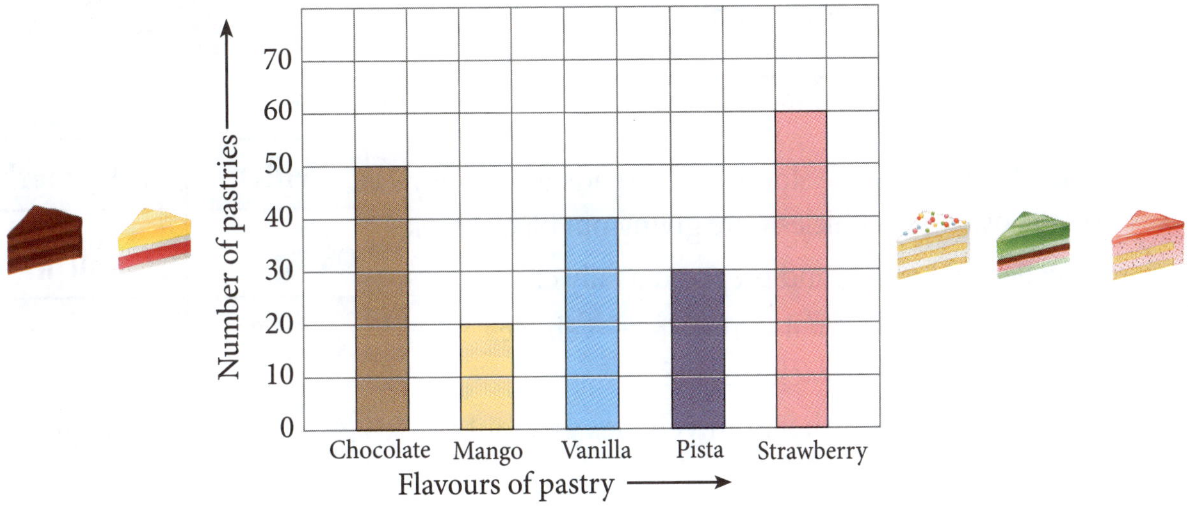

1. Name the different flavours of pastry sold by the bakery shop.

   ____

2. Which flavour of pastry was sold the most?

   ____

3. Which flavour of pastry was sold the least?

   ____

4. The number of chocolate pastries sold is equal to the total number of __________ and __________ pastries sold.

5. How many vanilla pastries were sold by the shop?

   ____

Skill Up!

A. 21 CS Communication, Information Literacy

Let us find out the number of birthdays of the students in your class for each month. Take a piece of paper and write down each student's birth date.

Now, make a tally chart like the one given below. Complete the tally chart for 12 months and display it on your class notice board.

Akshat	7	June
Samira	5	May

January	|||	February	||
March	卌	April	||
May	|||	June	||

This will make it easier for your teacher to know how many birthdays to expect each month.

B. 21 CS Critical Thinking, Information Literacy, Life Skills CC Integration with Science

Sanat did a survey. He stood on the roadside one day to see how many vehicles were giving out black smoke. He collected his data and prepared a tally chart.

1. What was the total number of vehicles which were giving out black smoke?
2. Is it good for our health if vehicles give out black smoke on the roads?

Vehicle	Tally marks
	卌 ||
	卌 ||||
	卌 卌 ||
	卌 卌 卌

C. 21 CS Critical Thinking, Information Literacy

Here is another interesting way of sorting out data.

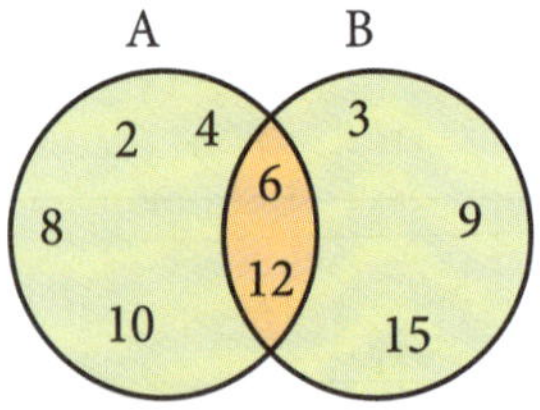

1. In circle A, we have the numbers which come in the table of 2.
2. In circle B, we have the numbers which come in the table of ______.
3. In the orange-shaded portion, we have the numbers which come in the tables of ______ and ______.

SUSTAINABLE DEVELOPMENT GOALS

Question B is in line with SDG 12 Responsible Consumption and Production and SDG 13 Climate Change. While making a lot of vehicles may be a sign of a rich country, these vehicles produce a lot of smoke. What would this smoke do to our health and the environment?

WORKSHEET 12

21 CS Information Literacy, Life Skills. CC integration with Science

13 CLIMATE ACTION

Trees are one of the most important natural resources. On the World Environment Day, the students of Class 3 decided to plant some saplings every week in the month of June. The pictograph shows the number of saplings planted in each week. Complete the table and answer the given questions.

Week	Number of saplings	
Week 1		7
Week 2		______
Week 3	________________	4
Week 4		______

Each  represents ___________.

1. What does the symbol  represent?

   ____

2. How many saplings were planted in Week 2?

   ____

3. In which week were the least number of saplings planted?

   ____

4. In which week were the most number of saplings planted?

   ____

5. Represent the above data using tally marks.

   Week 1 [ ] Week 2 [ ]

   Week 3 [ ] Week 4 [ ]

Reasoning Worksheet 3

1. Which of these shapes does not belong to this group?

   a. Triangle b. Circle c. Oval d. Sphere

2. If 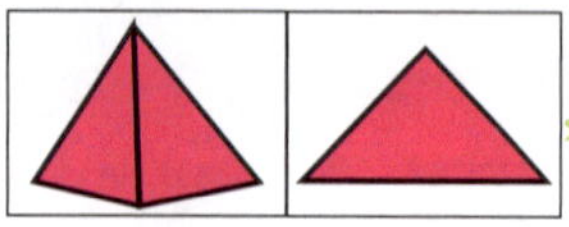, then 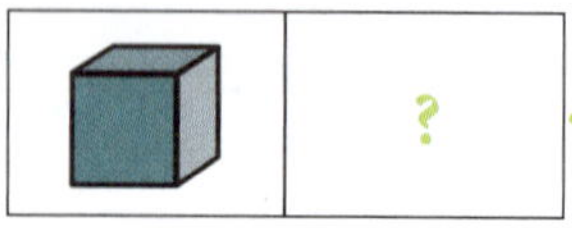

. Identify the missing part.

   a.  b. 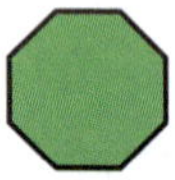 c.  d. 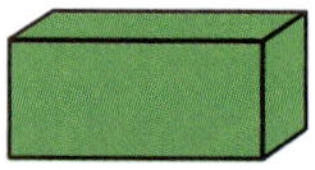

3. Look at the given pattern. Fill in the missing part from the given options.

    ____________

   a. 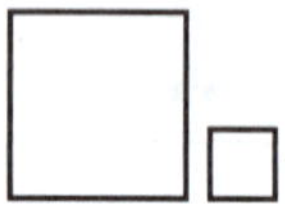 b.  c.  d. 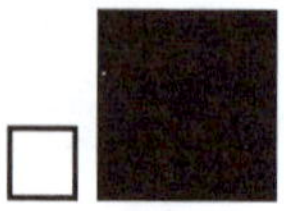

4. What should come next in the given number pattern?

   20 20 17 17 14 14 11 ____ ____

   a. 8 8 b. 11 11 c. 11 14 d. 11 8

5. Which month had the least number of rainy days?

   a. June
   b. August
   c. July
   d. September

Month	Number of rainy days
June	
July	
August	
September	

 = 3 rainy days

REVIEW CORNER

Review 1 **Chapters 1–3**

Maximum Marks = 40

A. Choose the correct option. **(3 × 1)**

1. The numeral for four thousand nine hundred seventy-two is __________.
   a. 4279 b. 4972 c. 4291 d. 4792
2. The place value of 8 in 5814 is __________.
   a. 8 b. 80 c. 800 d. 8000
3. The successor of 5679 is __________.
   a. 5680 b. 5678 c. 5681 d. 5679

B. Answer the following. **(3 × 1)**

1. Write the number names for the following.
   a. 5698 b. 1032
2. Write the number that comes in between the following.
   a. 2599 ______ 2601 b. 1011 ____ 1013
3. Counting in 100s, write the number that comes next:
   a. 4098 ______ b. 7903 ______

C. Solve the following. **(5 × 3)**

1. Estimate the sum of 243 + 119 to the nearest 10 and then 100.
2. Write the following numbers in ascending order.
   a. 5321, 937, 6100, 2493 b. 1987, 7707, 3002, 8191
3. Find the sum of the following.
   a. 1231 + 142 + 330 b. 4590 + 2065
4. Subtract the following.
   a. 4567 – 2771 b. 9309 – 5026
5. Estimate the difference between the following to the nearest 100.
   a. 255 and 123 b. 716 and 385

D. Solve the following word problems. **(4 × 4)**

1. Shaurya spent ₹959 on a shirt, ₹1450 on trousers and ₹148 on a pair of shorts. How much money did Shaurya spend in all? If he paid ₹3000 to the shopkeeper, how much money would be returned to him?
2. Form the greatest and the smallest 4-digit numbers using the digits 4, 7, 0 and 3. Write the number names for the numbers formed. Also, classify them as odd or even number.
3. Frame a word problem for the following subtraction: 1290 – 679. Also, solve the word problem.
4. Anoop saved ₹5420 in his bank account. He spent ₹1189 out of it. He saved ₹765 more. How much money does Anoop have now?

Review 2

Chapters 4–6

Maximum Marks = 40

A. Choose the correct option. **(3 × 1)**

1. 9 × 0 = ______

   a. 9 b. 18 c. 0 d. 1

2. 14 ÷ ___ = 14

   a. 1 b. 14 c. 0 d. 2

3. One-fourth = ______

   a. $\frac{4}{4}$ b. $\frac{1}{4}$ c. $\frac{1}{2}$ d. $\frac{1}{3}$

B. Fill in the blanks. **(3 × 2)**

1. 15 × 8 = ______; Division statements: ______________
2. 27 ÷ 3 = ______; Multiplication statements: ______________
3. $\frac{1}{5}$ of 25 = ______; Numerator: ______, Denominator: ______

C. Answer the following. **(3 × 5)**

1. a.

	H	T	O
	1	3	4
×			2

b.

	T	O
	5	6
×		2

2. a. 8 × 200 = ________ b. 321 × 3 = _____
3. a. 8762 ÷ 2 = ______ b. 3243 ÷ 10 = ____
4. Write the fraction for the shaded and unshaded portions in the given figures.

   a. 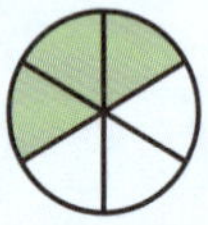

   b. 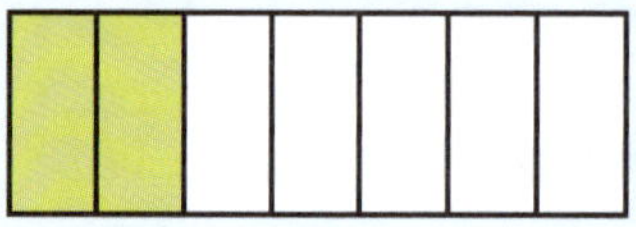

5. 675 ÷ 4 = Q ______, R ______. Also verify the answer.

D. Solve the following word problems. **(4 × 4)**

1. There are 23 students in class 3. Each student brought ₹50 for the class picnic. What was the total amount collected for the picnic?
2. Frame two word problems on the division problem: 18 ÷ 2.
3. Rita bought 8 pastries out of which 3 were chocolate pastries. What fraction of the pastries were chocolate? If half of the pastries bought by Rita were chocolate pastries, then how many chocolate pastries would be there?
4. Estimate the product of 208 and 48. Is the estimated product greater than or less than the actual product?

Comprehensive Review 1

Chapters 1–6

Maximum Marks = 80

A. Choose the correct option. **(6 × 1)**

1. The place value of 7 in 3719 is ______.
   a. 7 b. 70 c. 700 d. 7000
2. The predecessor of 6490 is ______.
   a. 6400 b. 7400 c. 6489 d. 6491
3. In $3 \times 4 = 12$, the product is _____.
   a. 3 b. 4 c. 12 d. 1
4. $12 \div 1 =$ ____
   a. 1 b. 12 c. 0 d. 11
5. One-third = ____
   a. $\frac{1}{1}$ b. $\frac{1}{2}$ c. $\frac{1}{3}$ d. $\frac{1}{4}$
6. $397 + 186 + 91 =$ ____
   a. 547 b. 674 c. 764 d. 667

B. Fill in the blanks. **(6 × 2)**

1. The number name for 2376 is ____________.
2. The numbers that come before and after 8173 are ________ and ________, respectively.
3. $6809 - 4012 =$ ______; Verify: ______ + 4012 = ______
4. $7 \times 9 =$ ______; Multiplicand: ______, Multiplier: ______
5. Divisor = 2, Dividend = 845: Quotient = ______, Remainder = ______
6. Fractions with the same denominator are called ______ fractions. An example is ______.

C. Answer the following. **(10 × 3)**

1. Write the numerals for the following.
   a. Three hundred twenty-one ________
   b. Seven thousand fourteen ________
2. Write the expanded form of the following.
   a. 3176 ______________________________
   b. 9076 ______________________________
3. Write >, < or =.
   a. 5698 ☐ 5700 b. 2534 ☐ 2534
4. a.

	Th	H	T	O
	2	4	5	7
+	3	5	1	4

   b.

	H	T	O
	4	8	3
+	1	2	2

5. a.

	H	T	O
	9	4	7
−	2	2	2

b.

	Th	H	T	O
	8	6	2	5
−	1	0	3	1

6. a. $6 \times 400 =$ ________ b. $123 \times 4 =$ ________
7. a. $316 \div 4 =$ ________ b. $240 \div 20 =$ ________
8. Write the fractions for the following.
   a. Three-fourths: ________ b. One-fifth: ________
9. Colour the figure to represent the given fraction.
   a. $\frac{1}{6}$  b. $\frac{3}{4}$ 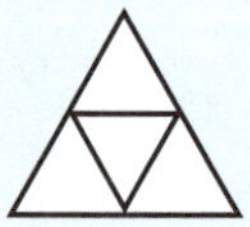
10. Name the type of fraction.
   a. $\frac{7}{4}$: ____________ b. $\frac{1}{3}$: ____________

D. Solve the following. **(8 × 4)**

1. A soap factory produced 2508 soaps in the first week, 1995 soaps in the second week and 3001 soaps in the third week. How many soaps were produced in the three weeks? Round off the answer to the nearest 100.
2. The sum of two numbers is 3033 and the difference between the same two numbers is 1011. If one number is twice the other number, then find the two numbers.
3. a.

	Th	H	T	O
		1	5	2
×			1	2

b.

	Th	H	T	O
	2	3	4	1
×				2

4. Frame a word problem for the multiplication: 28×9. Also find the actual product and the estimated product.
5. A fruit vendor bought 155 apples and 220 oranges. If 15 fruits can be packed in one box, how many boxes will be needed to pack all the fruits?
6. The teacher made 5 groups of 4 students each. Then she made them stand in two equal lines. How many students were there in each line?
7. Samira brought 12 toffees to school. She distributed $\frac{3}{4}$ of the toffees among her friends. How many toffees did she distribute?
8. Calculate:
   a. $7\overline{)529}$ b. $\frac{2}{9}$ of 36

Maximum Marks = 40

A. Choose the correct option. **(3 × 1)**

1. 1 m = ________ cm
   a. 1 b. 1000 c. 10 d. 100
2. 4:15 can be written as
   a. Half past 4 b. Quarter past 4 c. Quarter to 4 d. 5 minutes past 4
3. The given amount of money is equal to

a. ₹77 b. ₹50 c. ₹67 d. ₹70

B. Fill in the blanks. **(3 × 2)**

1. a. 5 m 26 cm = ___________ cm b. 9 kg = __________ g
2. In a year, ___________________________ months have 31 days.
3. a. 9 rupees 50 paise = ______ paise b. 1475 paise = ₹ ______

C. Solve the following. **(5 × 3)**

1. a. 8000 kg = __________ g b. 3000 mℓ = __________ ℓ
2. Reshma bought 1575 cm of cloth. How many metres of cloth is that?
3. Draw the hands of the clocks to show the given time.

a. 3:30 b. 7:45

4. Tick the correct option.
   a. It takes about 3 minutes/3 hours to brush teeth.
   b. It takes about 8 minutes/8 hours to drive from Delhi to Jaipur.
   c. It takes about 2 minutes/2 hours for a plane to fly from Delhi to Mumbai.
5. Find the following.
   a. ₹1000 + ₹500 + ₹10 b. ₹25.75 + ₹6.50 c. ₹93.80 – ₹28.55

D. Answer the following. **(4 × 4)**

1. Suman bought 2 kg 800 g of mangoes and 1ℓ 145 mℓ of liquid detergent. How much would that be in grams and millilitres, respectively?
2. Vijay went to play football at 5 o'clock and came back home after two hours. What time did he come back home?

3. Following are a few important events in Sejal's life.
   a. Sejal left school in March 2013. b. Was born in 1995.
   c. Became the head girl of the school in 2012. d. Took up a job in 2017.
   e. Joined college in July 2013. f. Got married in 2019.

   Sequence the above events in the correct order. Create a horizontal and a vertical timeline.
4. If one notebook costs ₹40.50, what will be the cost of 3 such notebooks? Write the amount in paise.

Review 4

Chapters 10–12

Maximum Marks = 40

A. Choose the correct option. **(3 × 1)**

1. A rectangle has ____________.
   a. 4 sides and 3 corners b. 3 sides and 4 corners
   c. 4 sides and 4 corners d. 3 sides and 3 corners
2. What will come next in the given pattern?
   2, 4, 6, 8, _____
   a. 9 b. 10 c. 11 d. 12
3. If  = 2 stars, then  = ____________.
   a. 1 b. 2 c. 3 d. 4

B. Solve the following. **(3 × 2)**

1. Name the following.
   a.  b. 
2. Mark the unit being repeated in the given pattern .

3. What is tessellation? Can the given pattern be called a tiling pattern?
    Yes or No

C. Answer the following. **(5 × 3)**

1. What are flat shapes? Name any two flat shapes and write their properties.
2. Match the following.
   a.  i. Line
   b.  ii. Line segment
   c.  iii. Closed figure
3. Does  form a pattern? Give reasons for your answer .
4. If  stands for 3 burgers, then
    stand for _______ burgers.

 stand for ________ burgers.

 stand for ________ burgers.

5. On Sunday, Jyoti ate the following: 

   Fill in the blanks.

   a. She ate _____ bananas. b. She ate _____ peaches. c. She ate _____ mango.

D. Solve the following questions. **(4 × 4)**

1. Draw the line of symmetry for the symmetrical figures.

   a.  b.  c.  d. 

2. The pictograph below shows the number of students from classes 1 to 5 in a school. Look at the pictograph and answer the questions given.

   Each ☆ = 8 students.

Number of Students	
Class 1	☆ ☆
Class 2	☆ ☆ ½☆
Class 3	☆ ☆ ☆
Class 4	☆ ☆ ☆ ½☆
Class 5	☆ ☆ ☆

   a. What is the title of the pictograph?

   b. How many students is ☆ equal to?

   c. What is the total number of students from class 1 to class 5?

   d. Which class has the maximum number of students?

3. The following tally chart shows the number of birthdays of students of class 3 in the given months. Study the chart and answer the following questions.

Month	Number of birthdays
July	𝍸 ||
August	||
September	||||
October	|||
November	𝍸 ||||

   a. In which month are there 9 birthdays? ____________

   b. In which month are there the least number of birthdays? ____________

   c. How many more birthdays are there in September than October? ____________

   d. In which two months are there the same number of birthdays?

4. The following bar graph shows the favorite colour of 20 students. Study the bar graph and answer the given questions.

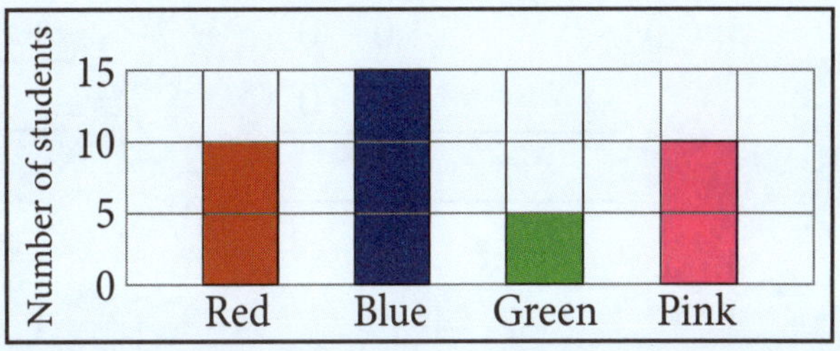

   a. What is the most favorite colour among the students of class 3?

   b. Which two colours are liked equally by the students?

   c. How many more students like blue than red? __________

   d. How many more students like pink than green? __________

Comprehensive Review 2

Chapters 7–12
Maximum Marks = 80

A. Fill in the blanks. **(6 × 1)**

1. 5:15 is also written as quarter _____ 5.
2. When the minute hand moves from 2 to 6, it takes _______ minutes.
3. 5 rupees 41 paise is equal to _______ paise.
4. A line of symmetry divides a shape into ________ equal parts.
5. In the given pattern
   20, 19, 18, 17, 16, 15 _______ is being subtracted every time.
6. In tally marks  represents ________.

B. Answer the following. **(6 × 2)**

1. a. 1 year = ___ weeks b. 1 hour = ____ minutes
2. How many days are there in a leap year? Name the month that gets an extra day in a leap year.
3. Convert: a. 23 rupees 7 paise to paise b. 4 km to m
4. How is a line different from a curve?
5. What is the repeated unit in 1 2 3 1 2 3 1 2 3 1 2 3?
6. In a pictograph if  = 6, then what is 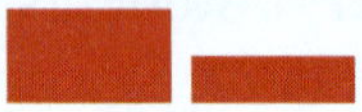 equal to?

C. Solve the following. **(10 × 3)**

1. 

   In the clock given alongside.
   a. The minute hand is pointing at _________.
   b. The hour hand is pointing at ___________.
   c. The time is __________.

2. It takes about
   a. 3 __________ (hours / minutes) to watch a movie.
   b. 15 __________ (hours / minutes) to eat breakfast.
   c. 6 _________ (hours / minutes) in school everyday.

3. a.
```
      ₹
  1 0 0 0
    5 0 0
+     2 0
---------
---------
```
   b.
```
      ₹
  9 2 . 7 5
+   5 . 2 5
-----------
-----------
```
   c.
```
        ₹
  1 5 0 . 8 0
–   9 2 . 6 0
-------------
-------------
```

4. a.
```
   ₹
  2 4
×   5
-----
-----
```
   b.
```
   ₹
  1 5 . 2 5
×         3
-----------
-----------
```
   c. ₹100 ÷ 10 = ______

5. If the cost of 1 pen is ₹5. What is the cost of:
   2 pens ______ 5 pens ______ 10 pens ______

6. Complete the following.
   a. A cuboid has _____ faces and _____ vertices.
   b. A cylinder has _____ flat faces and _____ curved face.
   c. A cone has _____ flat face, _____ curved face and _____ vertex.
7. Match the following.

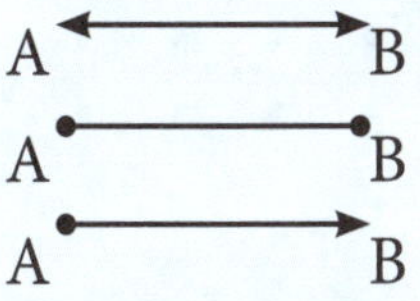

Line segment
Ray
Line

8. On the given dot grid, draw the following:
   a. Vertical line
   b. Horizontal line
   c. Diagonal line

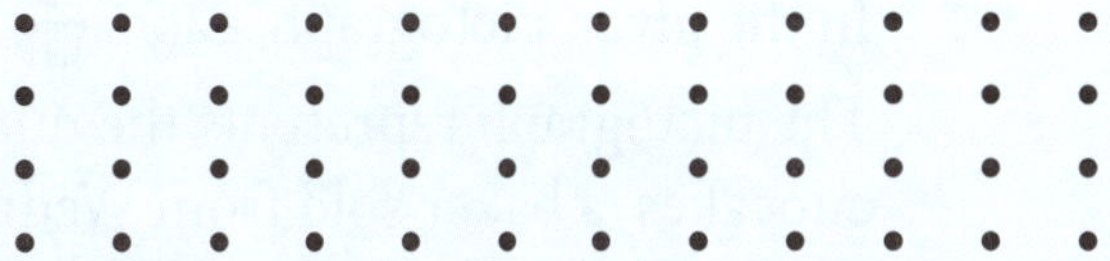

9. Complete the following patterns.
   a.  __________
   b.  ________
   c. 5, 10, 15, 20, __________
10. The number of pages of a storybook that Mihir read on Friday, Saturday and Sunday is given below in the form of tally marks.

Day	Number of pages
Friday	𝍸 𝍸 |
Saturday	𝍸 𝍸 ||
Sunday	𝍸 𝍸 𝍸

How many pages did Mihir read on the following days:
Friday ____ Saturday ____ Sunday _____.

D. Answer the following questions. **(8 × 4)**

1. If today is the 23rd of July (Thursday), what will be the date and day:
   a. after 1 week? b. 1 week ago?
2. Given below are some events from Komal's life.
   a. Komal joined high school in 2008.
   b. Komal completed class 1 in 2005.
   c. Komal completed class 12 in 2018.
   d. Komal was born in 2000.
   e. Komal became school captain of junior school in 2010.
   Create a timeline for all the events given above from Komal's life.
3. Alex bought the following stationery items. The shopkeeper made the following bill for him. Identify and circle the errors and correct them as well.

Universal Stationary Shop			
Item	Quantity	Rate per item	Amount
Pencils	5	₹4	₹30
Erasers	5	₹3	₹40
Pencil box	1	₹45	₹45
Ruler	3	₹12	₹56
		Total	₹171

4. A group of 5 friends wanted to collect ₹750. How much should each child bring? They want to buy a videogame for ₹900. Do they have enough money to buy it? If not, how much more money do they need?

5. In the dot grid given, draw:
   a. a rectangle
   b. a curve
   c. a triangle

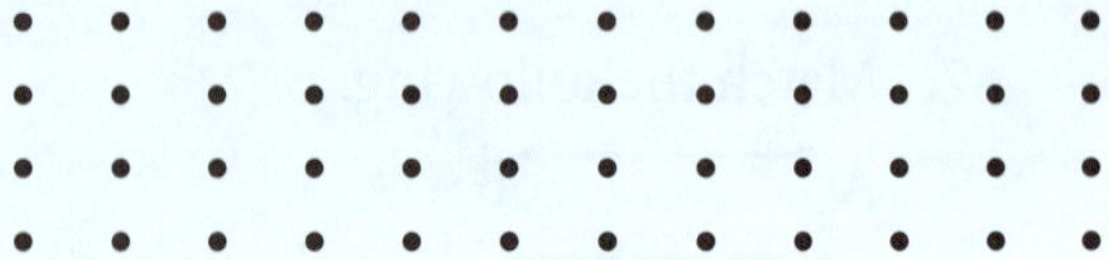

6. Name and draw two solid shapes that have the following features:
   a. 6 faces
   b. No vertices

7. In the given pictograph, each  = 6 cupcakes.
   The pictograph represents the numbers of cupcakes a baker sold from Wednesday to Sunday. Study the pictograph and answer the questions.

Cupcakes sold from Wednesday to Sunday

Days	Number of cupcakes sold
Wednesday	
Thursday	
Friday	
Saturday	
Sunday	

   a. How many cupcakes did the baker sell on Thursday?
   b. How many more cupcakes did the baker sell on Saturday than on Wednesday?
   c. On which day, did he sell the maximum number of cupcakes?
   d. What was the total number of cupcakes he sold in these 5 days?
   e. On which day, did he sell 18 cupcakes?

8. The given bar graph represents the number of some animals in a zoo.

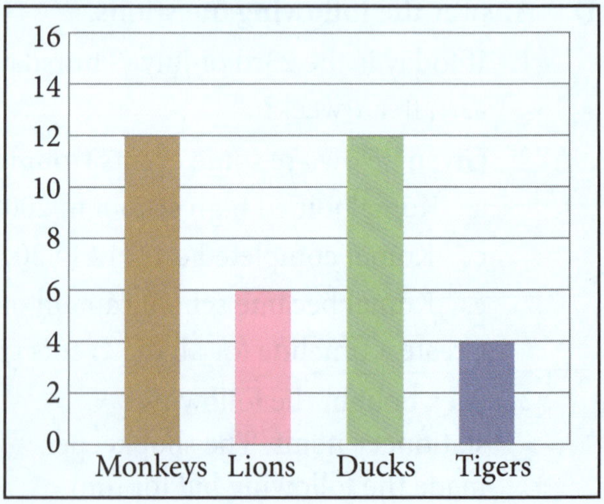

   Study the bar graph and answer the questions given below:
   a. Write the number of the following animals in the zoo
      Monkeys   Lions
      Ducks   Tigers
   b. How many more lions are there than tigers?
   c. Which animal is the least in number in the zoo?
   d. Are there more ducks or monkeys in the zoo?

CLASS 3

QUESTION PAPER SET A

IMO

SOF INTERNATIONAL MATHEMATICS OLYMPIAD 2020-21

DO NOT OPEN THIS BOOKLET UNTIL ASKED TO DO SO

Total Questions: 35 | Time: 1 hr.

Guidelines for the Candidate

1. You will get additional ten minutes to fill up information about yourself on the OMR Sheet, before the start of the exam.
2. Write your **Name, School Code, Class, Section, Roll No.** and **Mobile Number** clearly on the **OMR Sheet** and do not forget to sign it. We will share your marks / result and other information related to SOF exams on your mobile number.
3. The Question Paper comprises four sections:

   Logical Reasoning (10 Questions), **Mathematical Reasoning** (10 Questions), **Everyday Mathematics** (10 Questions) and **Achievers Section** (5 Questions)

   Each question in Achievers Section carries 2 marks, whereas all other questions carry one mark each.
4. All questions are compulsory. There is no negative marking. Use of calculator is not permitted.
5. There is only ONE correct answer. Choose only ONE option for an answer.
6. To mark your choice of answers by darkening the circles on the OMR Sheet, use **HB Pencil** or **Blue / Black ball point pen** only. E.g.

   Q.16: Sonia had 80 sweets. She gave 15 sweets to Danish and 15 sweets to Megha. How many sweets are left with her?

   A. 50 B. 30 C. 60 D. 40

   As the correct answer is option A, you must darken the circle corresponding to option A on the OMR Sheet. 16. ● Ⓑ Ⓒ Ⓓ
7. Rough work should be done in the blank space provided in the booklet.
8. Return the OMR Sheet to the invigilator at the end of the exam.
9. Please fill in your personal details in the space provided on this page before attempting the paper.

SOF
SCIENCE OLYMPIAD FOUNDATION
Inspiring Young Minds Through Knowledge Olympiads

Name:..

Section:........... SOF Olympiad Roll No.:.. Contact No.:..

1. Find the odd one out.

A. 

B. 

C. 

D. 

2. Select a figure from the options which will complete the given figure pattern?

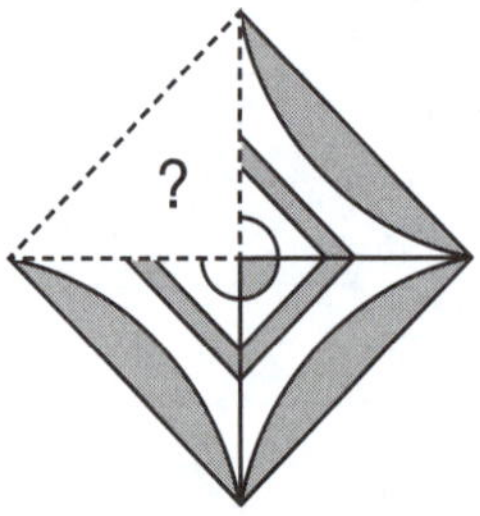

A. 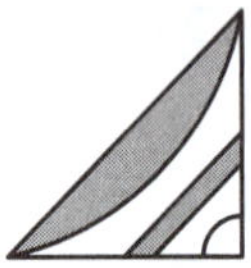

B. 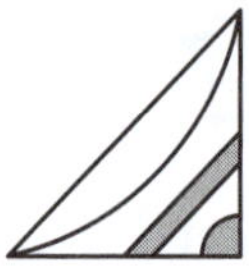

C. 

D. 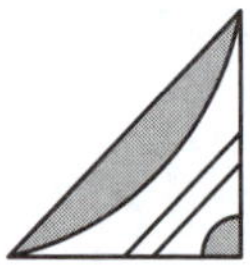

3. How many triangles are there in the given figure?

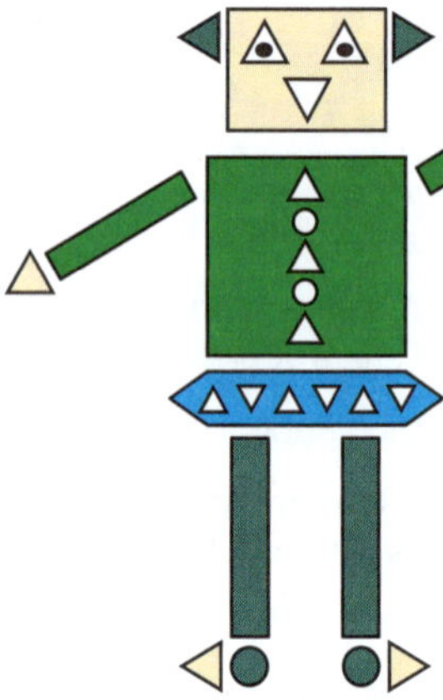

A. 20

B. 18

C. 16

D. 21

4. How many possible combinations of 1 wrist watch and 1 wall clock can be formed from the given watches and wall clocks?

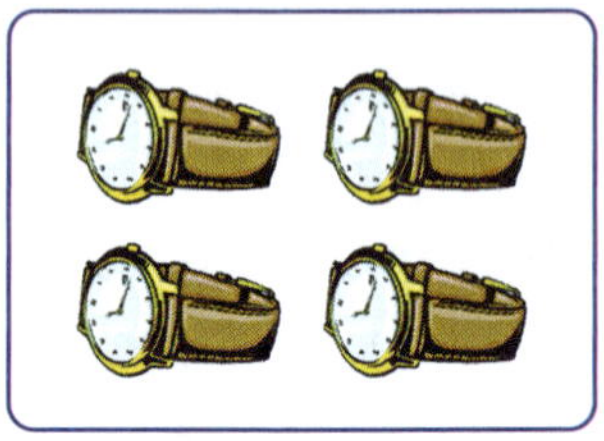

A. 7

B. 10

C. 14

D. 12

5. There is a certain relationship between the pair of figures on the either side of ::. Identify the relationship between the given pair and find the missing figure.

F : 12 :: I : ?

A. 14 B. 9 C. 18 D. 20

SPACE FOR ROUGH WORK

6. Which of the following words can be formed from the letters of the given word?

STATEMENT

A. TOAST B. TEASE C. MINES D. SNEAP

7. In which group does the number 30 NOT belong?

A. 5, 10, 15, 20, ...
B. 3, 6, 9, 12, 15, ...
C. 6, 12, 18, 24, ...
D. 4, 8, 12, 16, 20, ...

8. Which of the following figures will replace the question mark (?) in the given figure matrix?

A. 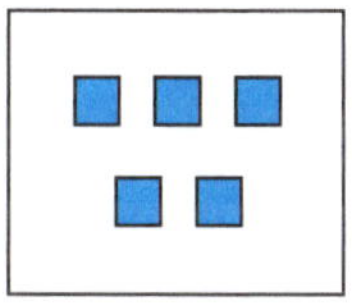

B. 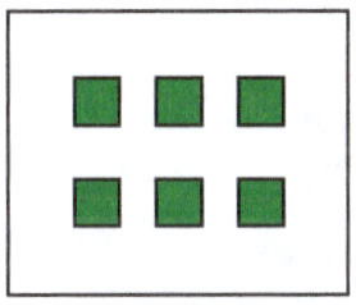

C. 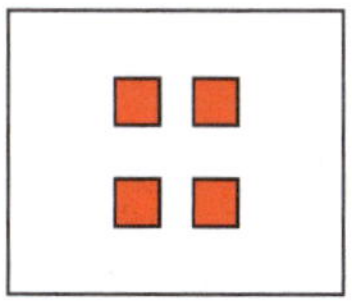

D. 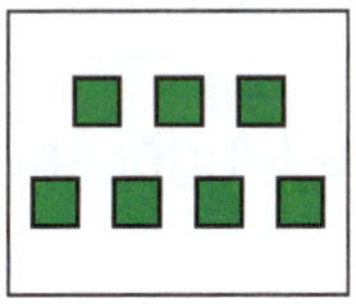

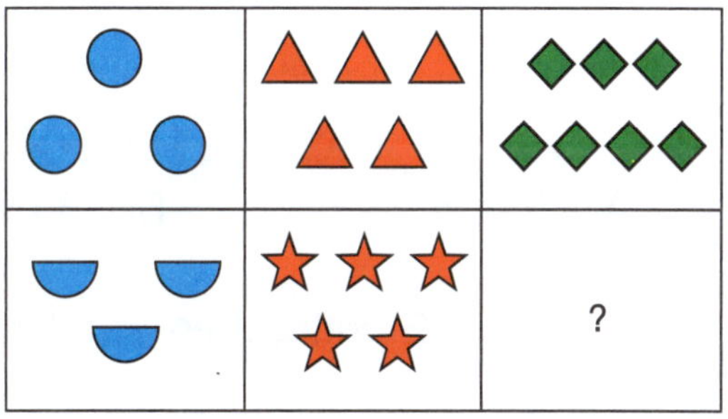

9. If yesterday was Friday, then sixth day from today will be ______.

A. Thursday B. Wednesday C. Friday D. Saturday

10. Find the mirror image of the given figure.

Mirror

A. 

B. 

C. 

D. 

MATHEMATICAL REASONING

11. Which of the following number names does NOT belong to the given figure?

A. Two hundred ninety nine
B. Seven hundred sixty five
C. One hundred two
D. Five hundred ninety seven

SPACE FOR ROUGH WORK

12. If  represents 4 books, then which of the following represents 18 books?

A. 

B. 

C. 

D. 

13. The value of 

− 

= ?

A. 9 tens B. 9 ones C. 91 hundreds D. 913 ones

14. If 1 □ = 2 units, then stapler is ________ units longer than the pencil.

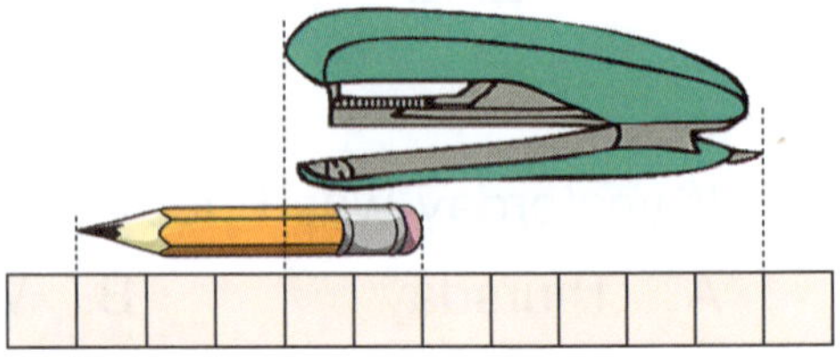

A. 2
B. 6
C. 4
D. 3

15. Weight of 2 such toy horses is ________ the weight of 1 laptop.

A. Less than
B. More than
C. Same as
D. Can't be determined

16. Himanshi has two ₹ 500 notes. Which of the following items can she buy, if she spends all her money?

A. Toy tiger and spinning bell
B. Toy tiger and violin
C. Spinning bell and violin
D. Toy tiger, spinning bell and violin

Toy tiger

Spinning bell

Violin

SPACE FOR ROUGH WORK

17. A concert started at 20:45. It lasts for 2 hrs 25 minutes. At what time did it finish?

A.  B.  C.  D. 

---

18. Find the total length of boundary of the given figure.

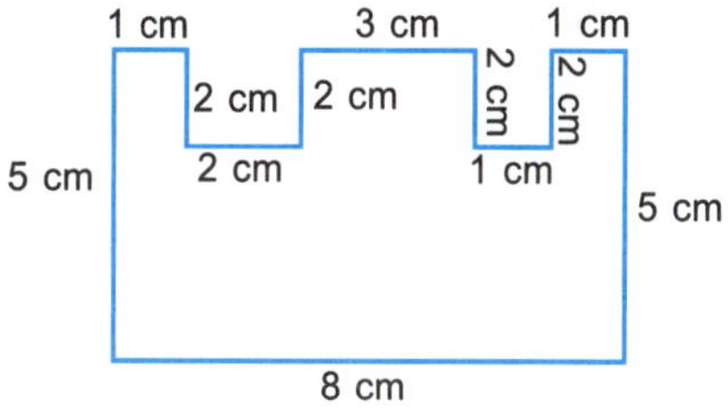

A. 30 cm
B. 34 cm
C. 36 cm
D. 38 cm

---

19. If the digit at tens place is interchanged with the digit at thousands place in the given number, then what is the difference between the new number formed and the given number?

A. 2997 B. 360 C. 1980 D. 297

---

20. If 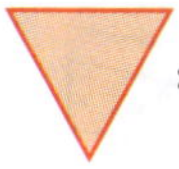 = 1 whole, then 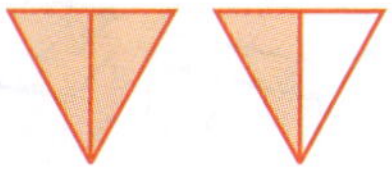 equals ____.

A. $1\frac{1}{2}$ B. $3\frac{1}{2}$ C. $2\frac{1}{2}$ D. $4\frac{1}{2}$

EVERYDAY MATHEMATICS

21. Riya has 8 clay balls and 12 toothpicks. She make a shape having six faces. Which of the following shapes she made?

A. 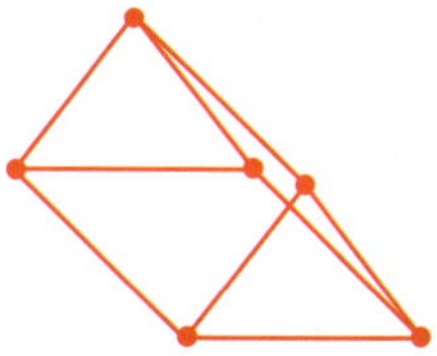 B. 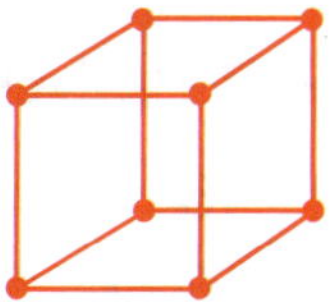 C. 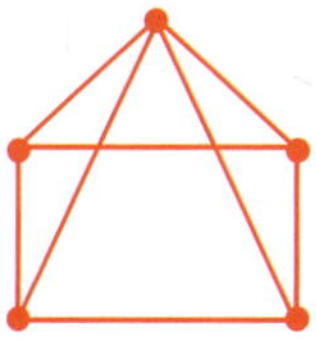 D. 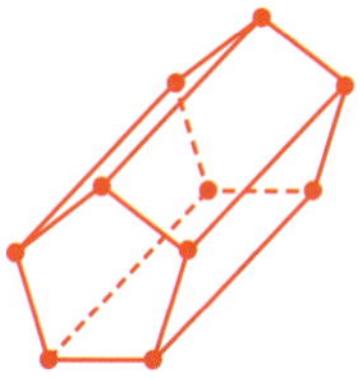

---

22. There are 9785 people in a party. Out of these 3245 are males, 1878 are females and rest are children. How many children are there in the party?

A. 4662 B. 5642 C. 4748 D. 5258

SPACE FOR ROUGH WORK

23. Garvit drinks given glasses of water every day. How many glasses of water will he drink in three weeks?

A. 36 B. 84 C. 252 D. 288

24. Nidhi buys two packets of flour as shown. If she uses 2 kg 875 g flour to bake a cake, then how much flour is left with her?

3 kg 50 g

A. 2 kg 575 g
B. 175 g
C. 4 kg 125 g
D. 3 kg 225 g

25. A cake was divided into twelve equal parts. Kritika ate $\frac{3}{12}$ of the cake and Arun ate $\frac{5}{12}$ of the cake. What fraction of the cake was left?

A. $\frac{8}{12}$ B. $\frac{4}{12}$ C. $\frac{2}{12}$ D. $\frac{7}{12}$

26. Kanika has 75 cookies. If she put them equally in the given boxes, then how many cookies are left with her?

A. 3 B. 4 C. 1 D. 2

27. Aman bought 5 shirts at ₹ 899 each. How much amount did he pay in all?

A. ₹ 4095 B. ₹ 4495 C. ₹ 4945 D. ₹ 6540

28. Monika puts exactly 4 stones in each of the vessels shown. How many stones she has used in all?

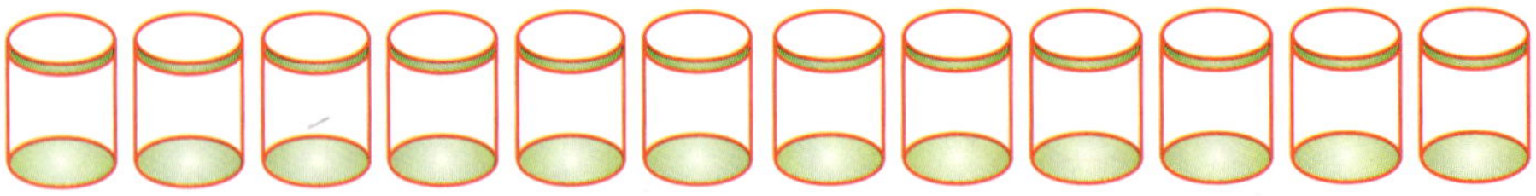

A. 60 B. 62 C. 46 D. 48

29. On Monday, 2476 cars crossed the toll. On Tuesday, 3298 cars crossed the toll and 1947 cars crossed the toll on Wednesday. How many total cars crossed the toll in these three days?

A. 5774 B. 7721 C. 9731 D. 6741

SPACE FOR ROUGH WORK

30. The temperature in Srinagar is 18°C less than the temperature shown in the given thermometer. Find the temperature in Srinagar.

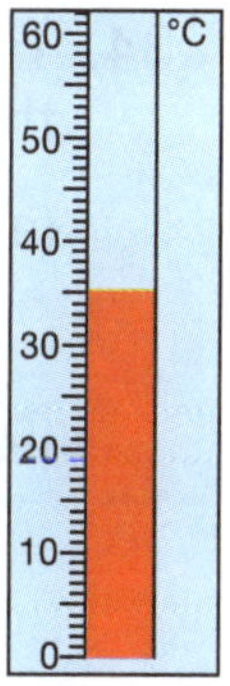

A. 35°C

B. 17°C

C. 18°C

D. 12°C

ACHIEVERS SECTION

31. Find the value of P, Q and R respectively.

	P	1	3
	×	1	Q
2	8	9	1
+4	1	3	0
Q	0	2	R

A. 3, 7, 4

B. 4, 5, 7

C. 4, 7, 1

D. 7, 3, 5

---

32. Niharika bought 2 bunches of bananas, 3 boxes of cookies and 4 baskets of strawberries. What is the total weight of the items she bought?

1 kg 25 g

975 g

1 kg 75 g

A. 8 kg 750 g B. 7 kg 75 g C. 9 kg 275 g D. 9 kg 125 g

---

33. Identify the number using the given clues.

- It is an even number.
- The digit at tens place is the largest odd number.
- The digit at hundreds place is the remainder obtained when 56 is divided by 7.
- The digit at tens place is thrice the digit at thousands place.

A. 3094 B. 3196 C. 3095 D. 6098

SPACE FOR ROUGH WORK

34. The given graph shows the number of pages read by five boys on a particular day. Study the graph carefully and answer the following questions.

(a) How many less pages Manav read than Nakul and Dev together read?

(b) Aayush and ________ read 28 pages together.

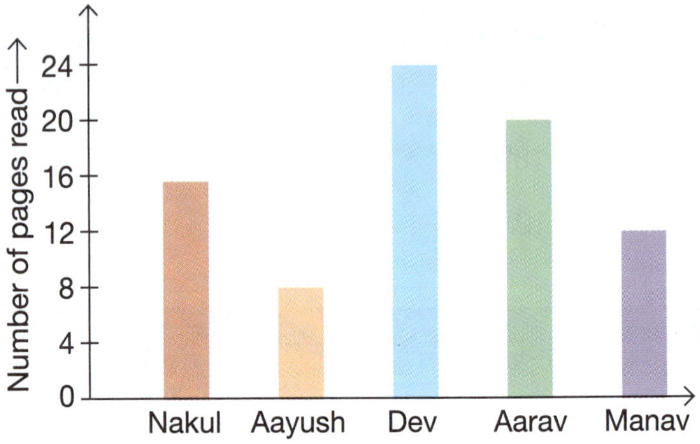

	(a)	(b)
A.	20	Manav
B.	20	Aarav
C.	28	Manav
D.	28	Aarav

35. Four girls Aaliya, Palak, Divya and Ekta each having ₹ 1000 went on shopping. If they bought the following items, then which girl has maximum amount left after the shopping?

A. Palak B. Divya C. Ekta D. Aaliya

SPACE FOR ROUGH WORK

SPACE FOR ROUGH WORK

ANSWER KEYS

1.	(D)	**2.**	(C)	**3.**	(B)	**4.**	(D)	**5.**	(C)	**6.**	(B)	**7.**	(D)
8.	(D)	**9.**	(A)	**10.**	(D)	**11.**	(D)	**12.**	(D)	**13.**	(D)	**14.**	(C)
15.	(A)	**16.**	(B)	**17.**	(A)	**18.**	(B)	**19.**	(C)	**20.**	(A)	**21.**	(B)
22.	(A)	**23.**	(C)	**24.**	(D)	**25.**	(B)	**26.**	(A)	**27.**	(B)	**28.**	(D)
29.	(B)	**30.**	(B)	**31.**	(C)	**32.**	(C)	**33.**	(A)	**34.**	(D)	**35.**	(B)

SOF
SCIENCE OLYMPIAD FOUNDATION

National Office: Plot 99, First Floor, Sector 44 Institutional area, Gurugram -122 003 (HR) India

Email: info@sofworld.org | Website: www.sofworld.org

Regd. Office: 406, Taj Apt., Ring Road, New Delhi-110 029

Note: Please address all communication to the National Office only.

Answers

Chapter 1

Exercise 1A

1. a. Two hundred thirty-five
   b. 200 + 30 + 5
   c. 2 hundreds 3 tens 5 ones
   d. 234 e. 236
2. a. 284 < 364 < 659 < 971
   b. 843 > 705 > 364 > 129
3. a. 125
   b. One hundred twenty-five

Exercise 1B

1. a. 600, 6 b. 7000, 7 c. 90, 9
2. Number: 4735
   Number name: Four thousand seven hundred thirty-five
3. a. Five thousand six hundred eighty-nine
   b. Two thousand one hundred seven
   c. Six thousand
4. a. 6281 b. 9367 c. 8154
5. a. 4000 + 0 + 20 + 9
   b. 8000 + 500 + 70 + 2
   c. 1000 + 300 + 60 + 4
6. a. 6429 b. 5138 c. 3240 d. 8653
7. a. 7695 b. 7000 c. 90 + 5 = 95

Exercise 1C

1. a. 3816 b. 2068 c. 9150
2. a. 5892 b. 2077 c. 1429
3. a. 1673 b. 3049 c. 7166
4. a. 7440, 7450, 7460, 7470
   b. 2591, 2601, 2611, 2621
5. a. 2200, 2300, 2400, 2500
   b. 9336, 9436, 9536, 9636
6. a. 4000, 5000, 6000, 7000
   b. 6929, 7929, 8929, 9929

Exercise 1D

1. a. < b. > c. > d. =
2. a. 7264 b. 8407
3. a. 1001 b. 2105

Exercise 1E

1. a. 1580 < 4891 < 7643 < 9621
   b. 1782 < 2814 < 5962 < 6432
   c. 2058 < 2431 < 3849 < 5143
2. a. 8726 > 8251 > 7592 > 7068
   b. 6214 > 5728 > 4816 > 4205
   c. 9432 > 9100 > 7640 > 7381
3. a. Greatest: 8542, Smallest: 2458
   b. Greatest: 9310, Smallest:1039
   c. Greatest: 8532, Smallest: 2358
4. a. Any one of the digits: 0, 2, 4, 6 or 8
   b. Any one of the digits: 0, 2, 4, 6 or 8
5. a. Any one of the digits: 1, 3, 5, 7 or 9
   b. Any one of the digits: 1, 3, 5, 7 or 9

Exercise 1F

1. a. 630 b. 420 c. 5350 d. 8580
2. a. 500 b. 1600 c. 6100 d. 7100

Chapter Revision

A. 1. c. 9897 2. d. 1547 3. b. 2466 4. b. 4843

B. Thousands = 3 Hundreds = 5
   Tens = 2 Ones = 9
   Number name: Three thousand five hundred twenty-nine
   Expanded form: 3 thousands 5 hundreds 2 tens 9 ones or 3000 + 500 + 20 + 9

C. 1. 3592, 3593, 3594, 3595
   2. 2764, 2765, 2766, 2767
   3. 6748, 6749, 6750, 6751
   4. 8004, 8005, 8006, 8007

D. 1. Seven thousand three hundred twenty-nine
   2. One thousand four hundred sixty-eight
   3. Three thousand two hundred fourteen
   4. Eight thousand three hundred fifty-two

E. 1. 4013 2. 7006 3. 2893 4. 5742

F. 1. 3593 2. 9279 3. 9999 4. 600 5. 6

G. 1. > 2. = 3. <

H. 1. 2440, 2450, 2460, 2470
   2. 1395, 1495, 1595, 1695
   3. 4947, 5947, 6947, 7947

I. 1. 1960 < 3425 < 8237 < 9054
   2. 1673 < 4700 < 8153 < 9046
   3. 1542 < 6208 < 7140 < 9873

J. 1. 9300 > 8471 > 6702 > 2064
   2. 9876 > 6400 > 5710 > 3498
   3. 5921 > 4382 > 3596 > 3420

K. 1. Greatest: 9763, Smallest: 3679
2. Greatest: 8541, Smallest: 1458
3. Greatest: 7420, Smallest: 2047

L. 1. Nearest 10 = 6500, Nearest 100 = 6500
2. Nearest 10 = 1700, Nearest 100 = 1700
3. Nearest 10 = 9910, Nearest 100 = 9900

Chapter 2

Exercise 2A

1. 637 2. 856 3. 967 4. 867

Exercise 2B

1. 875 2. 889 3. 973 4. 968

Exercise 2C

1. 952 2.496 3. 793 4. 694

Exercise 2D

1. 754 2. 912 3. 718 4. 835

Exercise 2E

1. 8598 2. 6054 3. 5430 4. 7718

Exercise 2F

1. 368 people 2. 723 marbles
3. ₹1453 4. 705 people

Exercise 2G

1. a. 30 b. 50 c. 60 d. 90
2. a. 900 b.600 c. 300 d.200

Chapter Revision

A. 1. F 2. T 3. F 4. F
B. 1.—c. 2.—d. 3.—a. 4.—b.
C. 1. 949 2. 380 399 170
D. 1. 746 2. 973 3. 800 4. 847
5. 785 6. 658 7. 6228 8. 8597
9. 6992
E. 1. 424 2. 641
3. 784 4. 1954

Chapter 3

Exercise 3A

1. a. 16 b. 485 c. 758 d. 385
2. 268

Exercise 3B

1. a. 2717 b. 6303 c. 3364 d. 882
e. 4837 f. 1119
2. a. 6554 b. 3168 c. 4028 d. 2889

Exercise 3C

1. 5232 2. 8141 3. 5271

Exercise 3D

1. 6541 2. 3654
3. ₹2350 4. 8398
5. 2320 6. 9100

Exercise 3E

(Suggestive answers.)

1. a. During the pandemic, a shopkeeper sold 157 masks out of 438 masks in a day. Find the number of remaining masks.
b. A baker baked 3985 fruit cakes. He sold 1472 cakes. How many cakes are left for selling?
c. Jenny had ₹8702. Gargi had ₹4596. Who had less amount of money and by how much?
2. a. 470, 400; actual: 463 b. 650, 700; actual: 654
c. 490, 500; actual: 484 d. 170, 200; actual: 176

Chapter Revision

A. 1. c 2. b 3. a 4. d
B. 1. e. 353 2. a. 8299 3. d. 455
4. c. 4347 5. b. 1921
C. 1. 591 2. 365 3. 186 4. 1813
5. 5367 6. 3846
D. 1. T 2. T 3. F 4. F 5. T
E. 1. 1055 2. ₹5850
3. 2825 4. 2514
F. 1. b. 490 2. a. 200 3. d. 450
4. a. 270 5. c. 3000

Chapter 4

Exercise 4A

1. a. 2, 9, 18 b. 15, 3, 45 c. 6, 7, 42
2. a. T b. F c. F d. T
3. a. 36 b. 0 c. 64 d. 22
e. 6 f. 21

Exercise 4B

1. a. 96 b. 116 c. 696 d. 820
2. a. 9 b. 8 c. 7 d. 6
e. 6, 0 f. 1, 9

Exercise 4C

1. a. 20 b. 360 c. 400 d. 4800
2. a. 180 b. 680 c. 260 d. 1000

Exercise 4D

1. a. 325 b. 368 c. 5486 d. 2938
2. a. 966 b. 945 c. 1134 d. 390
e. 8046 f. 6702

Exercise 4E

1. 46 2. 273 3. 175 4. 924

Exercise 4F

1. a. 325 b. 360
   c. 595 d. ₹3750

3. a. 500 b. 2400 c. 3600

Chapter Revision

A. 1. F 2. T 3. F 4. F 5. T

B. 1. 35 2. 81 3. 48 4. 48
   5. 200 6. 300

C. 1. d. 270
   2. a. 830
   3. e. 6950
   4. b. 9200
   5. c. 500

D. 1. 396 2. 406 3. 860 4. 390
   5. 804 6. 6750

E. 1. 840 2. 1161 3. 694 4. 2178
   5. ₹796 6. 325 7. ₹625
   8. If the cost of one notebook is ₹42, find the cost of 20 such notebooks. ₹840

CHAPTER 5

Exercise 5A

1. a. 3, $27 \div 9 = 3$ b. 4, $20 \div 5 = 4$
2. a. 3, $15 \div 5 = 3$ b. 10, $30 \div 3 = 10$
3. a. 8, $2 \times 8 = 16$, $8 \times 2 = 16$
   b. 3, $8 \times 3 = 24$, $3 \times 8 = 24$

Exercise 5B

1. Q = 5 2. Q = 3, R = 2 3. Q = 2
4. Q = 4, R = 3

Exercise 5C

1. Q = 12 2. Q = 13
3. Q = 11, R = 2 4. Q = 36
5. Q = 18, R = 1 6. Q = 12
7. Q = 21, R = 1 8. Q = 10

Exercise 5D

1. Q = 142 2. Q = 312
3. Q = 72 4. Q = 156, R = 1
5. Q = 62, R = 1 6. Q = 171, R = 1
7. Q = 240 8. Q = 120

Exercise 5E

1. a. 4, 8 b. 57, 3 c. 7, 90 d. 5, 8
2. a. 7 b. 12 c. 5 d. 7

Exercise 5F

1. a. 12 b. ₹10
   c. 6 packets, 5 biscuits left
2. a. If the cost of 4 erasers is ₹24. Find the cost of one eraser. ₹6
   b. If 16 pens are to be distributed equally among 3 children, how many pens would each child get and how many are left over?
   5 pens, 1 pen is left over

Exercise 5G

1. ₹15 2. 28 3. 25
4. 50

Chapter Revision

A. 1. c. 2. b. 3. c. 4. c. 5. d.

B. 1. 4, 2 2. 59, 0 3. 78, 9 4. 5, 26
   5. Dividend, Quotient

C. 1. 210 2. Q = 176, R = 2
   3. Q = 137, R = 1 4. 200
   5. Q = 131, R = 1 6. Q = 18, R = 26
   7. Q = 16, R = 20 8. Q = 7, R = 10

D. 1. 160 2. 40
   3. 12 4. 7
   5. 20 baskets, 5 apples left
   6. 25
   7. 40 cookies were packed equally in 5 boxes. How many cookies were packed in one box? 8 cookies
   8. 74

CHAPTER 6

Exercise 6A

1. b. one-fourth = $\frac{1}{4}$ c. three-fourths = $\frac{3}{4}$
   d. two-thirds = $\frac{2}{3}$

2.

Numerator:	2	1	3	5
Denominator:	5	6	7	9

3. a. $\frac{1}{2}$ b. $\frac{1}{3}$ c. $\frac{2}{3}$ d. $\frac{3}{4}$ e. $\frac{1}{4}$

4. a.  b. 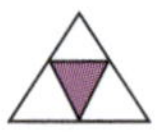 c. 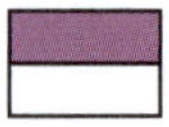

Exercise 6B

1. Red cars = $\frac{1}{6}$

2. a. 
   b. 
   c. 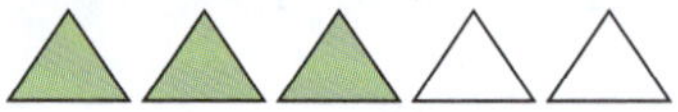

3. a. $\frac{2}{5}, \frac{3}{5}$ b. $\frac{1}{4}, \frac{3}{4}$ c. $\frac{1}{6}, \frac{5}{6}$ d. $\frac{3}{7}, \frac{4}{7}$

Exercise 6C

1. a. 4, circle 4 ice creams b. 6, circle 6 dice
   c. 6, circle 6 penguins
2. b. 3 c. 3

Exercise 6D

1. Unit fractions: $\frac{1}{2}, \frac{1}{7}, \frac{1}{34}$

   Like fractions: $\frac{4}{5}, \frac{3}{5}; \frac{17}{15}, \frac{18}{15}; \frac{13}{9}, \frac{8}{9}; \frac{8}{10}, \frac{9}{10}$

   Unlike fractions: $\frac{4}{5}, \frac{5}{3}, \frac{1}{2}, \frac{17}{15}, \frac{4}{12}, \frac{1}{7}, \frac{1}{34}, \frac{13}{9}, \frac{8}{10}, \frac{6}{4}$

   Proper fractions: $\frac{1}{2}, \frac{1}{7}, \frac{1}{34}, \frac{4}{5}, \frac{3}{5}, \frac{8}{9}; \frac{8}{10}, \frac{9}{10}, \frac{4}{12}$

   Improper fractions: $\frac{17}{15}, \frac{18}{15}; \frac{13}{9}, \frac{6}{4}, \frac{5}{3}$

2. a. $\frac{5}{9}$ b. 4 c. 8
   d. 4

Chapter Revision

A. 1. d. 2. b. 3. c. 4. b.

B. 1.  2. 

C. 1. $\frac{1}{4}, \frac{3}{4}$ 2. $\frac{3}{8}, \frac{5}{8}$ 3. $\frac{3}{6}, \frac{3}{6}$

D. 1. $\frac{1}{2}$ 2. $\frac{1}{3}$ 3. $\frac{2}{3}$ 4. $\frac{3}{4}$
   5. $\frac{2}{5}$ 6. $\frac{4}{9}$

E. 1. c. 2. d. 3. a. 4. b.

F. 1. $\frac{3}{10}$ 2. $\frac{2}{5}$ 3. $\frac{3}{8}$

G. 1. 9 2. 4 3. 3
   4. 4 5. $\frac{5}{12}$

Chapter 7

Exercise 7A

1. Centimetre < Metre < Kilometre
2. a. Height of a refrigerator e. Length of bed
3. a. cm b. m c. km d. m

Exercise 7B

2. a. 300 cm b. 900 cm c. 342 cm d. 459 cm
3. a. 3 m b. 4 m 69 cm c. 4320 m d. 1 km 596 m

Exercise 7C

1. a. g b. kg c. g d. mg e. kg
2. a. 100 g b. 1 kg c. 200 g
3. a. 5000 g b. 8000 g c. 1375 g d. 7130 g
4. a. 5 kg 0 g b. 7 kg 342 g
   c. 3 kg 581 g d. 2 kg 467 g

Exercise 7D

1. a. 500 mℓ b. 1 ℓ
   c. 30 mℓ d. 5 mℓ e. 100 ℓ
2. a. 2000 mℓ b. 5000 mℓ c. 3020 mℓ
   d. 4780 mℓ
3. a. 3 ℓ b. 7 ℓ c. 5 ℓ 278 mℓ
   d. 9 ℓ 346 mℓ

Exercise 7E

1. 700 cm 2. 2 m 49 cm
3. 7 kg 485 g 4. 2370 mℓ

Chapter Revision

A. 1. cm 2. m 3. kg

B. 1. length 2. mass
   3. litres, millilitres 4. kilometres

C. 1. c. 2. a. 3. b. 4. e. 5. d.

D. a. 2 m 0 cm b. 7 m 59 cm

E. a. 5068 g b. 2375 g

F. a. 1 ℓ 745 mℓ b. 6 ℓ 87 mℓ

G. 1. 200 cm 2. 3200 m 3. 5000 g
   4. 1 ℓ 500 mℓ 5. 2000 mℓ

Chapter 8

Exercise 8A

1. a. 1:00 or 1 o'clock b. 4:30 or half past 4
   c. 3:30 or half past 3 d. 2:45 or quarter to 3
2. a.  b. 
   c.  d. 

Exercise 8B

1. a. 10 minutes b. 15 minutes c. 35 minutes
   d. 50 minutes e. 55 minutes
2. a. 4:45 or quarter to 5 b. 9:05 or 5 minutes past 9
   c. 4:35 or 25 minutes to 5
3. a.  b.  c. 
4. a. 8:00 b. 6:30

Exercise 8C

1. e. 3 f. 4
2. a. 7 b. 12
   c. 52 d. 365 e. 366
3. a. 31 days b. 31 days
   c. 30 days d. 31 days
   e. 31 days f. 30 days
4. Correct order: b., e., d., a., c.

Horizontal timeline:

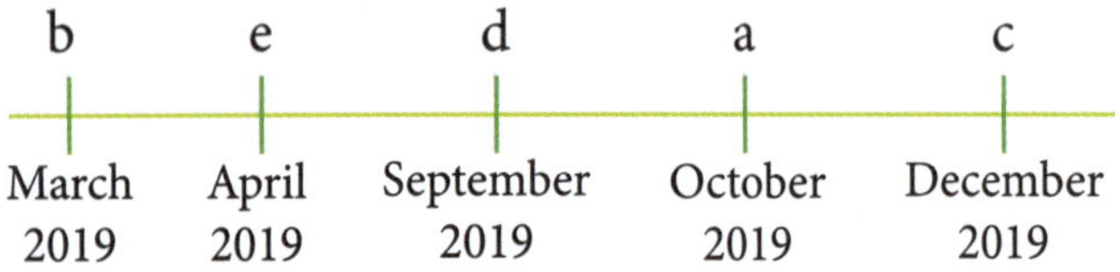

Vertical timeline:

March 2019 — Madhav completed class 2
April 2019 — His next year's classes began
September 2019 — Madhav went for a school picnic
October 2019 — Madhav visited Mumbai
December 2019 — His Christmas holiday began

Chapter Revision

A. 1. c. 2. a. 3. c. 4. d.
B. 1. b. 2. a. 3. d. 4. c.
C. 1.  2.  3. 
D. 1. a. 2. b. 3. b. 4. b.
E. 1. F 2. T 3. F 4. T 5. F
F. 1. 40 minutes 2. 01:40 3. 3:45
   4. Reach hometown: 26 October; Return home: 14 November
   5. Correct order: c, f, b, e, d, a

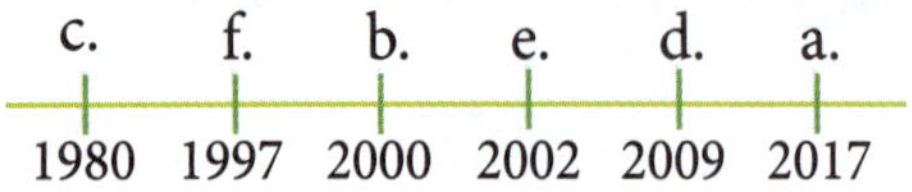

Chapter 9

Exercise 9A

1. a. ₹65.25 b. ₹130.50
2. a. 600 p b. 2300 p c. 1350 p d. 5207 p
3. a. ₹4.30 b. ₹13.05 c. ₹82.50 d. ₹19.02

Exercise 9B

1. a. ₹34.41 b. ₹237.47 c. ₹32.11 d. ₹273.52
   e. ₹216 f. ₹164.25 g. ₹42 h. ₹7
2. a. ₹93 b. ₹72 c. ₹125

Exercise 9C

1. Cupcakes: ₹96, Doughnuts: ₹10, Cookies: ₹1; Total: ₹486
2. Row 1: ₹350 should be ₹450
   Row 3: ₹220 should be ₹110
   Total: ₹1020 should be ₹1010.

Chapter Revision

A. a. 300 p b. 1700 p c. 670 p d.1989 p
B. a. ₹0.20 b. ₹19 c. ₹3.47 d. ₹18.08
C. 1. b. 2. d. 3. a. 4. c.
D. 1. ₹407 2. ₹145 3. ₹280 4. ₹112
   5. ₹123.25
E. Skirt: 90 × 2 = ₹180, Frock: 1 × 150 = ₹150
   Top: 1 × 75 = ₹75, Bellies: 1 × 112 = ₹112; Total: ₹517

Chapter 10

Exercise 10A

1. a. Sphere b. Cube c. Cone d. Cylinder
   e. Cuboid
2. a. Rectangle, 4 sides, 4 vertices, 1 face
   b. Cone, 1 curved side, 1 vertex, 1 flat face and 1 curved face
   c. Cube, 12 sides, 8 vertices, 6 flat faces
   d. Cylinder, 2 curved sides, No vertex, 2 flat faces, 1 curved face
3. a. C b. O c. O d. C e. O

Exercise 10B

1. a. Line AB b. Point A
   c. Ray AB d. Line Segment XY
   e. Line EY f. Curve GH
2. 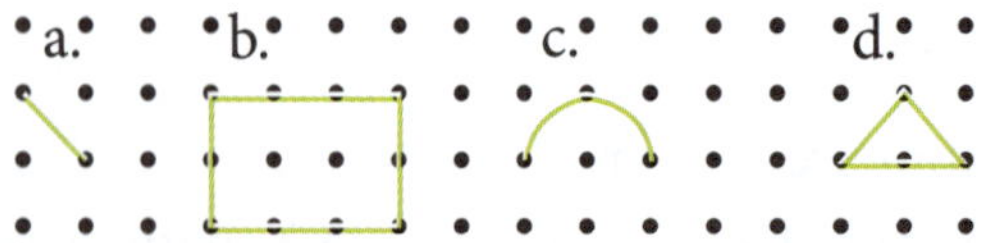

3. a. Airplane b. Candle c. Rocket d. Swan

Exercise 10C

1. a. Yes b. No c. Yes
2. a.  b.  c. 

Chapter Revision

A. 1. c. 2. b. 3. d. 4. a. 5. b.
B. 1. d. 2. c. 3. a. 4. b.
C. 1. cube 2. two- 3. cylinder 4. curve
5. cannot
D. 1.  Symmetrical b. Not symmetrical
2.  Symmetrical
3. 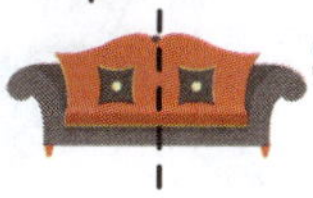 Symmetrical

Chapter 11

Exercise 11A

1. a.  b. 
2. a.  b. 
3. a.  b. 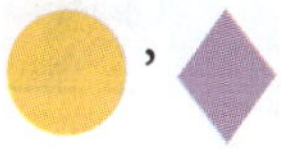

Exercise 11B

1.  2.  3.  4.  5. 

Exercise 11C

1. c and d

Chapter Revision

A. 1. 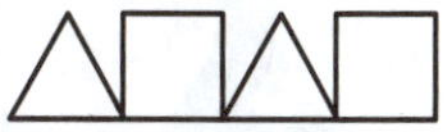 2. 16 19 22 25
3. 10 9 8 7 4. 50 40 30 20
5.  6. 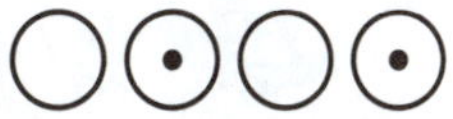
7.  8. 

B. 1.  2.  3.  4. 

C. 1.  2. 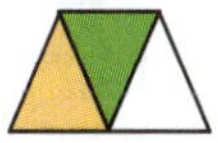 3. 

Chapter 12

Exercise 12A

1. a. 15 b. Mango c. Watermelon
d. 5 e. 70
2. a. 6 b. 8 c. Cricket d. Tennis
e. 6

Exercise 12B

1. a. Week 1: 3 Week 2: 5 Week 3: 1 Week 4: 4
Week 5: 3
b. Week 2 c. Week 3 d. 16 e. Weeks 1 and 5
2. Cat = 15 = 
Rabbit = 8 = 
Fish = 20 = 
Dog = 12 = 
Bird = 9 = 

Exercise 12C

1. a. Monday = 40 Tuesday = 70
Wednesday = 50 Friday = 50
b. Tuesday c. Thursday
d. Wednesday and Friday
e. Ice creams sold from Monday to Friday
2. a. 50 b. 40 c. Bicycle d. Bus
e. Mode of transport used by students and teachers

Chapter Revision

A. 1. 8 10 4 6
2. 2 3 6 7 5 15
B. 1. Pocket money saved
2. ₹18 3. Dulqar 4. Nick 5. ₹68
6. No, ₹32 more needed
C. Hazel = ₹18 = 
Nick = ₹12 = 
Dulqar = ₹24 = 
Jyoti = ₹14 = 
D. 1. Chocolate, Mango, Vanilla, Pista, Strawberry
2. Strawberry 3. Mango
4. Mango and Pista 5. 40

SEE Learning
Social
Emotional
Ethical

Donation Can Make A Change!

21 CS Critical Thinking and Communication

HQ Cooperation and Collaborative Living, Living in an Interconnected Society

My SEE Social Emotional Ethical Space

Answer the following questions.

1. What is the total amount of money collected by the children after 4 months?

   ____

2. Find the pocket money left with Harpreet, if he saves ₹150 monthly.

   ____

3. What is the difference between the amount of money that Latha and Zomawii get as pocket money?

   ____

4. Do you think donation is important? Share your thoughts in the space below.

   ____

   ____

   ____

   ____

Share the idea of donating stationery items with your parents and seek some help from them. Write the important points of the discussion below.

Maths Mela

21 CS Creativity and Innovation

EL AI

Let us build an abacus from a shoebox

All you need is... Empty shoebox, thin or narrow sticks, chart papers, scissors, beads of four different colours, sketch pens and an adhesive tape

Let's Start!

Note:
Do not use scissors or cutter yourself. Take help of an elder while cutting.

1. Take the shoebox and cover it completely with a chart paper.

2. With a scale and a pencil, mark four marks at equal intervals on one of the longer sides of the box.

3. With the pencil, punch a hole at each of these marks.

4. Rotate the tip of the pencil through each hole till it is wide enough for a stick to pass through.

5. Insert a stick in each hole.

6. Starting from the extreme right of the box, write O for ones, T for tens, H for hundreds and Th for thousands (below the sticks).

7. Your abacus is now ready for use.

8. Represent number 5496 using different coloured beads.

Do It Yourself!

Can you make a similar model for the addition of numbers? Give a brief idea about your model in the space given below.

Make the model that you have described above. Write the materials required and the steps of its construction. Take a picture of the model and paste it in the box.

All I Need Is:

Let's Start:

Eminent Mathematicians

Ada Lovelace (1815–1852)

Ada Lovelace is considered to be the mother of computing science and the world's first computer programmer. She contributed to the development of Charles Babbage's Analytical Engine (a mechanical general-purpose computer developed in 1837). She was the first person to see that computers could do more than mathematical calculations, recognizing that musical notes and letters of the alphabet could be turned into numbers for manipulation by computers.

William Oughtred (1574–1660)

William Oughtred is an English mathematician and is considered one of the world's greatest mathematicians because of his writings on the subject. He introduced many symbols for mathematical operations. Among those, only two symbols are still widely used; the multiplication symbol (×) is one of them.

Luca Pacioli (1445–1517)

Luca Pacioli was an Italian mathematician and accountant. He developed the field of accounting, and is also referred to as the father of Modern Accounting. Paciolo wrote a paper on magic and mathematics, notable for being the first known guide to performing card tricks. It also included a collection of mathematical puzzles. For unknown reasons, it was never published in Paciolo's lifetime.

T.A. Saraswati Amma (1918–2000)

T.A. Saraswati Amma was a scholar born in Kerala, India, who specialized in the geometry of ancient and medieval India. Her specialization is considered to be a significant event in the study of the history of Indian mathematics. Saraswati Amma's work was finally published in book form as *Geometry in Ancient and Medieval India* in 1979.

Dorothy Johnson Vaughan (1910–2008)

Dorothy Johnson Vaughan was an African–American mathematician and computer programmer who made important contributions to the early years of the U.S. space program.

In December 1943, she started working for National Advisory Committee for Aeronautics (NACA)'s West Area Computing unit, a group of African–American female mathematicians who were considered 'human computers', performing complex mathematical calculations and studying data for aerospace engineers. Vaughan is one of the women featured in the book and a biographical film named *Hidden Figures*, both released in 2016.